TEACHING ENGLISH CREATIVELY

D1152131

What does it mean to teach English creatively to primary school children?

How can you successfully develop pupils' engagement with and interest in English and communication?

Teaching English Creatively offers ideas to involve your children and demonstrates the potential of creative teaching to develop children's knowledge, skills, understanding and attitudes. Underpinned by theory and research, it offers informed and practical support to both students in initial teacher education, and practising teachers who want to develop their teaching skills.

Illustrated by examples of children's work, this book examines the core elements of creative practice in relation to developing imaginatively engaged readers, writers, speakers and listeners. Creative ways to explore powerful literary, non-fiction, visual and digital texts are offered throughout. Key themes addressed include:

■ meaning and purpose
■ play and engagement
■ curiosity and autonomy
■ collaboration and making connections
■ reflection and celebration
■ the creative involvement of the teacher.

Stimulating and accessible, with contemporary and cutting-edge practice at the forefront, *Teaching English Creatively* includes a wealth of innovative ideas to enrich literacy..

Written by an author with extensive experience of initial teacher education and English teaching in the primary school, this book is an essential purchase for any professional who wishes to embed creative approaches to teaching in their classroom.

Teresa Cremin (Grainger) is Professor of Education at the Open University, UK and President of the United Kingdom Literacy Association (2007–9).

LEARNING TO TEACH IN THE PRIMARY SCHOOL SERIES

Series Editor: Teresa Cremin, the Open University

Teaching is an art form. It demands not only knowledge and understanding of the core areas of learning, but also the ability to teach these creatively and effectively and foster learner creativity in the process. *The Learning to Teach in the Primary School Series* draws upon recent research, which indicates the rich potential of creative teaching and learning, and explores what it means to teach creatively in the primary phase. It also responds to the evolving nature of subject teaching in a wider, more imaginatively framed twenty-first century primary curriculum.

Designed to complement the textbook *Learning to Teach in the Primary School*, the well-informed, lively texts offer support for students and practising teachers who want to develop more flexible and responsive creative approaches to teaching and learning. The books highlight the importance of the teachers' own creative engagement and share a wealth of innovative ideas to enrich pedagogy and practice.

Titles in the series:

Teaching English Creatively
Teresa Cremin

Teaching Science Creatively
Dan Davies and Ian Milne

TEACHING ENGLISH CREATIVELY

Teresa Cremin with
Eve Bearne,
Henrietta Dombey and
Maureen Lewis

Routledge
Taylor & Francis Group

LONDON AND NEW YORK

First published 2009
by Routledge
2 Park Square, Milton Park, Abingdon, Oxon OX14 4RN

Simultaneously published in the USA and Canada
by Routledge
711 Third Avenue, New York, NY 10017

Routledge is an imprint of the Taylor & Francis Group, an informa business

© 2009 Teresa Cremin for text, editing and selection.
Eve Bearne, Henrietta Dombey and Maureen Lewis
their individual contributions.

Typeset in Times New Roman and Helvetica Neue by
Florence Production Ltd, Stoodleigh, Devon
Printed and bound in Great Britain by
TJ International Ltd, Padstow, Cornwall

British Library Cataloguing in Publication Data
A catalogue record for this book is available from the British Library

Library of Congress Cataloging-in-Publication Data
A catalog record for this book has been requested

ISBN10: 0–415–54829–2 (hbk)
ISBN10: 0–415–43502–1 (pbk)
ISBN10: 0–203–86750–5 (ebk)

ISBN13: 978–0–415–54829–8 (hbk)
ISBN13: 978–0–415–43502–4 (pbk)
ISBN13: 978–0–203–86750–1 (ebk)

CONTENTS

CONTENTS ■ ■ ■ ■

ILLUSTRATIONS

AUTHOR BIOGRAPHIES

Teresa Cremin (previously Grainger) is Professor of Education (Literacy) at The Open University, President of the United Kingdom Literacy Association (UKLA) (2007–9), Trustee of the Poetry Archive and of Booktrust and joint coordinator of the British Educational Research Association special interest group on creativity. Teresa has always been concerned to make learning an imaginatively vital experience and seeks to foster the creative engagement of both teachers and younger learners in her research and consultancy work. She views teaching as an art form and believes that in some way, all teachers should be creative practitioners themselves.

Teresa undertakes collaborative research and development projects with teachers as researchers. Her research has involved investigating teachers' identities as readers and writers and the pedagogical consequences of increasing their reflective and aesthetic engagement as literate individuals. She has also examined teachers' knowledge of children's literature, the relationship between drama and writing, the development of voice and verve in children's writing, storytelling, poetry and the role of 'possibility thinking' in creative learning.

Teresa has published widely in the fields of literacy and creativity, her most recent books, published with colleagues, include: *Jumpstart Drama!* (David Fulton, 2009); *Building Communities of Readers* (PNS/UKLA, 2008); *Creative Learning 3–11* (Trentham, 2007); *The Handbook of Primary English in Initial Teacher Education* (UKLA/NATE, 2007); *Creativity and Writing: Developing Voice and Verve in the Classroom* (RoutledgeFalmer, 2005) and *Creative Activities for Character, Setting and Plot 5–7, 7–9, 9–11* (Scholastic, 2004).

Eve Bearne's research interests while at the University of Cambridge, Faculty of Education have been children's production of multimodal texts and gender, language and literacy. She has also written and edited numerous books about language and literacy and children's literature and most recently co-authored *Visual Approaches to Teaching Writing: Multimodal Literacy 5–11* with Helen Wolstencroft (Sage, 2008). She is currently responsible for Publications for the United Kingdom Literacy Association (UKLA) and is a Fellow of the English Association.

Henrietta Dombey is Professor Emeritus of Literacy in Primary Education at the University of Brighton. Since the start of her teaching career, when she was confronted with a class of 7-year-olds with very little purchase on written language, she has been passionately interested in the teaching of reading and committed to a creative approach to it. This interest has encompassed attention to phonics, children's knowledge of the syntax and semantics of written language and the interactions between teachers, children and texts that appear to be productive of literacy learning. Henrietta has written extensively on many aspects of teaching reading.

Maureen Lewis currently works as an independent consultant and is an honorary Research Fellow at the University of Exeter. She has been a primary school teacher, researcher, university lecturer and writer and has published widely on all aspects of literacy, most recently on creative approaches to teaching reading comprehension. She is well known for her work on pupils' interactions with non-fiction texts and for the development of 'Writing Frames', arising from the influential Nuffield EXEL Project, which she co-directed with David Wray. In her role as a regional director for Primary National Strategy, Maureen wrote many teaching materials and led the development and writing of *Excellence and Enjoyment: Learning and Teaching in the Primary Years*. Maureen has also produced or been series editor for other classroom materials for literacy, including *Longman Digitexts*. She is currently working with Oxford University Press, developing the *Project X* reading programme aimed at engaging boy readers.

ACKNOWLEDGMENTS

This book has benefited from many conversations and collaborations with colleagues in classrooms, in universities, in arts organisations and in policy contexts. I would like in particular to thank my three contributing authors, Eve Bearne, Henrietta Dombey and Maureen Lewis for producing such engaging chapters at speed in response to my desperate request- almost overnight it seemed. Sometimes pressures beyond one's control emerge and then, as we all know, one's real colleagues and friends find the time to add to their evident talent and help out. I am indebted to them.

I am also keenly aware of the contribution of the many teachers with whom I have worked on research and development projects over the years, together our collective desire to play, innovate and open new doors on children's learning taught us a great deal about our own creativity and the children's. Our curiosity also enabled us to explore the pedagogical consequences of more creative approaches to English teaching. My colleagues Andrew Lambirth and Kathy Goouch from Canterbury Christ Church University also deserve a special mention, for many years we experimented with ideas and possibilities in professional development contexts, and I learnt much from this collaborative and iterative process.

Thanks are also due to the United Kingdom Literacy Association, the Esmée Fairbairn Foundation, the Qualifications and Curriculum Authority, Creative Partnerships (both Kent and Central), Canterbury Christ Church University, the Open University and the Arts Council England for awarding funding grants that have enabled me to work alongside teachers in classrooms, observe them in action, document their pedagogic practice and seek to understand the relationship between their own engagement and stance and that of the younger learners.

I would also like to thank Anna Clarkson, Helen Pritt and Catherine Oakley from Routledge whose long standing support and enthusiasm has helped this text become a reality, and my own family whose playful approach to life and language has fostered my own creative stance towards English and communication.

TEACHING ENGLISH CREATIVELY

INTRODUCTION

Teaching and learning English is, at its richest, an energising, purposeful and imaginatively vital experience for all involved, developing youngsters' competence, confidence and creativity as well as building positive attitudes to learning. At its poorest, English teaching and learning can be a dry, didactic experience, focused on the instruction of assessable skills, and paying little attention to children's affective or creative development as language learners and language users.

Following apparently safe routes to raise literacy standards, interspersed with occasional more creatively oriented activities, does not represent balanced literacy instruction. Such practice pays lip service to creative approaches and fails to acknowledge the potential of building on young children's curiosity, desire for agency and capacity to generate and innovate. Such practice also ignores government reports and policy recommendations that encourage teachers to teach more creatively (DfES, 2003; QCA, 2005a,b). It also ignores research that indicates the multiple benefits of teaching and learning literacy creatively (for example, Woods, 2001; Vass, 2004; Grainger *et al.*, 2005; Ellis and Safford, 2005).

Teaching literacy creatively does not mean short-changing the teaching of the essential knowledge, skills and understanding of the subject; rather it involves teaching literacy skills and developing knowledge about language in creative contexts that explicitly invite learners to engage imaginatively and which stretch their generative and evaluative capacities. Creative teachers work to extend children's abilities as readers, writers, speakers and listeners and help them to express themselves effectively, to create as well as critically evaluate their own work. Both the Early Years Foundation Stage (DCSF, 2008a) and the renewed Primary National Strategy (PNS) (DfES, 2006a) recognise the importance of creativity and highlight the role of teachers in fostering children's curiosity, capacity to make connections, take risks and innovate.

Creativity emerges as children become absorbed in actively exploring ideas, initiating their own learning and making choices and decisions about how to express themselves using different media and language modes. In responding to what they read, view, hear and experience, children make use of their literacy skills and transform their knowledge and understanding in the process. It is the aim of this book to encourage and enable teachers to adopt a more creative approach to the teaching of English in the primary phase.

THE LITERACY AGENDA

In the last decade, primary English teachers have experienced unprecedented prescription and accountability. The National Literacy Strategy (NLS), introduced in 1998, reconceptualised English as 'literacy', specified a specific core of knowledge to be taught and tested, and required teachers to employ particular pedagogical practices in a daily literacy hour (DfEE, 1998). Combined with the high stakes assessment system, this arguably led to an instrumental approach to teaching and learning literacy, dominated by content rather than process. Initially, many teachers interpreted the original framework very literally, assiduously seeking to ensure coverage of the teaching objectives. In addition, some educators, pressured by tests, targets and curriculum coverage, short-changed their pedagogical principles (English *et al.*, 2002) or found themselves continuing to dominate classroom interaction, leaving little space for the learners themselves (Mroz *et al.*, 2000).

Furthermore, in the early years of the NLS, concerns were expressed about the use of extracts and the decline in opportunities for extended writing (Frater, 2000). Professional authors too were critical of the backwash of assessment and the focus on textual analysis at the relative expense of pleasurable engagement in reading (Powling *et al.*, 2003, 2005). While the NLS brought many benefits, it also arguably constrained teachers' and children's experience of creativity and reduced professional autonomy and artistry in the process.

In a revisitation of the English curriculum (English 21, QCA, 2005c), the Qualifications and Curriculum Authority (QCA) identified four key strands, namely: competence, creativity, cultural understanding and criticality, suggesting that creativity is no longer seen as an optional extra, but a goal of the English curriculum and one that deserves increased attention. Additionally, the renewed PNS framework (DfES, 2006a) offers more autonomy to the teaching profession and endorses a more responsive and creative approach to literacy teaching. Its twelve strands of reading, writing, speaking and listening are now detailed in a more integrated and holistic manner, and the end of year objectives enable teachers to plan extended and flexible units of work. Influenced by the changing nature of twenty-first century communication, the new framework and the Rose review (Rose, 2009) recognise the emerging creativity agenda and explicitly encourages more creative literacy teaching.

THE CREATIVITY AGENDA

Since the publication of *Excellence and Enjoyment* (DfES, 2003), schools have been urged to be more innovative and flexible in shaping the primary curriculum. A plethora of policies and practices about creativity, influenced by economic and political goals, have become prominent in government policy, most of which seek to ensure creativity is recognised, fostered and promoted. These include the *Creativity: Find It! Promote It!* project run by the QCA (QCA, 2005a), which produced materials to support creativity and a useful policy framework for 4–16-year-olds; the inspection report *Expecting the Unexpected: Developing Creativity in Primary and Secondary Schools* (Ofsted, 2003); and the establishment of the Creative Partnerships (CP) initiative. The CP programme seeks to offer opportunities for the young to develop their creativity by building partnerships with creative organisations, businesses and individuals, and to demonstrate the role creativity and creative people can play in transforming teaching and learning. The report *Nurturing Creativity in Young People* (Roberts, 2006) and the government's response to this (DCMS, 2006) are also influencing the agenda.

The definition of creativity employed by these documents is that coined in the report *All Our Futures: Creativity, Culture and Education*, namely that creativity is 'imaginative activity fashioned so as to produce outcomes that are both original and of value' (NACCCE, 1999: 30). This report suggested that the curriculum needed rebalancing, and now, ten years later, primary schools are finally working to adopt more creative approaches to teaching and learning.

Recently, the secondary curriculum for 11–14-year-olds has been radically reconceived with personal, learning and thinking skills at its core. One of the six strands of this framework focuses on developing young people as creative thinkers, another on their capacity for independent enquiry (QCA, 2008). The Rose Review of the Primary Curriculum also clearly affirms the need to develop children as creative thinkers and independent learners (Rose, 2009), in literacy and across the curriculum.

EXPLORING CREATIVITY

In the light of this burgeoning policy agenda, it is crucial for teachers to clarify what creativity means to them in terms of teaching and learning, both in literacy and across the curriculum. The openness often associated with it may be unsettling, as one newly qualified teacher (NQT) recently observed, 'It's all changing and I can't cope with it – they're asking us to make the decisions now and be creative and I don't know how'. She appeared to feel safer delivering downloadable plans to ensure curriculum coverage in literacy and was unsure how to plan for creativity in literacy, for extended explorations and textual enquiries, based on children's interests and literacy objectives. Black *et al.* (2002) suggest that teachers need to shift from being presenters of content to becoming innovative 'leaders of explorations'. To achieve this, some may need to dispel any lingering myths that creativity is an arts-related concept, applicable only to those aspects of literacy that involve literature, drama or poetry for example. In addition, teachers need to accept that creativity is not confined to particular children, but is a human potential possessed by all and one that is open to development

Creativity, in essence the generation of novel ideas, is possible to exercise in all aspects of life. In problem solving contexts of a mundane as well as unusual nature, humans can choose to adopt a creative mindset or attitude and trial possible options and ideas. It is useful to distinguish between high creativity and everyday creativity, between 'Big C Creativity' (seen in some of Gardner's (1993) studies of highly creative individuals, for example, Einstein and Freud) and 'little c creativity' that Craft (2000, 2005) suggests focuses on agency and resourcefulness of ordinary people to innovate and take action. It is the latter, more democratic view of creativity that is adopted in this book, connected to literacy teaching and learning. Making original connections in thought, movement and language need to be recognised as creative acts, just as much as the production of a finished piece of writing or a poetry performance.

Creativity involves the capacity to generate, reason with and critically evaluate novel suppositions or imaginary scenarios. It is about thinking, problem solving, inventing and reinventing, and flexing one's imaginative muscles. As such, the creative process involves risk, uncertainty, change, challenge and criticality. Some schools, in planning for creativity in literacy, make use of the QCA framework, which characterises creativity in education as involving:

- posing questions
- making connections
- being imaginative
- exploring options
- engaging in critical reflection/evaluation.

(QCA, 2005a,b)

FINDING A CREATIVE WAY FORWARD

If teachers are to adopt innovative ways forward in their English teaching, they need to reconcile the tension between the drive for measurable standards on the one hand and the development of creativity on the other. As children move through school, they quickly learn how the system works and suppress their spontaneous creativity (Sternberg, 1997). Some teachers too, in seeking to achieve prescribed literacy targets, curb their own creativity and avoid taking risks and leading explorations in learning. More creative professionals, in combining subject and pedagogical knowledge, consciously leave real space for uncertainty and seek both to teach creatively and to teach for creativity. Teaching creatively involves teachers in making learning more interesting and effective, and using imaginative approaches in the classroom (NACCCE, 1999). Teaching for creativity, by contrast, focuses on developing children's creativity, their capacity to experiment with ideas and information, alone and with others. The two processes are very closely related.

In examining the nature of creative teaching in a number of primary curriculum contexts, Jeffrey and Woods (2003, 2009) suggest that innovation, originality, ownership and control are all associated with creative practice. More recent research has affirmed and developed this, showing that creative teachers, in both planning and teaching, and in the ethos that they create in the classroom, attribute high value to curiosity and risk taking, to ownership, autonomy and making connections (Grainger et al., 2006). They also afford significance to the development of imaginative and unusual ideas in both themselves and their students. This work suggests that while all good teachers reward originality, creative ones depend on it to enhance their own well-being and that of the children. They see the development of creativity and originality as a distinguishing mark of their teaching. Perhaps, therefore, the difference between being a good teacher and being a creative teacher is one of emphasis and intention. The creative teacher is one who values the human attribute of creativity in themselves and seeks to promote this in others (ibid.; Cremin, 2009). In the process, such teachers encourage children to believe in their creative potential and give them the confidence to try. Furthermore, they seek to foster other creative attributes in the young, such as risk taking, commitment, resilience, independent judgement, intrinsic motivation and curiosity.

Creative literacy teaching is a collaborative enterprise; one which capitalises on the unexpected and enables children to develop their language and literacy in purposeful, relevant and creative contexts that variously involve engagement, instruction, reflection and transformation. Such an approach recognises that teaching is an art form and that 'learning to read and write is an artistic event' (Freire, 1985), and one that connects to children's out-of-school literacy practices. Creative English teaching and teaching for creativity in English aims to enable young people to develop a questioning and critically reflective stance towards texts, to express themselves with voice and verve multimodally and in multiple media, and to generate what is new and original.

CORE FEATURES OF A CREATIVE APPROACH

An environment of possibility, in which individual agency and self-determination are fostered and children's ideas and interests are valued, discussed and celebrated, depends upon the presence of a climate of trust, respect and support in the classroom. Creativity can be developed when teachers are confident and secure in both their subject knowledge and their knowledge of creative pedagogical practice; they model the features of creativity *and* develop a culture of creative opportunities.

A creative approach to teaching English encompasses several core features that enable teachers to make informed decisions, both at the level of planning and in the moment-to-moment interactions in the classroom. The elements of creative English practice that are examined throughout the book are introduced here. They include:

1. profiling meaning and purpose;
2. foregrounding potent affectively engaging texts;
3. fostering play and engagement;
4. harnessing curiosity and profiling agency;
5. encouraging collaboration and making connections;
6. integrating reflection, review, feedback and celebration;
7. taking time to travel and explore;
8. ensuring the creative involvement of the teacher.

1 Profile meaning and purpose

Significant research into effective teachers of literacy, funded by the UK Teacher Training Agency in the late nineties, showed that effective professionals believe that the creation of meaning in literacy is fundamental (Medwell *et al.*, 1998, Wray *et al.*, 2002). As a consequence, they highlight the purpose and function of reading and writing in their classrooms. Explicit and focused attention is given to linguistic features, but these are taught in context and practised through meaningful activities, the purposes of which are clearly explained to the children. In a separate survey of practice in successful schools, Frater (2000) again found that effective teachers foregrounded the construction of meaning in literacy, and creatively extended and enriched the NLS framework of objectives. Work in the US also confirms that exemplary and creative professionals highlight the meaningful components in any learning process (Block *et al.*, 2002).

The meaning and purpose of literacy learning connects to the outcome sought, which may include, for example, a poetry anthology, a newspaper, a website, a PowerPoint™ presentation, a film, or a play. Young people need to be helped to read, produce and critically evaluate a wide range of texts and engage in English practices that make the world meaningful and imaginatively satisfying to them, and in fostering creativity in English, teachers need to be geared towards individual children's passions, practices, capabilities and personalities.

2 Foreground potent affectively engaging texts

Partly as a result of rapid technological advances and the increasing dominance of the image, the nature and form of texts has changed radically and many are now multimodal. They make use of sound and music, voice, intonation, stance, gesture and movement, as well as print and image, and exist in many different media such as a computer screen, film, radio and book. Children bring to reading and writing in school a wealth of multimodal text experiences, both screen-based and on paper, often showing a preference for the former in their reading (Bearne *et al.*, 2007). Their teachers may have experienced a smaller range of textual forms as young readers and writers, but need to recognise that children's creativity is often evidenced in their playful engagement with such contemporary textual forms and that their passion for popular cultural texts can valuably be harnessed (Marsh and Millard, 2000). So teachers need to connect the literacies of home and school, offering rich textual encounters that bridge the gap between the children's own 'cultural capital' (Bordieu, 1977) and the culture of school.

Texts play a critical role in creative English teaching, so teachers' knowledge of children's authors and poets is crucial (Cremin *et al.*, 2008a,b), enabling them to select texts for extended study and reading aloud that will evoke an imaginatively vital response. In profiling the learner above the curriculum, creative professionals respond to children's aesthetic and emotional engagement in learning, sharing their own responses to texts and inviting the learners to respond likewise. Children's affective involvement is central to creativity, since it encourages openness and fosters the ability to make personal connections and insights. Teachers seek out potent texts that offer both relevance and potential engagement; they know that fiction, non-fiction and visual texts can inform and expand the horizons of readers and writers, offering rich models, provoking a variety of creative responses and providing a context in which language skills can be taught (Ellis and Safford, 2005). As texts are perceived as integral to teaching English creatively and fostering the creativity of young learners, references to literature and other texts are made throughout this book.

3 Foster play and engagement

The importance of play and deep engagement is widely recognised in fostering creativity; the spontaneous nature of play, its improvisational and generative orientation is critical. A close relationship also exists between the ways in which real world literacy is used and the nature of play, since both are purposeful, meaningful and offer choices. The Early Years Foundation Stage Curriculum (DCSF, 2008a) in England leads the way in recognising the importance of play and playful approaches, which encompass learning through exploration and the evaluation of possibilities. Such playful endeavours need to be offered throughout the primary phase, perhaps in the context of investigating fictional scenarios, experimenting with different poetic presentations, creating a play script for performance or examining current issues to debate and discuss.

If the spirit of play and imagination is encouraged, then teachers and learners are more open to new and different opportunities, to trying new routes and paths less well travelled (Fisher and Williams, 2004). Creative English learning is a motivating and highly interactive experience involving a degree of playfulness and the potential for engagement in multiple contexts. In such contexts, creativity will not simply be an event or a product, although it may involve either or both, but a process involving the serious play of ideas and possibilities. In studying literature in depth, for example, time for deep immersion and engagement in the theme or genre will need to be provided, as well as dedicated time for play – engaged mental and physical play – with textual patterns, puzzles, conventions, materials and ideas. During this time children will also experience explicit instruction and tailored teaching. Through drama and storytelling, art, discussion, drawing and dance, children's outer play encourages the inner play of the imagination and develops their flexibility with ideas and language (Grainger *et al.*, 2005).

4 Harness curiosity and profile agency

At the core of creativity is a deep sense of curiosity and wonder, a desire to question and ponder; teachers need to model this questioning stance, this openness to possibility and desire to learn. In the context of the literacy classroom, developing opportunities for children to 'possibility think' their way forwards is therefore crucial (Craft, 2001). This will involve immersing the class in an issue or subject and helping them ask questions, take risks, be imaginative and playfully explore options and ideas as they work on extended purposeful projects. On the journey, knowledge about language and skills will be developed through their involvement as readers, writers, speakers and listeners.

Crucial to this exploration will be the development of children's self-determination and agency. Their capacity to work as independent enquirers and creative thinkers will be influenced by the degree to which teachers share the control of the learning agenda (Cremin *et al.*, 2006a). Offering elements of choice in reading and writing, in terms of texts to read and the subject matter or form of writing for example, can help construct literacy curricula that build on learners' interests as well as their social/cultural capital. Encouraging children to identify their own questions about texts, not just respond to those identified by the teacher, can also increase their involvement, intentionality and agency, but it is not enough. Self-directed learning and the agency of individuals and groups must be carefully planned for, reflected upon and celebrated in order to foster creativity.

Teachers need to be able to stand back and let the children take the lead, supporting them as they take risks, encounter problems and map out their own learning journeys, setting their own goals and agreeing some of their own success criteria in the process. In open-ended contexts, control is more likely to be devolved, at least in part to children, and they are more likely to adapt and extend activities in unexpected ways, adopt different perspectives and construct their own tasks. In this way innovation and creativity can be fostered. Such an approach resonates with both the personalisation agenda and the pupil voice movement and encourages children to take increased responsibility for their own education.

5 Encourage collaboration and making connections

The perception of both learning and creativity as collaborative social processes is gaining ground. While children engage individually, their endeavours are linked to the work of others and they support one another's thinking and creativity, fostering both individual and collective creativity (Vass, 2004). Creative English teachers seek to foster this and exploit the full range of collaborations available in and beyond the classroom, including, for example, pair work, small group and whole class work, as well as partnerships with parents, authors, poets, storytellers, dancers, actors, singers and others. Children will be involved in generating ideas through interaction and playful exploration, gathering knowledge with and from each other, seeking support from others, evaluating their work and that of others, and transforming their existing under-standing through a range of collaborative activities.

Creativity also critically involves making connections with other areas of learning, with other texts and experiences. Through their own questioning stance, creative teachers actively encourage pupils to make associations and connections, perhaps through connecting to prior learning, making links between subjects and/or across different media for example. Such teachers make personal connections in the context of literature discussions and share inter-textual connections to prompt children to make their own connections. Developing a spirit of enquiry and openness to ideas from different sources, such as people, texts of all kinds, objects and experiences can help children make lateral and divergent connections. In addition, a range of pedagogical strategies and diverse teaching styles and entry points can be used to enable new connections to be formed in the minds and work of the children.

6 Integrate reflection, review, feedback and celebration

Creativity not only involves the generation of novel ideas, but also the critical evaluation of them; it involves both selection and judgement as some ideas are rejected, while others may be pursued in more depth. Such evaluative reflection and review needs to be effectively modelled by teachers, as they seek to enable youngsters to make insightful self-judgements and to engage in small group peer-review and assessment of their creative endeavours. The creative process may involve rational and non-rational thought and may be fed by daydreaming and intuition (Claxton, 2000) as well as the application of knowledge and skills. So mapping in moments of reflection and contemplation and encouraging children to incubate their ideas and revisit earlier pieces of writing can, for example, support their development as creative learners.

The ability to give and receive criticism is an essential part of creativity, so teachers will want to encourage evaluation through supportive and honest feedback, as well as self-reflection and review. When learners are engaged in mindful, negotiated and interactive practices in English, they are more prepared to review their ongoing development work, as well as reflect upon the decisions they have made and the final outcome produced. This relates closely to the autonomy and agency offered, and the relevance of the activity in the learner's eyes. Teachers work towards a semi-constant oscillation between engagement and reflection as learners refine, reshape and improve their work, preparing perhaps for a storytelling festival or a publication deadline.

In addition, creative professionals seize opportunities to share and celebrate children's successes, in part through the actual publication of anthologies of work and festivals or assemblies for example, but also through informal class sharing of various kinds. Ongoing celebration and focused feedback is also significant; it can help children to reflect upon the creative process, their emerging ideas and unfolding work, and enriches learning.

7 Take time to travel and explore

Effective teachers work creatively to balance the teaching of skills, knowledge and understanding, through integrating teaching and learning about the language modes as children undertake extended units of work. Such learning journeys need to be imaginatively engaging, relevant and purposeful if children's creativity is to be developed. A ten-country European study on creative learning has demonstrated the importance of such extended open adventures, in which children explore and develop knowledge through focused engagement with their work, and review the process and outcomes of their engagement (Jeffrey, 2005, 2006). Additionally, in a United Kingdom Literacy Association (UKLA) project, which successfully raised boys' achievements in writing, it was found that taking time to travel enabled the disaffected boy writers to get involved in depth. The use of film and drama to drive the units of work also motivated them, helping raise their levels of commitment and persistence, their independence and motivation, as well as influencing the quality of the work produced (Bearne *et al.*, 2004).

Such extended work is now endorsed by the new PNS Framework (DfES, 2006), which adopts a more flexible stance and suggests planning extended opportunities to explore and investigate a particular text type or issue over a period of two to four weeks or more. This builds in increased time for creative exploration and engagement, and also allows emergent issues to be responded to. The lessening pace, which has been in the forefront in recent years, may additionally help teachers trust their instincts, deciding to divert the journey and/or follow the learners' interests, thus creating a more responsive and flexible curriculum. Creative pedagogues also plan significant 'critical events' as Woods (1994) describes them, holistic projects that often include external specialists and have ambitious long-term goals: the production of a film or play perhaps. In such projects, children are encouraged to initiate activities and direct more of their own work, which can nurture both interest and commitment – potent fuel for a journey of extended exploration (see Chapter 12).

8 Ensure the creative involvement of the teacher

In schools where standards in English are high, teachers' passions about English and their own creativity are also valued and given space to develop (Frater, 2001). Creative teachers, as Sternberg (1999) suggests, are creative role models themselves; professionals who continue to be self-motivated learners, value the creative dimensions of their own lives and make connections between their personal responses to experience and their teaching. Such teachers are willing and able to express themselves, even though this involves taking risks and being observed in the process. Wilson and Ball (1997) found risk taking is a common characteristic of highly successful literacy teachers, not merely in relation to their artistic engagement, but also in their capacity to experiment and remain open to new ideas and strategies that may benefit the learners. Creative teachers plan with specific objectives in mind but, as the QCA (2005a) guidance notes, may spontaneously alter the direction of the exploration in response to children's interests and needs.

The kinds of pedagogical approaches that the QCA framework suggests teachers should employ to foster creativity include:

- establishing criteria for success;
- asking open questions;
- encouraging openness to ideas and critical reflection;
- capitalising on the unexpected without losing sight of the original objective;
- regularly reviewing work in progress.

(QCA, 2005a,b)

Through their own imaginative involvement in classroom endeavour, teachers' creative potential can be released and their confidence, commitment and understanding of the challenge of using literacy for one's own expressive and creative purposes can grow. As artists in their classrooms, telling tales, responding to texts, performing poems, writing and taking roles in drama, teachers are freed from the traditional patterns of classroom interaction and are more personally and affectively involved, using their knowledge and skills, as well as their creativity and experience. The experience and practice of the teacher as artist/composer needs to be reinstated 'at the heart of the pedagogic activity of teaching writing' and of teaching literacy (Robinson and Ellis, 2000: 75). If teachers themselves are imaginatively involved, they are better placed to develop children's creativity, working alongside them as co-participants in the learning process.

CONCLUSION

Good practice exists when creative and informed professionals respond flexibly to current curricula and develop coherent and imaginative approaches underpinned by pedagogical and subject knowledge *and* knowledge of individual children. This book seeks to support such practice by offering practical advice and ideas for taking a creative approach to English and showing how knowledge, skills and understanding can be developed through engagement in meaningful and creative contexts. In order to ensure that teachers are able to develop principled practice in teaching English creatively, research and theoretical perspectives are woven throughout. In reflecting upon the combination of practice and theory offered, it is hoped that teachers will appreciate more fully the potential of teaching English creatively and teaching for creativity in English.

FURTHER READING

Craft, A. (2005) *Creativity in Schools: Tensions and Dilemmas*, Oxford: RoutledgeFalmer.
Cremin. T. (2009) Creative Teachers and Creative Teaching, in A. Wilson (ed.), *Creativity in Primary Education*, Exeter: Learning Matters
Jeffrey, B. and Craft, A. (2004) Teaching Creatively and Teaching for Creativity: Distinctions and Relationships, *Educational Studies*, 30(1): 47–61.
Maybin, J. and Swann, J. (eds) (2006) *The Art of English: Everyday Creativity*, Basingstoke: Palgrave Macmillan.

CHAPTER 2

DEVELOPING SPEAKERS AND LISTENERS CREATIVELY

INTRODUCTION

When children use language to learn and to communicate in creatively engaging and motivating contexts, they experience its powerful provocative, as well as evocative, potential. This chapter, alongside Chapter 3 on drama, focuses on talk as a highly accessible and potent medium for learning, literacy and personal development. The creative nature of talk is highlighted and the role of the teacher as a model of curiosity and creative engagement is examined. The chapter also shares practical strategies to develop children's confidence and competence as language artists through activities such as oral storytelling, both personal and traditional and in the context of other small group activities that offer opportunities for engagement and reflection. By the end of the Early Years Foundation Stage (DCSF, 2008a), it is expected that children will be able to listen with enjoyment to a variety of texts, sustain attentive listening, use talk to organise, sequence and clarify thinking, interact with others, and imagine and recreate roles and experiences. These core aims are related to the four strands of speaking and listening noted in the PNS (DfES, 2006a), which are:

Speaking
■　Speak competently and creatively for different purposes and audiences, reflecting on impact and response.
■　Explore, develop and sustain ideas through talk.

(PNS, Strand 1)

Listening and responding
■　Understand, recall and respond to speakers' implicit and explicit meanings.
■　Explain and comment on speakers' use of language, including vocabulary, grammar and non- verbal features.

(PNS, Strand 2)

Group discussion and interaction

■ Take different roles in groups to develop thinking and complete tasks.
■ Participate in conversations, making appropriate contributions building on others suggestions and responses.

(PNS, Strand 3)

Drama

■ Use dramatic techniques, including work in role to explore ideas and texts.
■ Create, share and evaluate ideas and understanding through drama.

(PNS, Strand 4)

PRINCIPLES

Oracy is a vital foundation for the development of literacy. In their early encounters with language, young children learn to take part and to negotiate meaning, actively solving problems and making sense with and through others. Adults, as their conversational partners, engage in highly contextualised talk arising out of activities in which both engage. In their homes, the amount and quality of the dialogue that children experience is highly significant and the quality of the dialogue in school contexts is therefore no less important. As Britton (1970) observed, 'reading and writing float on a sea of talk'; oracy is the basis of much literate behaviour. Talk enables learners to think aloud, formulate their thoughts and opinions, and refine and develop their ideas and understandings through engaging in meaningful dialogue with others. Talk also enables learners to relate new experiences to previous knowledge and understanding, and to value their own and others' ideas.

While talk is a rich resource for learning, it is also a mode of communication with considerable artistic power and potential. Research into everyday talk affirms that creative language use is not a special feature of some people, but is common to all (Carter, 2004). This research suggests that playful use of language is typically co-produced and is most likely to develop in dialogic and intimate conditions. Maybin (2006: 413) also asserts that '. . . the seeds of artistic and literary uses of English, are all to be found in everyday uses of language'. Through telling stories and taking part in drama, for example, children can experience the potential of the spoken word and enrich their oral artistry. Their creativity, understanding and imagination can also be engaged and fostered through discussion and interaction. So teachers need to value, appreciate and develop children's spoken language and enable them to learn collaboratively and creatively through interaction. Furthermore, Meek (1985: 47) suggests that as children learn to handle the language of the taken-for-granted in their culture, they become wordsmiths, whose voices creatively experiment with existing forms and functions.

TALKING AND LEARNING

Arguably, the predominant model of learning in western societies has been one of information transfer, in which children are seen as empty vessels, passive learners who receive information from their teacher. In this model, learning is viewed as an individual cognitive activity and teaching centres on individual performance, and emphasises personal expression and individual skill development. Yet teachers intuitively know that learning is often a mutual accomplishment and that collaboration is a critical way to build intellectual insight and understanding. Today, many educationalists, leaning on the work of Vygotsky (1978), argue for a pedagogy in which talk plays a central role and believe that humans learn through guided participation and the support of more competent others (Wells, 1999; Mercer and Littleton, 2007). Recent research into development through dialogue proposes that learning is a product of interthinking, and that for a teacher to teach and a learner to learn, they must use talk and joint activity to create a shared communicative space, an 'intermental development zone' (Mercer, 2000). In this way cognitive development has been re-viewed as a dialogic process, a transformation of participation.

As a consequence, an interactive pedagogy needs to be built in the classroom, one which highlights collaboration and joint knowledge construction, ensuring children's active involvement in a community of learners. In such a community, quality oral interaction and full pupil participation, now widely regarded as central elements of learning (Cambourne, 1995; Geekie *et al.*, 1999) play a central role, and children are creatively engaged in their own learning, talking their way forwards and making connections as they travel. In such contexts, the adult 'leads by following' (Woods, 1995), offers contingent instruction and ensures that the responsibility for managing the problem solving involved is gradually handed over.

In dialogic teaching and learning, language is used as a tool, a social mode of thinking, employed for the development of knowledge and understanding, and questions are structured so as to provoke thoughtful answers, which in turn provoke further questions (Alexander, 2004). In the following extract, from an extended discussion between six 10-year-olds about one image from Shaun Tan's book *The Rabbits*, the children's voices demonstrate their focused engagement and tentative thinking as they reflect individually and collaboratively:

Martha: 'I think the rabbit's looking into the sky.'

Tim: 'But it's underneath him.'

Liam: 'Maybe it's a puddle'

Martha: 'Yeah but like a portal hole or something. If every star is a rabbit, he could be counting.'

Tim: 'Or maybe that's where lots of rabbits have died since they got there and they dug a hole in the ground and put all their dead bodies down there. So that could be where all the dead rabbits are dead and buried.'

Eloise: 'There's a padlock or key or twig there, so maybe that keeps it shut so they can hide.'

Tim: 'Maybe they've stolen some of the kangaroo things and put them down there.'

Liam: 'I was thinking that was a puddle of water and they're looking at the reflection.'

Josh: 'It looks like a bucket.'

John: 'It could kind of like be digging to get water.'

Eloise: 'But you can't see his shadow in the water.'

In generating almost endless possibilities before turning the page, the children engage in sustained shared thinking, although they do not reach a shared understanding at this point in their conversation. However, as their teacher observed, a 'consensus of uncertainty' (Beckett, 2006) is created, which motivates their desire to read on and seek further illumination about the meanings and messages offered. Their shared discussion, undertaken independently of their teacher, allowed them to talk through ideas and engage in genuinely exploratory talk. Such talk involves children in using language to explore ideas and options, share information and give reasons for their views, constructively criticising other's ideas as possible insights are tested and agreement is sought. Mercer and Littleton (2007), drawing on considerable research, argue that the benefits of dialogic teaching include improvement in learning, in reasoning and in problem solving in groups and individually. However, in order to accrue these benefits the research indicates that children need support. Teachers need to model such exploratory talk, thinking and inter-thinking and need to help children see 'how' they talk in groups, setting ground rules for effective group work.

TEACHER TALK AND ORAL ARTISTRY

Despite the high profile given to interactive whole class teaching in recent years, research suggests that that there are still few opportunities in such contexts for children to question and explore ideas, and that the teacher-led recitation format (question–response–feedback) remains prevalent (Mroz *et al.*, 2000). In addition, it is clear that the pressure of pace, the desire to cover the curriculum and to raise standards, often prompts teachers to short change their pedagogical principles and understanding of the role of talk in learning (English *et al*, 2002; Burns and Myhill, 2004). Earlier work also suggests that teachers tend to dominate classroom interaction patterns and use mostly closed or factual questions in whole class contexts (Galton *et al.,* 1999).

However, teachers can modify their talk and many creative teachers actively seek to model a more speculative and hypothetical stance, employing a range of open-ended questions that raise the level of cognitive demand and facilitate children's analytical thinking. Such professionals try to use their voices and their imaginations to offer open invitations to learn and negotiate the curriculum content with young learners, whose own voices play a significant role in the learning process. They tend to place the learners above the curriculum and combine this with a positive disposition towards creativity, which actively encourages young people to learn and think for themselves (Beetlestone, 1998; Craft, 2000). Such teachers respond to children's feelings and interests, allow them considerable scope to work together, maintain their individual identities/ autonomy and foster their capacity to reflect critically (Jeffrey and Woods, 2003). The spoken word plays a highly significant role in such creative practice, in which teachers seek to allow children real thinking time, model tentativeness and show genuine interest in what the learners have to say.

If teachers develop their own creative potential and value the creative dimensions of their own lives, this can help them extend the children's development as oral language artists and creative language users (Prentice, 2000). The powerful art forms of drama and storytelling both support the oral artistry of the spoken word and involve teachers in working alongside children, spontaneously using language to generate ideas and express themselves. If teachers are to contribute imaginatively to the construction of confident and curious individuals, their ability to interest and inspire, tell stories and take up roles in drama, using words flexibly and creatively, deserves development. In addition, teachers need to be able to bring an author's voice to life evocatively and need to develop an ear for the colour, movement and drama of the language used by both professional writers and by the children themselves. Through inviting their participation and experiential engagement in the process of learning, teachers can help children hear, notice and experience language emotionally, aesthetically and artistically.

FOSTERING CURIOSITY AND AUTONOMY THROUGH GROUP WORK

When teachers and learners embark on a collaborative learning journey, which focuses on exploration and playful engagement, the role of curiosity and identifying genuine questions of interest or puzzlement come to the fore. Jeffrey and Craft (2004) describe this as an 'inclusive approach to pedagogy', one which involves posing questions, identifying problems and issues, and debating and discussing thinking together. Such questions are the building blocks of dialogic classrooms in which time is made for discussion and collaboration in whole class and small group contexts right across the curriculum (Alexander, 2004). But in order to foster children's curiosity and develop their questioning stance, teachers need to demonstrate their own curiosity and desire to learn (Cremin, 2009). They also need to show they are interested in and curious about the children, both as people and as learners. As children realise their questions make a difference, they begin to ask more, ponder longer and reflect upon other ways to achieve a task or represent their learning.

The questioning perspective of creative teachers demonstrates that the formulation of a problem is as important as the resolution of one; such professionals make extensive use of generative questions, creating further interest, enquiry, talking and thinking. Research into children's 'possibility thinking' (Craft, 2001) suggests that teachers who foster this 'what if' frameset make extensive use of large framing questions and employ an explicitly speculative stance in the classroom (Chappell *et al.*, 2008). Possibility thinking, which is seen to be at the heart of creative learning, is driven by curiosity, question posing and question responding (Burnard *et al.*, 2006; Cremin *et al.*, 2006a; Craft *et al.*, 2007). Teachers' open-ended questions tend to push children back on their own resources, encouraging knowledge sharing and increased autonomy. In explicitly encouraging children to identify and share their own questions about a text, for example through thought showers or pair work on what puzzles them, teachers foster children's curiosity and affirm their questions as valid and valuable, demonstrating interest in and respect for learners' ideas.

One teacher, employing a 'bookzip' strategy, suggested to a group of 5–6-year-olds that the book *Dinosaur Time* by Michael Foreman was zipped up tight and could not be opened, without that is, endangering the lives of the book fairies. The group, not able to read the book, examined the front and back covers and generated a number of questions. Their thoughts were rich and varied, reflecting both prior knowledge and connections, and offering their teacher an insight into their interests and imaginings before the book had even been opened. These included:

'Are there any dinosaurs in the water?'

'Why is his hair blue?'

'Did the person actually kiss the dinosaur?'

'Do you know what it is about?'

'Do you know the kids' name?'

'Do the monster and the boy make friends?'

'What do the bedrooms look like in the houses?'

'Do the leaves make noises . . . shish . . . in the book? That would make it scary.'

'What's in the sea?'

'Are there any flaps in the book?'

'Have you seen the pictures?'

'Where does the story happen?'

'Have you read it before?'

'Does the boy really have blue hair in the story?'

In addition to fostering their curiosity about stories, creative teachers encourage children to undertake collaborative research and other activities that enable them to pursue their own enquiries. This can foster the learners' sense of autonomy and responsibility, and may involve framing challenges in which, as the DfES (2003: 9) recommend, there is 'no clear cut solution and in which pupils can exert individual and group ownership'. Creative teachers, when invited to respond to children's problems during collaborative work, frequently employ reverse questioning, passing back the responsibility for resolving difficulties to the learners, enquiring for example 'How could you deal with this problem do you think? What ideas have you got?' (Cremin *et al.*, 2006a). This particular micro-strategy appears to nudge children back on their own resources, encouraging both knowledge sharing and problem solving. Despite children's willingness to engage in small group activities, they need encouragement and support in order to work effectively together, using language to generate ideas, solve problems, reason and construct knowledge (Mercer and Littleton, 2007). Relevant support strategies for effective group work include:

■ *Ground rules*: Create a poster with ground rules for working in groups. Highlight particular elements in different group tasks.
■ *Roles for group members*: Groups decide on roles such as leader, reporter and scribe, and review these during the extended activity.

- *ARQ*: Teach the Aim, Review, Question technique to help the groups monitor their progress and keep on task. Any member of the group or the teacher can play the ARQ card if they feel uncertain of where the group is heading or want to recap work so far.
- *Setting targets*: Groups decide what goals they are setting themselves and a timescale to work towards.
- *Review time*: Build in time to review the work itself, to consider how the group is operating, and for the group to set targets.

FOSTERING IMAGINATIVE ENGAGEMENT: STORYTELLING

All children have stories to tell: family stories, reminiscences, hopes, warnings, explanations, jokes, televisual tales and tales read, heard and created. Humans use narrative as a way of making sense of the complexity of existence, for narrative is a major means of thinking, communicating and constructing meaning; 'a primary act of mind' (Hardy, 1977). The creative social process of telling tales offers pleasure and satisfaction and fosters the creative sculpting of language at the very moment of utterance. Words and phrases, intonation and feeling, gesture and eye contact, pace and humour are all employed. This traditional oral art form can be woven into literacy teaching as a valuable medium to foster creative language use. Oral storytelling builds on children's narrative competence, fosters their imaginative engagement in learning and enriches their oral confidence and competence. As the children's writer David Almond (2001) observed:

> The roots of story are internalised through the circle of reading, writing, telling and listening.

Yet, too often, storytelling is viewed only as an early years practice and the potential of the art form remains undeveloped in school. In orally retelling tales, teachers and children can develop their verbal artistry and extend their creativity capacity that they may find more difficult to demonstrate or develop in writing.

Personal oral stories deserve a central role in the curriculum. As children retell chosen anecdotes and incidents from their lives, they are involved as active agents, making spontaneous choices about vocabulary, style and language while leaning on the natural writing frame of lived experience. The work of Rosen (1988) and Zipes (1995), among others, has shown the significance of autobiography and of individual, as well as collective, memory in the formation of identity. Through affording space for children to share their personal stories in different curriculum contexts, as well as in literacy time, teachers demonstrate their respect for individuals, and offer the chance for learners to make connections, reflect upon their lives, and enhance their narrative capacity and spoken fluency. Children can create timelines or emotions graphs of significant events in their own lives, for example, and use these to prompt oral recounts, which may later be recorded as diary entries or autobiographical extracts. Additionally, they can make personal story boxes, using shoe boxes and adding items from their homes that convey something of themselves, their families and interests. Such storyboxes can prompt personal storytelling.

Traditional tales also deserve a prominent role in a creative approach to literacy teaching. Originally moulded for the ear, those with a strong oral orientation still retain considerable repetition, rhythm and sometimes rhyme, which make them easier for children to recall. If teachers tell, as well as read, traditional tales and enable children to become storytellers, then over time the young learners will tacitly learn to use the oral patterns and strong narrative structures of such narratives, as well as rich and memorable story language. The process of preparing to tell a tale to others is not a memory test however, but an opportunity to share the soul of the story, leaning on the narrative structure and enticing listeners to imagine and respond. Over time the creative experience of oral storytelling and re-voicing known tales can have a marked impact on children's literacy learning and their creative capacity to transform texts (Fox, 1993a,b; Grugeon and Gardner, 2000) and can make a rich contribution to their narrative writing (Barrs and Cork, 2001; Grainger *et al.*, 2005). As well as listening to their teacher tell tales, reading traditional tales trapped in books can enrich children's repertoires and the structures and language upon which they draw. Leaning on powerful storytellers in this genre, such as Kevin Crossley Holland, Mary Medlicott and Fiona French, can help, as can purchasing rich anthologies such as *South, North, East, West* edited by Michael Rosen or *Breaking the Spell* edited by Sally Grindley.

Oral storytellers are language artists, who, whether they are telling personal or traditional tales, make full use of their voice and other visual and/or musical strategies to share their tale. Tellers choose how to share the essence of the story, using skills to assist their telling, which suit the tenor and temperature of the tale. Through retelling tales, children experience the fluency, flow and feel of their words, and can try out their own and others' tunes and receive a response. Through experimenting with using pause, pace and intonation, as well as gesture and facial expressions for example, children can develop their ability to use language and paralinguistic features to create effects and experience the role of the audience in reshaping the tale (Grainger, 1997). In retelling tales, teachers and younger learners release their potential to play with sounds and words, hear their own tunes and refine their skills.

Support for remembering story structures

In preparing for a storytelling festival or story sharing event with another class at the end of an extended learning journey, various strategies can be used to enrich children's memory of the structure and events in their chosen story, including:

- *The three seeds of story*: These indicate the beginning, middle and end of the tale. Pictures are drawn on three paper seeds of different sizes to deconstruct a tale (or plan a new one), and are then watered in the retelling by the storyteller's words.
- *Story mountains*: These paper mountains reflect the trajectories of stories and are particularly useful for climactic stories. Symbols, pictures or words that represent key events in the tale are drawn on different parts of the mountain range.
- *Skeletal summaries*: These are keyword summaries that are listed on the body of a drawing of a skeleton. Significant phrases from the story can also be included to aid recall (see Figure 2.1: 'Story skeleton').

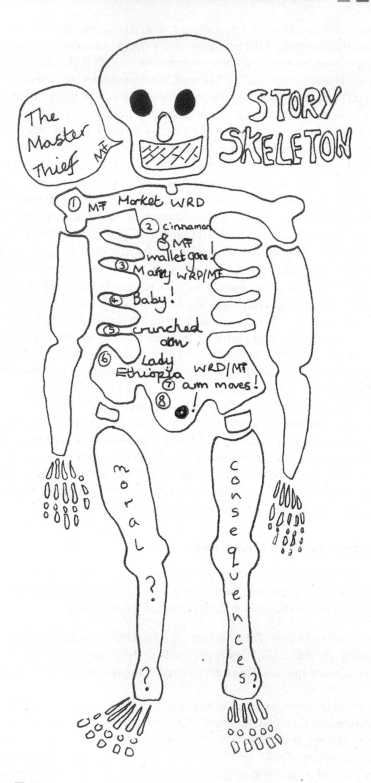

■ **Figure 2.1** A 'story skeleton'

■ **Figure 2.2** A story plate of 'The Tailor's Button'

■ *Story plates*: Paper plates, once drawn upon, can reflect the key elements of a tale. The children's drawings may be drawn as structural prompts anywhere or may be placed clockwise around the plate (see Figure 2.2: 'The Tailor's Button').

■ *Emotions graphs*: These focus on the characters and involve the learners in recording in map or graph form, a character's journey though the narrative. The vertical axis represents the emotions of the character from low to high and the horizontal graph represents the timeline of the tale. They are particularly helpful for retelling the story from a character's perspective.

There are also a range of organisational strategies, in which children retell their tale or part of it to others. These help to embed the narrative in the mind and foster fluency and confidence, including:

■ *Storytelling pairs*: In A and B pairs, tellers retell their tale to their listening partner, taking turns and focusing on improving their telling.

■ *Whole class story circle*: As a class, perhaps using a story icon, retell the tale, avoiding taking turns around the circle, but encouraging children to step forward spontaneously.

■ *Rainbow regroup*: When a group has worked to predict the ending to a partly told tale, each member is given a colour and new groups are formed, in which each child retells their own group's ending to the others.

■ *Story conferences*: These are opportunities for children to retell a tale or part of one in preparation for a story event to a small group of listeners who offer support and feedback to the teller. The comments from one group of 7-year-olds indicate the value of this evaluative activity.

> 'You were great at gestures, each time the king came in I knew it was him 'cos of the crown thing you did.'

> 'I couldn't hear it all, you could make the wizard shout that might help – he's meant to be angry.'

> 'When you described the butterfly that was good but you keep saying "and then and then" and that makes it boring!'

> 'Your eyes told the whole story – they make it real and brilliant.'

> 'I liked it when you made the king fierce, it was kind of scary.'

In addition, it is worth paying attention to traditional story beginnings, which can be collected, displayed and imitated as a resource for explicit and implicit use and for children to innovate with when telling or writing traditional tales. The examples in Figure 2.3 are drawn from a class of 8–10-year-olds who had engaged in a six-week learning literary journey focused on storytelling. The influence of the oral in the written is evident and effectively invites the reader in, capturing their interest and indicating a sense of fluency and creative flow.

The benefits that accrue from inviting children to engage creatively as oral language artists and integrating oral storytelling into the curriculum include the following: an increase in children's motivation and pleasure, oral fluency and confidence, and an enlarged awareness of audience, as well as a wider vocabulary and knowledge and use of different literary conventions and story structures. Combining their experience of oral storytelling and their knowledge of stories, children can experiment with parody, as a group of 10-year-olds creatively did in producing their own broadsheet *The Daily Crime*. (See Figure 2.4 for the front cover spread.)

REFLECTING UPON TALK

Children benefit from recognising their own oral creativity, their capacity to play with words and ideas and imagine other worlds and places. If they become aware that they are much more creative in their talk than they realise, they can begin to appreciate their artistic capacity, and the value in generating as well as evaluating their talk. They need opportunities to verbalise what they know and what they have learnt, and to share their discoveries with each other, evaluating themselves and each other in positive,

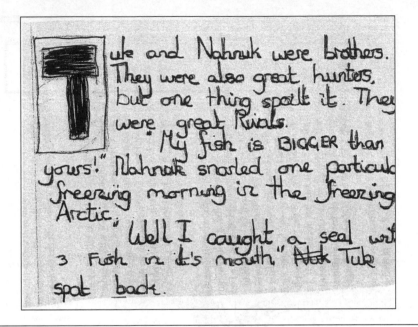

■ **Figure 2.3** Two different story beginnings

constructive ways. As Corden (2000: 178) observes, a crucial element of successful group work is 'the development of children's metadiscoursal awareness: that is their understanding of group interaction and their ability to monitor, control and reflect on their use of language'. To achieve this, teachers may need to raise the profile of talk for learning in the children's eyes, and find supportive ways to help them to reflect critically upon their own and others' oral contributions in a range of contexts. These might include:

- *Talk detective work*: Individuals take it turns to be a Talk Detective and listen to a group at work, making notes and commenting on their interaction afterwards.
- *Report back*: Individuals take it in turns to create a summary of their group's work and then review this with their group to see if they represented the discussion fairly.
- *Group talk on tape*: Groups listen to short taped extracts of their work and comment on their own and each others' contributions.
- *Characteristics of good talkers and listeners*: Children identify individuals who are skilled as both talkers and listeners and create classroom posters for reference and review.

Figure 2.4 Front cover of *The Daily Crime*, a group newspaper

In seeking to widen children's understanding of how talk is used in society, teachers may make use of different technologies in the classroom, using drama to recreate and review such language use. For example, watching a children's show such as *Art Attack* or *Blue Peter* can enable the class to focus on and discuss the presenters' skills during a demonstration about how to make a particular craft item, which could then be recreated as an oral procedural text in drama and the role of talk reviewed in this context. Alternatively, a documentary debating the presence of UFOs or climate change could be watched, considered as an oral text and recreated around another topic and then reviewed in groups. Talk within the Houses of Parliament, radio programmes, chat shows, reality shows, adverts and a wealth of other oral texts can also be used in the classroom, to offer real world relevance and help children reflect upon how people use language for different purposes, in different situations and social groups.

In addition, teachers will wish to assess children's growing confidence and competence as talkers and listeners, and gather information from a range of contexts, which can be summarised to make judgements about the progress of each child. Focusing on a couple of children each week to ensure systematic coverage of the whole class, and building opportunities for assessing talk across the curriculum, can help as teachers identify and review targets with and for children.

CONCLUSION

The oral artistry of the spoken word is important to recognise and develop in the classroom; it can enrich children's confidence and competence as effective language users and creative thinkers who talk and listen and employ their imaginations to find ways forward in collaboration with others. As language artists in the primary classroom, creative teachers stretch their own voices and seek to model the capacity to question, generate and evaluate ideas, as well as play with words. Such professionals, alert to children's creative and poetic language use, build on the youngsters' playful oral potential by providing opportunities to develop their curiosity and imagination in collaborative group work, and in storytelling and drama. They also profile learning through talk and encourage children.

FURTHER READING

Carter, R. (2004) *Language and Creativity: The Art of Common Talk*, London: Routledge.

Marsh, J. (ed.) (2005) *Popular Culture, New Media and Digital Literacy in Early Childhood*, London: RoutledgeFalmer.

Maybin, J. and Swann, J. (eds) (2006) *The Art of English: Everyday Creativity*, Basingstoke: Palgrave Macmillan.

Mercer, N. and Littleton, K. (2007) *Dialogue and the Development of Children's Thinking: A Sociocultural Approach*, London: Routledge.

CHILDREN'S BOOKS

Foreman, M. (2002) *Dinosaur Time*, Walker.

Grindley, S. (1997) (ed.) *Breaking the Spell*, Kingfisher.

Rosen, M. (1995) *South, North, East, West*, Walker.

Tan, S. (2002) *The Rabbits*, Ragged Bear.

CHAPTER 3

DEVELOPING DRAMA CREATIVELY

INTRODUCTION

Drama, the art form of social encounters, offers children the chance to engage creatively in fictional world making play. Such play, whether in the role-play area or in classroom drama, involves making and shaping worlds, investigating issues within them and returning to the real world with more understanding and insight. While drama is associated with speaking and listening, it can also make a contribution to children's reading and writing as it offers rich opportunities for their purposeful use. By the end of the Early Years Foundation Stage (DCSF, 2008a), it is expected that children should be able to 'use language to imagine and recreate roles and experiences'. Within the PNS framework (DfES, 2006a), children are expected to:

■ use dramatic techniques, including work in role to explore ideas and texts;
■ create, share and evaluate ideas and understanding through drama.

(PNS, Strand 4)

The key features of creative literacy practice are evident in drama: it fosters play, collaborative engagement and reflection, is often based on a powerful text and harnesses children's curiosity and agency. It also enables them to lead their own class explorations accompanied by the Teacher in Role (TIR).

PRINCIPLES

Drama is imaginatively and intellectually demanding, a highly motivating tool for learning. It encompasses a very wide selection of practices, ranging from free play on the playground to more formal theatre trips (see Figure 3.1). Most of the activities noted, such as improvising with puppets and performances in assemblies, trigger children's imaginative involvement and involve an act of pretence. However, the most valuable form of drama at this phase is improvisational classroom drama. This involves

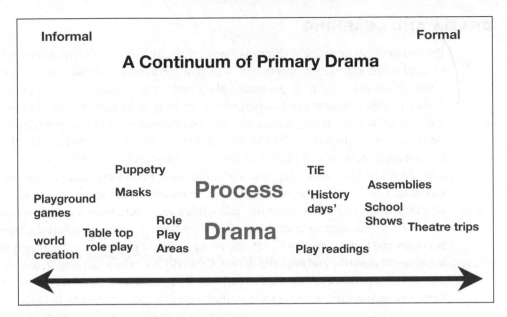

Figure 3.1 The primary drama continuum

children in exploring issues in role and improvising alongside their TIR, building a work in the process. It is commonly referred to as process drama (O'Neill, 1995), story drama (Booth, 1994) and/or classroom drama (Grainger and Cremin, 2001). Language is an important component of this symbolic and dramatic play, in which, through the use of TIR and other drama conventions, alternative ideas and perspectives are voiced. Classroom drama can help children dig down into the substrata of texts, increase their involvement and insight, and enhance their related written work, often undertaken in role.

The PNS (DfES, 2006a) objectives mirror the artistic processes of 'making, sharing and appraising' and encourage improvisational work, although several of the drama objectives interpret the 'sharing' component as 'performing', arguably giving an undue emphasis to the theatre end of the drama continuum and perpetuating a limited and limiting notion of drama as 'acting'. As the original NC stated:

> Good drama is about discovering the unknown, rather than acting out what has already been decided.
>
> NC (DfEE, 1989: 81)

This is not to suggest that acting a tale of *Goldilocks and the Three Bears*, for example, is inappropriate, but that investigating the consequences of Goldilocks' behaviour, through a court scene perhaps, or meeting her as a young adult in full-time employment demands different skills. Improvisational drama challenges children to imaginatively make, share and respond to each others' ideas, collaboratively co-authoring new narratives linked to the old. It makes use of structures and drama conventions, but significantly also encompasses considerable spontaneity and playfulness.

DRAMA AND LEARNING

Rooted in social interaction, drama is a powerful way to help children relate positively to each other, experience negotiation, and gain confidence and self-esteem as well as confront ethical principles, personal values and moral codes of conduct (Winston, 1998). Drama also offers rich opportunities for imaginative development through the creation of a questioning stance and the exploration of different possibilities and perspectives (Cremin *et al.*, 2006b). In each drama, children will be learning about the chosen content, the life of Mary Seacole or the evacuees in World War II for example, and should be able to develop, use and refine their knowledge and understanding of this area. Children are not just drawn to the content or plot, however, but also to the dramatic forms and conventions that allow them to explore meaning and express their ideas. They can learn to select, shape and transform these conventions for their own purposes and become more adept at discussing them, employing an increasingly critical language to describe and evaluate drama. Crucially too, since learning in drama arises out of the experience alongside the children's personal and social reflection upon it, drama enhances their reflective and evaluative capacities and ability to make connections. The key areas of learning in drama include: the imagination, personal and social issues, literacy, reflection, the content of the drama, and the form itself.

IMPROVISATIONAL CLASSROOM DRAMA

Creative teachers often use drama in literacy time as part of shared reading or as preparation for shared and independent writing. They also offer children extended drama sessions; longer dramatic explorations based on literature and linked to a cross curricular focus. Drama makes use of a range of conventions (see Figure 3.2), which can be combined and adapted to suit the dramatic exploration. Teachers take part in role in classroom drama and also need to develop the widest possible repertoire of other drama conventions, also employing metaphors and symbols, objects or icons as signifiers.

In classroom drama, no script is in evidence, although literature is often used to support, and shared fictitious worlds are created through the imaginations of both the children and their teacher (Taylor and Warner, 2006). Such drama focuses on the process of meaning making, has no immediate audience and is spontaneous, unpredictable and emergent. It frequently creates motivating contexts in which reading, writing and speaking, and listening are natural responses to the various social difficulties and dilemmas encountered. It also invites children to exchange ideas, experiment with alternative perspectives and raises questions rather than answers them. Significantly, it leaves room for ambiguity and challenges young learners to cope with open-ended scenarios and live with uncertainty (Grainger, 2003c).

When literature is used to trigger classroom drama, fictional moments need to be carefully chosen to ensure they involve a degree of tension, ambiguity or misunderstanding. Many such moments will be present in the text, others can be evoked through examining unmentioned conversations, nightmares, premonitions, a character's conflicting thoughts on a particular issue, and/or earlier or later problematic events that

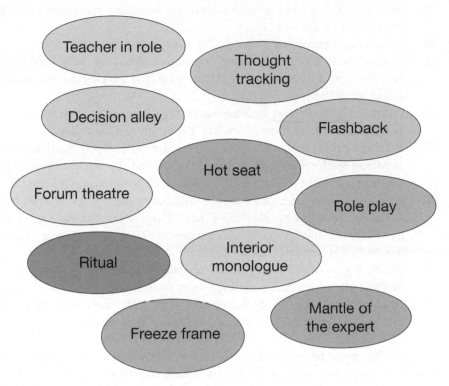

■ **Figure 3.2** Drama conventions

connect to the present situation. Fiction is packed with unresolved conflicts to choose from and non-fiction also contains contested issues to construct, investigate and examine. When selecting potentially rich moments it is important to consider:

- ■ What tense moments in the text would help reveal more about the theme, the characters, their motivation and relationships?
- ■ What possible scenarios might occur as a consequence of, or as a precursor to, the current difficulty that could usefully be brought to life?
- ■ What drama conventions could be employed at these moments to open up the text?
- ■ How much of the text needs to be revisited/read aloud immediately prior to the drama to contextualise the action?

For example, in planning a drama around the picture book *Giant* by Juliet and Charles Snape, in the context of a unit of work on the environment, teachers could select a number of moments within the tale to explore using different drama conventions. In this tale the Mountain Giant realises that the humans take her for granted and the combined effects of pollution and erosion wear away her desire to remain on the earth. Teachers could read the story aloud, stopping intermittently along the way to examine the issues though drama. The moments of dramatic exploration could include:

- examining the front cover with the title removed and generating possibilities in pairs based on the visuals;
- discussing these and making connections to other texts and tales;
- reading the beginning and in small groups creating sound collages and visual representations of the Mountain Giant when she realises that the humans have not cared for her;
- creating a decision alley as Giant walks into the ocean to leave and considers her options. Should she leave or has Lia, the young girl, persuaded her to stay?
- examining this further through half the class representing the humans and half in role as her forebears, the giants of the sea and sky, each seeking to persuade Giant to join them. What are their arguments? How persuasive can they be?
- at the end of the tale, small groups could create improvisations of one of the following or their own idea: a TV news items about the disappearance of the Mountain; the myth about how Giant and her relatives first came to dwell upon the earth; the consequences for the community ten years after the event;
- generating possible written communications about the incident, these might include: plans for a documentary, a letter from Lia to Giant found by her grand-children years later, the myth, the auto cues of the news item, or a newspaper article (see Figure 3.3 for 10-year-old Mark's example).

A wide range of picture fiction texts can be used to support drama in this way with teachers reading some of the texts and then stopping to open up the tale for the children to inhabit in role. Often the text will be left behind as a new narrative based around the children's interests emerges, built upon the shoulders of the old. Quality examples of such texts include *Quetta* and *The Watertower* by Gary Crew, *The Snow Dragon* by Vivian French, *Death in a Nut* by Eric Maddern, *Nobody Rides the Unicorn* by Adrian Mitchell, *The Wolves in the Walls* by Neil Gaiman, and *My Uncle is a Hunkle says Clarice Bean* by Lauren Child. Creative teachers will find their own favourites that offer a degree of tension and ambiguity, interest and challenge.

TEACHER IN ROLE

The most significant convention in classroom drama is Teacher in Role (TIR). This does not involve teachers in acting, but involves them in imagining themselves to be someone else, taking on this role and participating with the children from this perspective. It requires teachers to model the commitment and belief involved, adopting various roles in the drama. In extended classroom drama in particular, when teachers assume roles they unite the class and engage them in collaborative world making play. TIR is central to successful classroom drama, for as Bolton observes, 'seeing the teacher as a fellow artist in a shared endeavour is the key to relationships in the drama classroom' (1998: 76). Through TIR, teachers help shape and direct the imagined experience, negotiating this with the learners and supporting, extending and challenging their thinking from inside the fictional context. Positioned within the fictional context, the TIR influences and shapes the dramatic enquiry, and maintains control, in part by helping the children consider the consequences of their actions.

EVENING HERALD

'Mountain village' Debate the future

Following the recent spectacular disappearance of the mountain 'Giant', members of Littertown on the Ouse, have been holding urgent meetings to debate their future. Villagers are devastated that 'Giant' has left, wrenching up trees and plants and part of the river bed. A rare breed of badgers is also missing, presumably they fled as the Giant demolished their sets. Old Mr hogwart, who lived on the edge of

the mountain, is now forced to take lodgings in a nearby town. The council are seeking permanent accomodation for him somewhere safe and peaceful.

All the village are worried and frantic to know whether the Giant will come back. if she doesn't their grazing land will be gone forever with there orchards and their crop. "What have we done to deserve this?" exclaimed Mr Derby, a local councillor. Others felt that it was their fault, and said "we made it happen - we polluted her with insecticides and litter -

WE MUST CHANGE our ways on pay the price

J. Snape

■ **Figure 3.3** A newspaper article

Within the motivating world of drama, however, children often monitor their own behaviour, reflecting the commitment and involvement that their TIR demonstrates. TIR is key to developing the educational potential of drama. Rather than always adopting high-status roles, teachers can experiment with a variety of equal and/or low-status roles, which create new opportunities. They can take up oppositional roles, roles of those who have been affected by the children's actions, roles as messengers, shadows and storytellers. The spontaneous improvisational nature of these roles can create productive tensions that need to be resolved. When not in role, teachers can offer children opportunities to reflect upon and evaluate the drama, discussing the emerging situation and making connections. This pattern of oscillating between full involvement in role, and then separation from the role – as decisions are discussed and options considered and reflected upon – is typical of classroom drama. It deepens children's commitment and involvement, and extends their learning about the issues being explored. In this way, the TIR fosters the interrelated modes of children's creative thinking: enabling the 'imaginative–generative' mode, which involves process and outcomes, and the 'critical-evaluative' mode, which involves consideration of originality and value (NACCCE, 1999). Teachers also take significant roles in role-play areas, as described later in this chapter.

DRAMA AND SPEAKING AND LISTENING

Since extended classroom drama is oriented towards investigating problems and opening up issues, talk is an essential part of its currency. Drama creates imaginative and motivating contexts, which are often experienced as real and which provoke a variety of oral responses. In the context of improvising a decision alley or planning, discussing and evaluating a freeze-frame, for example, children spontaneously talk and listen to one another's ideas and often need to negotiate and make decisions together. So a number of forms of talk are used as well as gestures, facial expressions and movements to convey meaning. Learners adapt their speech for different purposes and audiences, using language styles and registers appropriate to both their role and the imaginary scenario. The opportunity to reflect upon these language choices can contribute to a growing command over the spoken word. Feelings, intuitions and a playful imagination come to the fore in drama, enabling both purposeful and creative language to be generated and a wider than usual range of vocabulary. The emotional engagement that drama triggers also influences the children's spoken contributions, which may be freer than in more conventional or formal classroom contexts.

Different drama conventions create different demands and prompt particular kinds of talk. For example, a class of 8–9-year-olds investigating *The Minpins* by Roald Dahl might be involved in the following activities:

■ Creating interior monologues and the desperate thoughts of young Billy, who, trapped indoors, dreams of adventuring into the forest – *using reflective introspective talk*.

■ Role-playing the conversation between Billy and his mother – *using persuasive talk* (see below for an example, created by Sam and Kaz, aged 9). This could also be improvised with TIR as Billy and the class as mum:

> Mum please can I go out, it's so hot in here – please?
>
> Then take your jumper off and I'll open the window a little.
>
> But I want to go out, I'm bored.
>
> Then read a book and before you ask – no you can't go on your playstation.
>
> Oh mum, the forest looks so exciting – I wouldn't go far, honest.
>
> I told you before it's not safe.
>
> Why, what's in there? What are you afraid of?

I'm not afraid, but we don't know who'll be out there and I've told you before about strangers.

In school Simon said 'Strangers don't come out 'til after dark'.

What rubbish that boy talks. Woods are not safe places.

I promise I won't talk to any strangers.

You are not going and that's that. And if you carry on arguing with me young man you'll be grounded.

Oh mum you're *so* unfair.

■ Whispering into Billy's ear in role as the devil – *using descriptive talk* to tempt and interest him in the Forest of Sin (see Figure 3.4 for an example of a note from the devil).

■ Voicing Billy's thoughts in role in a decision alley as he approaches the door and has to decide whether to slip out against his mother's wishes – *using discursive reflective inner talk*.

■ Creating a freeze-frame of Billy encountering someone or something in the Forest of Sin – *using generative talk* to share ideas and then negotiating to decide on one, and discussing as a group how best to convey this.

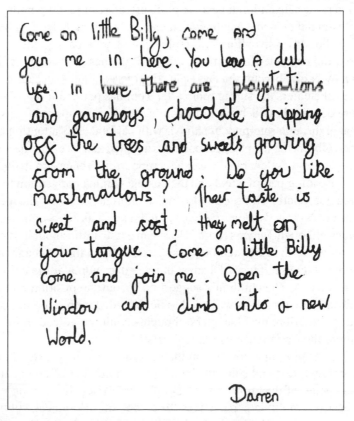

Come on little Billy, come and join me in here. You lead a dull life, in here there are playstations and gameboys, chocolate dripping off the trees and sweets growing from the ground. Do you like marshmallows? Their taste is sweet and soft, they melt on your tongue. Come on little Billy come and join me. Open the window and climb into a new world.

Darren

■ **Figure 3.4** Writing in role

These ideas merely relate to the first few pages of the text, before Billy meets the Minpins themselves. It is clear a wealth of opportunities for talk are available, some of which may lead to writing. If extended drama is developed based on this introduction, then the class might decide on the creature/person Billy met and explore the consequences of this with their TIR. Oral improvisational work can also be based on non–fiction texts; for example, children could create their own persuasive adverts to be filmed and reviewed, make news broadcasts about real world events, past or present, and improvise documentaries about cross curricular issues, with scientists, world experts and local people's views being sought. In each context the type of talk used will be different.

DRAMA AND READING

Drama offers a valuable context for enriching inference and deduction; it prompts textual interrogation and 'speaks the silence of stories' (Hendy and Toon, 2001: 76). In drama, an 'aesthetic' reading of the text is created, in which the focus is on the insights and satisfaction gained from the textual encounter (Rosenblatt, 1978). During drama children employ a number of strategies that are also central to reading, including: prediction, image construction, making imaginative connections, co-authoring the text, developing empathy and engaging emotionally and reflectively (Grainger, 1998). Drama can help children become more effective at reading both text and subtext, and can extend their understanding of characters' motives, behaviour and possible histories.

If drama conventions are employed in shared reading, then more may be revealed about the characters, narrative events and themes. For example, in *The Time it Took Tom* by Nick Sharratt, the class can – in role as mum – speak out loud simultaneously when she enters the sitting room after Tom has painted it red. This will help generate more details about her reaction. Tom's views and response to his mum could also be created through role-play in pairs or with half the class adopting one role and half the other. Observing the physical positions adopted and freezing the action to add the inner thoughts of these characters can also support inference and deduction.

Reading part of a text and then using a drama convention to explore the implied character relationships can also aid comprehension. In the beginning of Valerie Flournoy's *The Patchwork Quilt*, grandma is making a quilt for her granddaughter Tanya, although Tanya's Mum is less than enthusiastic about it. If only the early visuals are shown to the class, they will have to lean upon the language of the text in order to build a single sculpture of Tanya, mum and grandma at the point when mum arrives with cookies. The children's suggestions about the positioning of the characters and their facial expressions will need to be defended with reference to the silent sculpted text. In addition, the characters' thoughts could be voiced in interior monologues to explore their relationships in more detail.

In exploring a non-fiction theme, drama can help extend children's reading of the context, text and subtext. For example, a number of contrasting images could be constructed of the rainforest through freeze-frames. In creating these as photographs taken from multiple perspectives for a book on the subject, subtitles and paragraphs could be added to highlight the diverse positions and standpoints held. This will draw upon the children's understanding of the issues and motivate their comprehension of each other's representations.

DRAMA AND WRITING

Drama provides meaningful contexts for writing, both individual and collaborative. In-role work can lead to emotive writing from different stances and perspectives, and can make a real contribution to children's development as writers (McNaughton, 1997; Grainger *et al.*, 2005). Through orally rehearsing and refining ideas for writing and sharing these with one another, children can enrich their written work, adding both passion and pace to their prose. Both qualitative (Crumpler and Schneider, 2002) and quantitative studies (Fleming *et al.*, 2004) demonstrate that if drama is used in literacy sessions and in extended units of literacy work, it can make a significant contribution to children's writing. In the former, the focus will be on using drama to help generate and sculpt a particular genre of writing; in the latter, the drama not the writing will take precedence and teachers will 'seize the moment to write' in response to the imagined context (Cremin *et al.*, 2006b). Both approaches are valuable and are explored further in the following sections.

Combining drama and writing in literacy time: a genre-specific approach

When drama is used as a prompt in shared writing, to support the writing of a specific genre for example, then thoughtful bridges need to be built between the actual drama conventions used and the form of writing desired. While several conventions may be used to percolate ideas and involve children, the final convention employed needs to link closely to the chosen genre. In this way the last improvised scenario acts as a kind of dress rehearsal for writing and an oral writing frame. This has been described as a 'genre specific' approach to combining drama and writing (Cremin *et al.*, 2006a). Suggested links between different drama conventions and different genre are noted in Figure 3.5.

For example, in Jacqueline Wilson's *Cliffhanger*, young Tim makes it clear he does not wish to go an adventure holiday. His father, however, is determined that he should go to strengthen his physique and character, while his mum is worried for her beloved son. A family row ensues. If this is initially improvised in threes, the class can then engage in thinking out loud in role as Tim, pondering his options, his parents' views and his own fears. In this way the children will be prepared to undertake diary writing in reflective mode, since the convention interior monologue, is in oral form close to the first person narrative writing found in diary recounts.

In non-fiction shared writing, if the class are exploring the genre of instructional texts for example, children can lean upon TV programmes such as *Blue Peter* or *Art Attack* and work in role as presenting teams, demonstrating how to make cheese nachos or Christmas crackers. Watching programmes to observe the oral genre in action can help children analyse the structure and purpose of such presentations and highlight options. Their eventual improvisations can be watched and evaluated for ease of

Recount	Storytelling in role TV interview recounting an event
Diary	Thought tracking/interior monologue Telephone conversation
Report	Freeze-frame Hot-seating
Poetry	Group sculpture on theme Ritual
Instructions	Group improvisation Freeze-frames of process
Story structure	Freeze-frame significant events as a storyboard Improvised flashback/flash-forward
Explanation	Documentary improvisation by a scientist/ historian, etc.
Dialogues	Role-play Interviews
Notes/minutes	Hot-seating in role Formal meetings
Persuasive/discursive	Decision alley Formal meetings
Advertisement	Group improvisation – spontaneous or planned Freeze-frames brought to life
Play script	Role-play in pairs for conversation Small group play-making

■ **Figure 3.5** Making connections between drama and specific genres of writing

communication and interest. Alternatively, the TIR could demonstrate an instructional text in the style of one of the TV presenters, while the class make notes and write up the instructions for the programme's website. This operates as a formative assessment activity, since it helps to identify what the class know about the structure, organisation and language features of procedural texts. For more examples of drama and fiction/non-fiction writing links see Chapters 6 and 7 and Grainger (2001a,b; 2003a,b; Grainger and Pickard, 2004).

Combining extended drama and writing: a seize the moment ' approach

When classroom or process drama is integrated into an extended unit of work in literacy and in cross curricular contexts, it can energise the children's imaginative engagement and help to sustain their sense of focus and interest. It can also operate as a supportive scaffold for writing and help young writers develop what they want to say, find their position and perspective, and prepare them to commit this to paper or screen. In process drama, which in essence involves the creation of shared fictitious worlds, literature is often used as a catalyst or trigger and a range of drama conventions are employed to explore the ideas, issues and themes in the narrative. While a lesson plan with learning intentions will exist, process drama prompts teachers to respond to the interests of the children and venture into the unknown. In its openness to possibility and the generation of new worlds, classroom/process drama is a highly creative medium, through which children build belief and deepen their involvement in the fictional world frame as they try on various roles and perspectives.

When teachers engage as artists alongside children and engage emotionally in the tense scenarios being investigated, they learn to trust themselves and the children and recognise opportunities to seize the moment and write. In employing a 'seize the moment' approach to drama and writing (Cremin *et al.*, 2006b), teachers need to remain open to possibilities as the drama unfolds, living with the uncertainty of what might happen next in the fictional world and encouraging children to suggest moments in which purposeful writing might be undertaken. In involving children in the often conflict-driven, open-ended contexts that are typical of such extended classroom drama, teachers offer children considerable choice in terms of perspective, purpose and form in writing; this fosters their commitment and concentration, and frequently results in high-quality writing (ibid.).

Improvisational classroom drama has the potential to contribute markedly to composition and effect in writing and helps children create writing that captures the reader's interest and attention. It is critical, however, that time is taken to journey and that the drama is foregrounded, not any particular form of writing. This will ensure that at a moment of dramatic tension, when the emotional engagement of all involved is assured and the perspectives of many have been examined, the teacher can 'seize the moment' to write. At such moments, children's writing seems to flow from the imagined context with relative ease and is frequently full of 'stance and scenario' (Bruner, 1984: 98), reflecting their engagement in the issues and showing considerable attention to detail.

FOSTERING IMAGINATIVE ENGAGEMENT IN ROLE-PLAY AREAS

The imaginary contexts of role-play areas enable children to converse, create and draw on their experience, knowledge and understanding of the world to make meaning. In order to develop children's agency and ownership of learning, creative teachers negotiate possible options for role-play areas with them. Role-play areas are frequently established in early years classrooms, but inventive teachers of older learners also make good use of them, creating police stations, Egyptian archaeological digs and Victorian workhouses for example, offering children opportunities to use their knowledge and understanding in other areas of the curriculum (Cremin *et al.*, 2009a).

Role-play areas tend to mirror real world settings, such as doctors' surgeries, cafés and garden centres, but over time children also need to be challenged by a range of more imaginary open-ended contexts, including fictional book-based contexts and more generic open-ended themes. In addition, connecting to popular cultural themes

■ **Figure 3.6** An invitation to Percy

such as creating Bob the Builder's yard can be motivating and effective. In these contexts children can be prompted to become engaged as speakers, listeners, readers and writers. See Figure 3.7 for an example of a piece of writing that emerged spontaneously from a greenhouse role-play area based on the *Percy the Park Keeper* books by Nick Butterworth. Child initiated, this invitation to Percy from the fox drew on Callum's knowledge of the stories and provoked an interesting dilemma for Percy. Later the same day, when this had been discussed, the class engaged in improvisational classroom drama and held fox's party, which Percy and many animals attended. In exploring connections between role-play areas and fictional texts, as well as role-play and extended classroom drama, children expand their understanding of different settings, make inter-textual links and use literacy and language purposefully in imaginary contexts. It is therefore useful for teachers to read related tales so they can be revisited, re-enacted and recreated imaginatively, and for teachers to provide related literacy resources. For example, if the area is a desert island, texts such as under-sea maps, diagrams of shipwrecks, fiction and non-fiction books, a captain's log, a ship to shore radio, bottles for messages and sand can all help. Planning involves considering the place, the people, the predicaments and literacy opportunities with the children. See Figure 3.7 for planning both a café and a forest role-play area and Cremin *et al.* (2009a) for more ideas.

Physically co-creating the area helps to build interest and involvement, as does visiting a vet's surgery or estate agents, for example, prior to constructing one. However, while planning how to create the area and collecting resources is important,

A CAFÉ

■ PLACE and resources

Tables and chairs and stools, cloths and
napkins

Cutlery, cruet sets, menu holders, a till

Kitchen area, stove, cooking materials

■ PEOPLE, living/working and visiting

Waitresses and waiters

Chefs and managers

Cleaners and customers

Health/food inspectors and delivery
people

Plumbers and electricians

Telephone engineers and vermin control
personnel

■ PREDICAMENTS and TIR options

Chef is sick but children's themed
birthday party is due to begin

Health inspector finds mouse droppings

Electricity officer visits – imminent power
cut

Complaining customers

Phone call announces celebrity arriving

Menus not arrived in time for the grand
opening

■ READING/WRITING opportunities

Menus, notepads for food orders

Receipts, cheques, letter-headed paper,
money, computer

Telephone and notepad

Miss Wobble the Waitress (Alan Ahlberg)

This is the Bear and the Bad Little Girl
(Sarah Hayes)

Cookery books and party texts

Promotional materials for today's
specials

Adverts/ posters for the café

A FOREST

■ PLACE and resources

Crepe paper hangings, tree trunks for
sitting on

Branches, twigs and leaves, paper
campfire

■ PEOPLE, living/working and visiting

Tourists and walkers

Birdwatchers and wildlife specialists

Children on school outing and families
camping

Fictional characters: Three Bears and
Goldilocks, Hansel and Gretel, The
Animals from Farthing Wood, Harry
Potter characters

Forestry management workers

Arboretum inspectors, local farmers, fire
brigade

■ PREDICAMENTS and TIR options

Campfire gets out of hand

Walker lost, mobile broken

Trapdoor found in tree

Countryside commissioner visits

Forestry worker has accident

Poacher seen stealing eggs

Gate left open and cows stray

Someone stranded up a tree

■ READING/WRITING opportunities

Countryside code posters

Maps with walks

Secret message found in tree

Notices on gates

Book on flora and fauna of forests

Arboretum guide about trees

Camper's diary

Forestry worker's report

■ **Figure 3.7** Planning for role-play areas

considering the people who might live, work or visit the area and the difficulties they might encounter, is much more important. Without a real sense of possible characters and their problems, the children's socio-dramatic play will lack imaginative involvement. Planning possible people and their predicaments also offers multiple TIR options. The TIR, TAs or children from older classes can offer valuable models of the various scenarios generated and can engage in using reading and writing in the process. While direct imitation of these problem solving contexts is not sought, such modelling, can, like involvement of the TIR, extend and challenge children's play in the area.

In these small worlds, children lean on the support of the environment and are challenged by their TIR as they use language to imagine and create roles and experiences. Although allowing children to initiate their socio-dramatic play is important, and over-zealous TIR interventions are to be avoided, the presence of an adult can enhance role-play. The teacher, teaching assistant (TA) or parent helper needs to observe carefully and select an appropriate moment to play alongside the children, modelling and demonstrating their own engagement and challenging the learning (Cook, 2002). In addition to adopting high-status roles, such as the king of a castle or the manager of MacDonald's for example, teachers and TAs can adopt equal or low-status roles to create new opportunities for learning. They can also develop the literate potential of the area through the TIR, requesting advice and a map of the ocean for example, when visiting an undersea cave as a mermaid from foreign seas. The TIR can also offer new knowledge to support children in their role-play, such as warning tales of sharks and sightings of humans investigating a shipwreck. The spontaneous improvisational qualities of TIR work can create productive tensions and challenge children to resolve these problems through their play.

As with all creative learning, reflection and feedback are essential; children need to be given the chance to share the imaginary scenarios and difficulties they encounter and their responses. Sometimes guided and challenged by their TIR, they will be improvising and imagining as a small group in the area and benefit from sharing the resultant narratives with the class. This can help develop their pleasure in role-play and enrich the ideas and possibilities on which other groups can draw.

CONCLUSION

The multimodal art form of drama, which draws on the 'dramatic literacies' (Nicholson, 2000) of facial expression, body language, intonation, gesture, mime, movement and space, has the potential to create motivating contexts for powerful literacy learning. Creative literacy teachers plan opportunities to link drama and literacy and let each enrich the other; they also work flexibly, responding to children's interests and letting them lead as they imagine unknown territory together and learn from living in another space and time. Both in literacy time and in extended classroom drama sessions right across the curriculum, drama offers purposeful contexts for reading, writing, speaking and listening. It is an essential pedagogic tool in a creative teacher's repertoire.

FURTHER READING

Cremin, T., Goouch, K., Blakemore, L., Goff, E. and Macdonald, R. (2006b) Connecting Drama and Writing: Seizing the Moment to Write, *Research in Drama in Education*, 11(3): 273–91.

Grainger, T. (2003c) Exploring the Unknown: Ambiguity, Interaction and Meaning Making in Classroom Drama, in E. Bearne, H. Dombey and T. Grainger (eds), *Classroom Interactions in Literacy*, Maidenhead: Open University Press, pp. 105–14.

Nicholson, H. (2000) Dramatic Literacies and Difference, in E. Bearne and V. Watson (eds), *Where Texts and Children Meet*, London: Routledge.

Taylor, P. and Warner, C.D. (2006) *Structure and Spontaneity: The Process Drama of Cecily O'Neil*, Stoke-on-Trent: Trentham.

CHILDREN'S BOOKS

Ahlberg, A. (1981) *Miss Wobble the Waitress*, Puffin.

Butterworth, N. (2001) *Percy the Park Keeper Collection*, Ted Smart.

Child, L. (2000) *My Uncle is a Hunkle*, Orchard.

Crew, G. (1994) *The Watertower*, Era.

Crew, G. (2002) *Quetta*, Era.

Dahl, R. and Benson, P. (1993) *The Minpins*, Puffin.

Flournoy, V. (1991) *Patchwork Quilt*, Walker.

French, V. and Fisher, C. (2000) *The Snow Dragon*, Walker.

Gaiman, N. and Mckean, D. (2003) *The Wolves in the Walls*, Bloomsbury.

Garland, C. (1994) *Clive and the Missing Finger*, Black.

Hayes, S. and Craig, H. (1993) *This is the Bear and the Bad Little Girl*, Walker.

Maddern, E. and Hess, P. (2007) *Death in a Nut*, Frances Lincoln.

Mitchell, A. (1999) *Nobody Rides the Unicorn*, Doubleday.

Sharratt, N. (2000) *The Time It Took Tom*, Scholastic.

Snape, J. and C. (1999) *Giant*, Walker.

Wilson, J. (1995) *Cliffhanger*, Corgi.

CHAPTER 4

DEVELOPING READERS CREATIVELY – THE EARLY YEARS

INTRODUCTION

Teaching children to read is neither a trivial matter nor just a technical task. It is probably the most momentous achievement of the early school years, so primary professionals should approach it thoughtfully and creatively. This chapter focuses on teaching reading creatively to 4–7-year-olds and looks at how teachers can support the questioning stance of young learners, helping them to apply this to lifting the words off the page and making sense of what they read. It also reflects on teachers as readers, on enriching children's responses to reading and encouraging their independence.

The strands of reading within the revised PNS framework (DfES, 2006a) most relevant to fostering the creative development of young readers, on page and on screen, include:

Understanding and interpreting texts
■   Retrieve, select and describe information, events or ideas.
■   Deduce, infer and interpret information, events or ideas.
■   Explain and comment on writers' use of language, including vocabulary, grammatical and literary features.

(PNS, Strand 7)

Engaging with and responding to texts
■   Read independently for purpose, pleasure and learning.
■   Respond imaginatively, using different strategies to engage with texts.
■   Evaluate writers' purposes and viewpoints, and the overall effect of the text on the reader.

(PNS, Strand 8)

In relation to these strands, the PNS framework states, that by the end of the first three crucial years of schooling, children aged seven will be expected to make sense of what they read and be able to:

- draw together ideas and information from across a whole text;
- give some reasons why things happen or characters change;
- explain organisational features of texts;
- use syntax and context to build their store of vocabulary when reading for meaning;
- explore how particular words are used.

(PNS, Strand 7, Year 2)

It also states that children will be expected to:

- read whole books on their own, choosing and justifying selections;
- engage with books through exploring and enacting interpretations;
- explain their reactions to texts, commenting on important aspects.

(PNS, Strand 8, Year 2)

PRINCIPLES

Children have to learn how to make the black marks speak – out loud at first, and later in their heads. However, English, with its complex spelling, makes this much more difficult than it is in other languages, such as Italian or Finnish that are fortunate in having more regular spelling systems. So if children are to persist, teachers need to make reading and learning to read both pleasurable and creatively engaging. Unfortunately, England's primary schools are less successful at building positive attitudes to reading than those in most other comparable countries (Twist *et al.*, 2007), and this has an impact on children's decoding proficiency and their readiness to make the most of the written word. If teachers are to help children understand themselves and the world around them in complex ways, then reading must be made a creatively engaging activity for them – one that they will choose to do outside school as well as inside it.

Becoming familiar with the language of written texts is an essential part of this early learning, for written language is very different from spoken language. It tends to be more tightly constructed both at the level of the sentence and over large stretches of text. This is true for texts ranging from shopping lists to novels, and is certainly true of texts written for young children. Extensive written texts also tend to use a wider range of vocabulary. So if they are to become effective and enthusiastic readers, children need to become familiar with the language of books, to experience making sense of the world through this language, and to take pleasure in its power. Learning to read in English is hard and children need to taste its fruits and experience its rewards if they are to invest the necessary energy, commitment and focused attention that learning to read requires:

> Learning to read is fundamentally a task of learning how to orchestrate knowledge in a skillful manner.

(Bussis *et al.*, 1985: 113)

To achieve this orchestration requires both creative teaching and creative learning. But it is certainly not a matter that anything goes: all teaching acts should be shaped by principles arising from knowledge and understanding about how children learn most richly. In reading, these include the following:

■ *Learning to read, write and talk are interdependent*
As the PNS planning documentation states, the twelve Literacy strands 'feed into each other and support well-rounded development' (DfES, 2006b: 1). So teachers need both to plan specific activities that encompass reading, writing and talk, and also work to make the school day a ceaseless interplay of language in all its modes.

■ *Reading is an active, creative process from the earliest stages*
In order to make sense of the text in front of them, children need to make creative use of both their knowledge of letters and spelling patterns, and also their knowledge of other texts and the wider world. Making imaginative links to their own experiences and engaging as active constructors of meaning is important from the earliest stages.

■ *A rich experience of stories and poems has a central role to play*
While it is essential that children learn how to read non-fiction texts, it must be acknowledged that poetry and stories have a particular power. Through literature we can experience other ways of looking at the world and savour the heightened use of language. Through reading poetry children can take pleasure in the patterns and rhythms and the evocative power of memorable language. In re-reading their favourites, they gain practice in decoding words and making deeper meanings from them. Narrative enables us all to shape and give meaning to experience, and can inspire and excite, giving children a powerful incentive to read and offering deep satisfaction. Such experience is essential if children are to persist and engage in the large quantity of text that is necessary if they are to become effective readers.

■ *The experience of hearing stories has particular importance*
For decades it has been established that listening to stories enriches children's literacy learning in powerful ways (Bussis *et al.*, 1995 provides a survey of this research). Creative teachers read aloud frequently, offering children a rich experience of narrative and providing common points of reference.

■ *The texts that children experience out of school are significant*
Print pervades children's out-of-school lives. Most learn early to 'read' signs such as McDonalds and the labels on the coffee jar and their favourite sweets, as well as comic titles and their own names. Teachers need to find out more about children's preferences and their experiences of the techno-literacy practices of their homes and communities, to work to build on these in school (Marsh, 2004), and to introduce children to other texts that extend their grasp of the world.

■ *Assessment of children's experience, strengths, needs and interests is central*
Numerous research projects show that successful early teaching of reading always takes account of individual learners' literacy skills and experiences (Pressley *et al.*, 2001; Taylor and Pearson, 2002).

These principles connect to the conception of creative practice permeating through this book. Their implications are explored in the following sections. Adopting a creative approach to early reading involves a variety of classroom experiences, including the teaching of both letter–sound relationships and comprehension. It is also concerned to foster children's imaginative engagement in meaning making.

Teaching phonics creatively

There may be a temptation to view teaching phonics as the antithesis of creative teaching, as an exhaustive and exhausting drilling in phonic rules. But phonics can be conceived of and taught as a creative enterprise. Such teaching needs to be set in the context of a rich and rewarding experience of written text. Given the vagaries of English spelling, children need a commitment to the language and meanings of written text if they are to make phonics work for them. The most effective teaching places it in the context of making meaning from text (Medwell *et al.*, 1998). Books such as *Tanka Tanka Skunk* by Steve Webb, *Wriggle Piggy Toes* by John Agard, or *Baby Bird* by Joyce Dunbar, as well as many by Dr Seuss and others, can make this learning fun-filled. Such enticing and highly patterned books enable children to participate in playing with the sounds of words as they read and make meaning.

Treating children as active learners makes the process more enjoyable for both teachers and children. So while phonics teaching needs structure, it is also necessary to appeal to children's inventiveness and make use of their interest in language play. Useful guiding structures are provided by *Letters and Sounds* (DfES, 2007a), which sets out a sequence for teaching the correspondences between spoken and written English that operate at the level of the phoneme. It also includes activities for teachers and teaching assistants to use to implement this teaching. However, a number of these are fairly rule-bound, with little appeal to children's inventiveness, and need to be supplemented with activities of a more engaging and open-ended nature. Collaboratively constructed class alphabet books or friezes for example, can give children a greater sense of possession of their own learning than commercial ones. This is especially true if children's own interests and experiences, their 'funds of knowledge' (Moll *et al.*, 1992) are drawn upon in the creation of the book or frieze. Additionally, playing with magnetic letters can involve children in inventing nonsense words and their meanings, the most interesting of which can be displayed on the classroom wall.

Rhyme and analogy have a key role to play in learning to read English spelling. It is not infallible, but rhyme is often a better guide to a word's pronunciation than synthetic phonics on its own, often providing a more direct route to decoding than sounding and blending each phoneme. So drawing an analogy with a familiar word such as 'ball' is more helpful to a child trying to work out an unknown word such as 'fall', than sounding it out letter by letter. Children in Reception need experience of playing with language through rhyme and alliteration (Bradley and Bryant, 1983) and instruction in onset and rime (Goswami, 1999). Songs, rhymes and tongue twisters can all develop children's phonological awareness and are extensively used by creative teachers who seek to adopt a playful approach to language, highlighting pattern, sound and rhythm. In addition to introducing children to memorable examples of language play in books such *Chicky Chicky Chook Chook* by Cathy MacLennan, and playground rhymes and chants, teachers can help children construct their own and play their own phonic games. This could include 'silly registers', where the teacher adds a rhyming epithet to children's names, or creating alternative variations to 'Two Little Dicky Birds' and other rhymes.

Many children have reliable phonic knowledge but do not always put it to use in reading. They need extensive demonstrations of how this is done and opportunities to do it themselves in supported situations. Perhaps the most creative aspect of teaching phonics involves teachers in seizing unexpected opportunities to draw children's attention to letters, words and sounds, as they seek to make learning to read a positive and engaging experience. In this way they help children see how identifying the words enables you to take pleasure in them and to make sense of what it is they mean.

Reading and learning

Outside school, young children like to read jokes, magazines, comics, fiction, TV books and magazines, signs, poetry and websites (Clark and Foster, 2005) Many children show a preference for multimodal screen texts (Nestlé Family Monitor, 2003). Bearne *et al.* (2007) shows children as young as five demonstrating sophisticated expertise in on-screen reading, influenced in many cases by experience gained at home, through friends and family. Extensive use of DVDs and videos also appears to contribute to children's early awareness of screen conventions (Bearne *et al.*, 2007). So classrooms need to be hospitable to a wide range of texts, reflecting the range available in twenty-first century digital homes. The texts teachers choose for inclusion should all have something interesting to say and be capable of opening new doors as well as making connections between home and school. Encouraging children and parents to add to the class collection can make the classroom a lively meeting place for the children's different out-of-school experiences.

However, stories and poems in books still have a potent role to play in teaching children to read: nothing else offers such a rich experience of language, such an infectious demonstration of its powers. Reading stories and poems aloud in an inclusive and involving way makes this language available to children and is an essential daily practice throughout primary school. Creative practitioners draw extensively from literature, and invite children to engage in other worlds and imagine other possibilities through sharing a wealth of powerful narratives and poetry with them.

Some children come to school having experienced over a thousand story-readings, many of which will have been tuned to their particular interests and experiences by people who mean a lot to them. As well as enlarging their sense of the world and how people live in it, this daily encounter with the language of written text widens their vocabularies, extends their command of sentence structures and gives them a sense of the shapes of stories and poems (Purcell-Gates, 1988). So these children approach the business of learning to read with a strong sense of the rewards it can yield and also a familiarity with books and the language of stories. They know the kinds of things books say and the sort of language through which they are said. Put this together with phonic knowledge and they can move forward with assurance.

However, others may have their first experience of books in school. So teachers need both to value the experience of print with which children are familiar, the environmental print, words on household labels, TV guides and DVD covers for example, and also initiate them quickly into the pleasure of hearing stories and poems read aloud. Many effective teachers choose to start with inviting wordless texts that involve high drama and encourage the reader to turn the page. When such 'reading' is established, teachers will want to read reverberative texts that speak to the children and bear considerable rereading, ensuring that the experience of listening is an active one. But such reading aloud needs to be fully interactive. Through joining in, speculating on what might happen next and checking to see if this is the case, children can identify with the characters and situations, and make connections to their own lives in the process. This is possible well before the start of primary school, as the following example demonstrates:

It is towards the end of the summer term in a nursery class where only one child has been read to at home before school. But since the start of the school year the three and four year olds have been involved in active exploration of picture books through a daily 'story-time'. They have learned to predict what will happen on the next page and to check carefully to see whether they are right. Today Lee is wriggling, as his teacher, Nicky, is reading a carefully chosen text for the first time – Leo Lionni's *Fish is Fish*, a story of friendship between a minnow and a tadpole. Lee is successfully re-engaged as Nicky comments:

'Fancy that, Lee, fancy waking up in the morning to find you'd grown two little legs in the night!' A few pages later, the minnow, having leapt out of the water in imitation of his friend, lies stranded on the bank.

'He began to die' reads Nicky.

'But the frog might push him back!' shouts out Lee. Instead of asking him not to call out, Nicky responds

'D'you think he might? Let's find out and see.'

This sort of approach to reading has a value that endures throughout the primary school. The texts will change, but the teacher's open invitation to the children to join with her (or him) and the author in constructing meaning from them should ensure that reading is a truly creative activity, both when children are engaged in shared reading and when they are reading independently. Part of the significance of a story is always that it might have been otherwise. In Pat Hutchins' *Rosie's Walk*, for example, each time Rosie the hen sets off on her odyssey around the farm, her life is at risk, as she is unknowingly being followed by a fox. The enduring pleasure of the text lies in the tension between the possible, as presented in the pictures, and the actual, as presented in the verbal text. Texts such as this and the work of picture fiction creators such as John Prater, Colin McNaughton, Jeanne Willis, Lauren Child, and Philippe Dupasquier, offer considerable imaginative scope. Novels too offer similar pleasurable tensions and rich possibilities for readers to imagine, create visuals in the mind's eye, ask questions and engage affectively.

Shared reading of Big Books, whether in paper or electronic format, gives an unrivalled opportunity for children to combine their growing knowledge of the language of books and how stories work with their developing skill in word identification, and to make meaning together. 'Home made' posters of poems provide similar opportunities. Books with a simple repetitive text, such as *We're Going on Bear Hunt* by Michael Rosen, *Mrs Wishy Washy* by Joy Cowley, and Quentin Blake's *All Join In*, bear repeated rereading. And even in Reception, children can be helped to identify key words such as 'mud' with the aid of their phonic knowledge, as well as some of the more common 'tricky words' such as 'the' and 'to'. The aim should be to ensure that reading the text is not a laborious exercise in word identification, but a quest for pleasurable meaning in which word identification contributes to the process, rather than distracting from it.

TALK AND CREATIVE ENGAGEMENT

Children need to establish connections between their own experience and the texts they encounter in school. Life to text and text to life connections enhance the significance of both. 'Is your bedroom like that?' asked a Nursery teacher as she showed the children the forest growing in Max's bedroom in Maurice Sendak's *Where the Wild Things Are*. Leaving space for children to think, connect and voice their thoughts is a crucial element of creative practice. Teachers' questions and comments can guide children to identify their own connections, but in addition the voicing of children's own questions and puzzlements needs to be actively encouraged.

Moving around in an imaginary world can greatly enhance children's pleasure in text. If the role-play area is turned into the Three Bears' kitchen, the 'Zoopermarket' from Nick Sharratt's book or a magical castle, children can get right inside the story. More informally, hats or masks for outdoor play may help young learners re-enact the week's key book. Props of all kinds, as well as puppets and storybags, can also support retellings, and in improvised classroom drama children can explore gaps in the story, and deepen their understanding of the particular text and their larger awareness of the possibility of texts in general. Powerful texts provide rich spaces for all forms of improvisation. For more ideas on developing children's creativity in role-play areas and through drama see Chapter 3.

But perhaps the most important talk happens as teachers read and explore powerful stories with children. The meanings of written texts can only be fully realised through active engagement, through connections with first-hand experience, identification with the characters, wonder at their circumstances or moral judgement about their actions. Making story-time the site of such open explorations is a rich and thoroughly enjoyable way of initiating children into reading for significant meaning.

By engaging in this process together children can support one another and so learn more than they could on their own (Vygotsky, 1978; Mercer and Littleton, 2007). To do this, children need to listen to and build on each other's contributions. This means that teachers need to take a less dominant role in the process than they usually do. They need to listen to a ... children's comments and questions, creating an atmosphere in which all obs... are welcome, provided they enrich the process of making sense of the text... s can repeat or expand a pertinent observation in a way that invites other c... ᴵs. 'What does anyone else think?' asked his teacher, when Charlie, aged ... preted one of the early pages in *Farmer Duck* by Martin Waddell as indicating a flood. This prompted close examination of the picture and consideration of the story so far, in an interchange in which three other children made overt contributions, leading another to make an apt prediction.

Teachers have privileged access to printed text, but it can be highly productive to relinquish an all-knowing role, handing it over to the children to decide whether a particular prediction was right, and encouraging them to use the evidence of both words and pictures. Once the children have a purchase on phonics, it can even be useful for teachers to make carefully chosen errors in their Big Book reading, provided they are confident that a child will correct them. When a Reception teacher read, 'No, said his mum', Freddy, in outraged tones, corrected her saying 'Look, it's got a "the" in it, so it says "mother", not "mum".' The teacher acknowledged her error and reminded herself out loud how important it is to look at all the letters.

Teachers as readers

Teachers' attitudes to reading and their knowledge about children's literature and other texts can markedly influence their capacity to teach reading creatively, their ability to engage learners in extended units of work based on texts and their ability to foster independent reading for pleasure. Unfortunately, many primary professionals feel less than confident in this area and tend to rely on the books they enjoyed as children (Cremin *et al.*, 2008a,b). In a survey of 1,200 teachers, the UKLA found there was evidence that teachers relied on a narrow canon of children's authors, and in particular had very limited repertoires of poetry and picture fiction (ibid.).

In relation to picture books, when asked to name six picture fiction creators, only 10 per cent of the teachers could do so, while a worrying 38 per cent named only two or one. Remarkably, 24 per cent named none at all (Cremin *et al.*, 2008b). The highest number of mentions by far was for Quentin Blake (423) while four others were mentioned over a hundred times: Anthony Browne (175), Shirley Hughes (123), Mick Inkpen (121) and Allan Ahlberg (146). Some of these picture book makers were also named in the 'authors' list. There were also 302 specifically named books whose authors were seemingly not known or could not be recalled while the teachers were completing the questionnaire. These included, for example, multiple mentions of various Martin Waddell and Jez Alborough titles. But without knowing the authors, teachers cannot seek out more of their books, or recommend the writer or illustrator to children.

So many teachers are not in a position to encourage children to branch out and taste the powerful texts produced by a wide range of authors, nor to teach as creatively as they could with the invaluable support of contemporary writers and illustrators. To widen their repertoires, teachers can use a number of strategies, including regularly visiting the local library with the class, working with librarians and other teachers to share texts, reading Saturday review sections in newspapers and browsing in book-shops. There are also a number of excellent printed guides and websites to help teachers extend their knowledge of good books for children. These include:

- *Simply the Best! 0 to 7* (CLPE, 2002) – a book giving a brief sketch of every title included.
- *Books for Keeps* (www.booksforkeeps.co.uk) – a magazine, packed with book reviews and recommendations, published six times a year.
- Booktrust (www.booktrusted.co.uk/books) – a free access website that constantly updates their recommendations.
- Write Away (www.writeaway.org.uk) – a free access website with information on a wide range of new books.
- Seven Stories – the centre for children's books in Newcastle-upon-Tyne, which has a good recommendations area on its website (www.sevenstories.org.uk).

Most teachers do some reading for pleasure. To extend their knowledge of children's literature it can be useful and enjoyable when reading at home to alternate adult fiction with books written for children. This may rekindle some of the pleasures of childhood reading and will certainly help teachers to share new books more effectively with their children, to tempt them into new texts and guide their choices. It is also certain to make the process of exploring literature in class more varied and enjoyable for all concerned.

This argument is supported by research evidence. In a careful and wide-ranging survey, Medwell *et al.* (1998) found that knowledge of children's literature was one of the key features distinguishing the most effective literacy teachers from their less effective colleagues.

RESPONDING TO READING

Learning to read, as already outlined, is about learning to orchestrate knowledge on a number of different levels, from word to sentence, to whole text. It is a complex process, but in the most successful classrooms, children encounter engaging texts and learn how to put their technical knowledge to use in making sense of them (Medwell *et al.*, 1998; Frater, 2000). Reading in these classrooms always involves response, both the reader's response to the words and the teacher's response to the reader's attempt to make sense of them. To develop active engaged readers who approach reading with enthusiasm, carry it out effectively and relate what they read to what they have learned elsewhere, both kinds of response are crucial.

So whenever teachers model reading they need to model a response to the text, whether it is 'That sounds tasty!' to the dinner menu, or 'I'm not sure I would wish for that!' to one of the desires expressed by *The Fish that Could Wish* by John Bush and Korky Paul. Whenever children read to teachers, their responses should be invited. Sometimes predictions may be appropriate, sometimes it may make more sense to ask for genuine clarification, as I did to my 7-year-old daughter: 'I don't understand.

Is Robin Hood outside the castle trying to get in, or inside trying to get out?' Frequently it will be important to make connections with the children's own experience, 'Have you played a game like that?' Teachers voicing their own responses can elicit responses from children and prompt questions that are central to learner creative engagement in the activity of making meaning.

There is a danger that responding to text orally is not perceived as a legitimate literacy activity because it does not look like work. But it serves three essential purposes. Through refocusing the reading on meaning, it promotes comprehension in all its complexity. Through helping children make personal sense of texts, it makes reading more enjoyable and fosters the positive attitudes that children in England lack. Through encouraging reflection on such matters as moral issues and the writer's skill, it enables children to become more discerning readers, meeting many of the requirements of Strand 8 in the Framework (DfES, 2006a). So responding to text is a central part of learning to read, not an optional extra.

Formative assessment of children's reading requires a rather different kind of response. Effective teaching is always informed by continuous assessment of how the children are doing, against identified learning goals and targets. This involves watching what they do and talking with them. Many teachers use notebooks with pull-out grids of the relevant strands, to make brief, concrete, dated observations about each child's reading. These might include comments on a spelling pattern the child is finding problematic or surprisingly easy, the child's need to slow down and look at words more carefully, or to speed up and focus more on meaning. Effective teachers also note how a child copes with complex sentence structures, their readiness to read for pleasure, their persistence in doing so and their newly acquired interest in a particular author. The richer teachers' conceptions of reading are, the more creative their responses are likely to be to individual children.

Such day-to-day observations help teachers decide when to wait, when to intervene and what to point a child towards. This knowledge is useful in whole class, small group or one-to-one contexts. There is little point, for example, in sending a child off with the teaching assistant to play a game involving a spelling pattern that she has already mastered. It is helpful to go through the notebook systematically once a week or so.

Children need both to hear their teachers' reflections on their progress and to make their own. They need to be helped to appreciate and articulate their strengths and areas in need of attention. This can be formalised in jointly agreed target-setting that takes into account the importance of engaging with and responding to texts. An agreed response target might, for example, be 'find three books that I would want to read again and recommend these to others'. There should be a time when the child's progress towards this target is reviewed.

Assessing Pupils' Progress (APP) (DCSF, 2008b) is altogether a more formal business. This aims to help make teacher assessments thoroughly comprehensive, valid and reliable. It is an infrequent procedure, carried out by classroom teachers after training, in order to inform larger decisions about which aspects of reading need more emphasis for the whole class, particular groups or individuals. Based on assessment focuses from the National Curriculum, the APP process informs teachers about children's competences in many aspects of reading, but does not involve their attitudes or responses to reading. So these essential elements of the process need to be considered and recorded through more informal observation.

FOSTERING CHILDREN'S INDEPENDENCE AS READERS

In a sense, all of the activities mentioned above are about fostering independence. From the nursery on, however, children also need time when they read self-chosen books, individually or in twos or threes. At first they may just turn the pages, commenting on the pictures. As they become familiar with the language of books, they will start to 'talk their way through' them, drawing on their knowledge of how stories work. Children in all age groups can choose texts and read them for pleasure: it's not the time to urge a child to choose a 'harder' book. Rereading a much-loved text can have a number of positive effects.

While younger children cannot be expected to be silent, as they have to talk to think, teachers tend to aim for a quiet hum, and model the process by reading themselves, or use the time to work with an individual or group. Many teachers working with 6–7-year-olds introduce quiet reading with a daily 10 minute session, expanding this by degrees to 30 minutes across a year. Teachers also often include a short plenary, in which readers can share enjoyable incidents or pictures. Effective teachers of reading use word searches or maths puzzles as a filler activity for children who finish other tasks early, rather than reading, as this does nothing to encourage concentration.

Taking books home, some to be read by the child and some by the parent, helps strengthen connections between home and school and fosters independence. Here, again, choice matters. The more familiar teachers are with children's books, and the better they know the children, the more they will be able to guide their choices effectively, first of all by the selection of books available in the classroom, secondly by whole class 'taster' sessions of these books, and thirdly by individual recommenda- tions. A number of other activities can actively foster children's growing independence as readers, some of which are noted below.

- *Offer guidelines in making choices*: 'Look at the cover. Is this an author/illustrator you know? What do you think it might be about? Read the blurb on the back. Still interested? Read the first page and see if you want to turn over' can be useful advice. The books teachers read aloud, however, may have the biggest influence on children's choices.
- *Offer a diverse range of texts*: Create boxes with comics and magazines, joke and poetry collections and non-fiction books on subjects that interest the children. Offer these for quiet reading and to take home in addition to any other school reading books.
- *Involve children in book ordering*: It is important to involve the children in selecting new books, perhaps through voting for favourite authors, or examining websites and publishers' catalogues.
- *Create a class library/ book area*: Class libraries and book areas should be both orderly and highly appealing. Boxes are easier to rifle through than shelves.

Comfortable book areas, which the children help to plan and create, can make reading more inviting, as can book displays and comments encouraging children to try new authors and titles.

■ *Promote book ownership*: It is hardly surprising that possessing books is connected to reading proficiency. Developing a parent and child-friendly way of selling books increases the potential for commitment to reading. A school bookshop run by parents, with savings cards available and stock from a local bookshop on a sale or return basis, can help, publishers' book clubs can be successful too. For other possibilities, see Lockwood (2008).

■ *Join Reading is Fundamental (RIF)*: This charity enables children to choose up to three free books a year to take home and keep. Children choose from a wide range of texts, but to take part the school has to raise some funding. Go to www.literacytrust.org.uk/Rif/ to find out more.

■ *Connect to the local library*: Signing children up as members and taking them on visits can help, as can encouraging them to register on the library's Summer Reading Challenge and inviting the librarian to visit and share new titles.

■ *Organise a Book Swap Day*: Everyone, teachers and parents included, brings a book to exchange for a book ticket, the books are spread out in the hall and classes visit to choose different books. Class books swaps are also worthwhile.

■ *Organise a Book Week*: This needs to be planned well in advance, and preferably include the involvement of a children's author. But the benefits of a well organised Book Week are enormous in terms of raising the profile of reading.

■ *Shadow a children's book award*: Buying or borrowing the shortlist of the Kate Greenaway award or the UKLA book award for children's picture fiction, can help introduce new books and engage the children in the process of text selection.

CONCLUSION

Teaching young children to read can be a tiresome and frustrating business if a rigid phonics programme dominates and if reading instruction is not concerned with reader engagement. But if teachers treat it as a joint voyage of creative exploration, in and out of the spelling patterns of English as they travel through stories and poems, sharing inventions, wonder and laughter along the way, it can be a source of pleasure and satisfaction for teacher and taught. And the children are much more likely to become committed, engaged, imaginative and successful readers.

FURTHER READING

Bussis, A.M., Chittenden, E.A., Amarel, M. and Klausner, E. (1985) *Inquiry into Meaning: An Investigation of Learning to Read*, Hillsdale, NJ: Lawrence Erlbaum Associates.

Marsh, J. (2004) The Techno-Literacy Practices of Young Children, *Journal of Early Childhood Research*, 21(2): 51–6.

Taylor, B.M. and Pearson, P.D. (eds) (2002) *Teaching Reading: Effective Schools, Accomplished Teachers*, Mahwah, NJ: Lawrence Erlbaum Associates.

Woods, P. (2001) Creative Literacy, in A. Craft, B. Jeffrey and M. Liebling (eds), *Creativity in Education*, London: Continuum, pp. 62–79.

CHILDREN'S BOOKS

Agard, J. and Bent, J. (2008) *Wriggle Piggy Toes*, Frances Lincoln.

Blake, Q. (1998) *All Join In*, Red Fox.

Bush, J. and Paul, K. (1998) *The Fish that Could Wish*, Oxford.

Cowley, J. and Fuller, E. (1980) *Mrs Wishy-Washy*, Shortland.

Dunbar, J. and Ayto, R. (1998) *Baby Bird*, Walker.

Hutchins, P. (1970) *Rosie's Walk*, Puffin.

Lionni, L. (1974) *Fish is Fish*, Random House.

MacLennan, C. (2008) *Chicky Chicky Chook Chook*, Boxer.

Rosen, M. (1989) *We're Going on a Bear Hunt*, Walker .

Sendak, M. (1970) *Where the Wild Things Are*, Puffin.

Sharratt, N. (1995) *I went to the Zoopermarket*, Scholastic

Waddell, M. and Oxenbury, H. (1991) *Farmer Duck*, Walker.

Webb, S. (2003) *Tanka Tanka Skunk*, Random House.

CHAPTER 5

DEVELOPING READERS CREATIVELY – THE LATER YEARS

INTRODUCTION

Once children have learnt to read, the continuing challenge for teachers is to help them become engaged, enthusiastic and fluent readers who understand the pleasures and usefulness of reading, and who choose to read beyond the demands of the curriculum. Helping children develop into such readers requires more than simply giving children the opportunities to read longer and increasingly complex texts, although such experiences are important. This chapter focuses on teaching reading creatively to 7–11-year olds; the primary focus is on supporting deeper engagement with texts through creative approaches that build a reflective reading culture within the classroom, develop children's understanding of the texts they read and encourage personal responses, including critical readings. It also looks at how teachers can support children as they develop and expand their reading preferences and highlights the importance of teachers' own experiences and knowledge of children's books and reading.

The renewed PNS framework comments that: 'The revisions emphasise the importance of reading independently and reading for pleasure' (DfES, 2006a: 15). This suggests an acknowledgment of the importance of the reader developing personal preferences and responses to reading. In a creative classroom, as well as independent, private reading, these elements should be developed by experiencing reading as a social activity where readers share their responses and experiences within a community of readers. The strands of reading within the framework, most relevant to fostering the creative development of a fluent reader (on page and on screen), include:

Understanding and interpreting texts
■   Retrieve, select and describe information, events or ideas.
■   Deduce, infer and interpret information, events or ideas.
■   Explain and comment on writers' use of language, including vocabulary, grammatical and literary features.

(PNS, Strand 7)

Engaging with and responding to texts
- Read independently for purpose, pleasure and learning.
- Respond imaginatively, using different strategies to engage with texts.
- Evaluate writers' purposes and viewpoints, and the overall effect of the text on the reader.

(PNS, Strand 8)

PRINCIPLES

Creative teachers of reading who teach to promote children's engagement with and response to texts, and who seek to build reading fluency at this age use pedagogical practices underpinned by a number of principles. These include:

- valuing reading and reflection;
- knowing that understanding (comprehending) texts is critical to engagement, enjoyment and learning;
- providing potent and engaging texts;
- recognising the importance of talk around and in response to texts;
- building a reading culture within the classroom (including reading aloud to children);
- encouraging independent reading and personal choice (including texts from children's twenty-first century culture);
- offering clear modelling through their own reading experiences, responses and expertise;
- giving supportive feedback and suggestions for further development.

Various factors have been identified as important in teaching reading. Based on an extensive research review, Pressley (quoted in Harrison, 2002: 16) listed those factors he regarded as 'research proven' in the teaching of reading. Removing the use of decoding skills from his list as being largely used in the early reading stages, the list contains the following:

- encourage extensive reading;
- explicit work on sight vocabulary;
- teach the use of context cues and monitoring meaning;
- teach vocabulary;
- encourage readers to ask their own 'Why?' questions of a text;
- teach self-regulated comprehension strategies (for example, activating prior knowledge, visualisation, summarising);
- encourage reciprocal teaching (teacher modelling of strategies and scaffolding for independence);
- encourage transactional strategies (an approach based on readers exploring texts with their peers and their teacher).

The teaching approaches of reciprocal teaching and exploring texts with peers and teachers that Pressley (ibid.) identifies are central to the collaborative, reflective and supportive ethos found in creative and playful classrooms. However, the specific teaching strategies he mentions, such as teaching comprehension strategies and vocabulary, need to be embedded and contextualised in the extensive reading of exciting and affecting texts (see, for example, Lewis and Tregenza, 2007a,b). This is because becoming a fluent reader does not just mean getter quicker and more accurate at automatic word recognition and recognising an increasing number of words. While fluent reading – being 'the ability to read with comprehension, accuracy, speed and appropriate expression (prosody)' (Johns and Berglund, 2006: 3) – involves using cognitive skills, becoming an engaged and motivated fluent reader means much more than this.

Cambourne (1988, 1995) describes four essential elements of engagement. He suggests learners must:

- see themselves as potential 'doers', as must those around them;
- see the task as personally meaningful;
- perceive the learning as a low risk endeavour (that is, not be afraid of failure or ridicule);
- have the opportunity to bond with others.

Children who are not engaged and motivated to read do not benefit from reading teaching (Guthrie and Wigfield, 2000; Kamil, 2003). Becoming an engaged and motivated reader has social, emotional and cultural dimensions and involves the reader in seeing a purpose for reading. This is supported by children positioning themselves as a reader within a social, collaborative community with shared practices and expectations. It also involves readers in responding to the feeling and emotions in texts. Sensitive and creative teachers of reading seek to create a community of readers within their classrooms, providing a context in which children's diverse cultural capital and home literacies are acknowledged and creativity, speculation, experimentation, play, risk taking and reflection on reading are all encouraged.

READING AND LEARNING

Reading is central tool of learning and one that underpins learning across the curriculum. In order to learn from reading, readers must engage with the text they are reading in a way that ensures that what they read connects with and stays in their minds afterwards; that is, readers need to read actively, making links with what is already known and expanding or adjusting schema to include the new information (Rumelhart, 1980, 1985; Wray and Lewis, 1997). But readers come to texts with many different purposes – they may want to identify specific information, get a sense of what it was like to live in a particular time, entertain themselves, and so on. The purpose of the reading will influence what and how readers read. Rosenblatt (1985) distinguishes between two ways of reading a text, claiming that 'The difference between . . . kinds of reading lies . . . in what the reader does, where he or she turns his or her attention during the transaction with the text'. She identifies two different kinds of reading: efferent and aesthetic. In efferent reading, the reader's attention is centred on what should be retained after the reading, such as information to be acquired or a process to be followed. In aesthetic transactions, readers focus on what they are living through during the reading. They pay attention to the 'qualitative overtones of the ideas, images, situations and characters that they are evoking under the guidance of the text'.

Of course, either kind of response is possible to most texts depending on the stance the reader takes. Creative teachers of reading seek to maintain a balance between these two kinds of responses in literacy sessions and across the curriculum; for example, seeing the aesthetic potential within information texts, as well as using them for information gathering and textual analysis. (See Chapter 10 for further discussion of non-fiction texts.)

A study of World War II at KS2, for example, will involve reading information books on the topic, watching film materials, exploring written and visual artefacts such as ration cards and posters, and searching the Internet for relevant websites, which need multimodal literacies to read them. These reading events offer opportunities for efferent transactions and – in creative classrooms – aesthetic transactions. A ration card, for example, could be viewed as an information source, but it could also prompt discussion, drama and role-play about queuing for supplies, the desire for rare foodstuff and the struggle to feed a family. In planning to work creatively, teachers need to consider their purposes for examining texts as this will prompt different stances.

Learning about this period should also involve reading narrative, poetry and first person accounts. These offer rich opportunities for the reader to engage with the emotions, sights, sounds and smells experienced. Emotionally engaging stories about this period include, for example, the novels: *Goodnight Mr Tom* by Michele Magorian, *Johnnie's Blitz* by Bernard Ashley, *Tamar* by Mal Peet, *Once* by Morris Gleitzman and *Blitzcat* by Robert Westall and the picture fiction books: *War Boy* by Michael Foreman, *My War Diary* by Marcia Williams, *Luba: The Angel of Bergen-Belsen* as retold to Michelle McCann, *The Lion and the Unicorn* by Shirley Hughes *and Rose Blanche* by Christophe Gallaz and edited by Ian McEwan. Each of these offers powerful opportunities for readers to be involved in aesthetic transactions with the text. Creative teachers often offer a summary of several such texts and then negotiate with their class which of these or others might become the core book in an extended unit of work.

TALK AND PLAYFUL ENGAGEMENT

Talk is central to learning. It is the medium that allows learners to articulate and share their thoughts, feelings and ideas, and listen to those of others. Talking about and questioning a text enables children to share their understanding and puzzlements. Hearing the ideas of others may deepen their understanding and offer new insights since social inquiry promotes metacognition and reflection. Teachers who encourage conversation allow children 'to internalize cognitive strategies, construct meaning, feel ownership of the learning process, collaborate, communicate, gain empathy for other viewpoints, explore and expand their developing thinking, and engage in the curriculum' (Ketch, 2005: 11).

Through book discussion circles, book groups, book buzz sessions, book swaps, 'I love this book' slots, book judging panels, guided reading and so on, creative teachers of reading develop an ethos where talking about books is given high status and taken as the norm in the classroom. Talk may be the precursor to reading and may arise from it. Creative teachers encourage and support talk by asking open-ended, higher order questions and spend considerable time encouraging children to ask these too. Their questions and enquiries, their interests and confusions can lead to discussions around texts, supported by their teacher who will help the learners make connections both to their lives and to the text. The 'Tell me' approach advocated by Chambers (1993) and the use of literature circles (King, 2001) offer examples of how such discussions can be organised and guided. See Chapter 8 for more details.

Spending time on a powerful, affecting book can enhance the quality of the talk as discussion becomes more informed and complex over time. If this is picture fiction, it can be revisited and new insights discovered; highly potent examples include *The Wolves in the Walls* by Neil Gaiman and David Mckean, *Falling Angels* by Colin Thomson, *The Arrival* by Shaun Tan and *The Birdman* by Melvin Burgess and Ruth Brown. Spending time on whole texts also enables teachers to teach reading skills in context (see Grainger *et al.*, 2004a,b,c for practical ideas). The PNS (DfES, 2006a) has moved away from promoting the use of text extracts to endorsing extended units of work over several weeks and the class novel has seen a welcome revival. The following example shows how one creative teacher used her class novel, *King of the Cloud Forest* by Michael Morpurgo with a class of 10–11-year-olds over several weeks to encourage aesthetic responses and talk and teach comprehension skills in context. The result was a high level of motivation, understanding and engagement.

The text was chosen as it was a rich story full of action, emotion and dilemmas. It offered plenty of opportunities for discussion, drama, encouraging personal and critical responses, and building understanding through creative activities to develop empathy, inference and deduction. The text also linked to the theme of mountains being studied in other parts of the curriculum, enabling children to make links in their learning and to any personal experiences. The children were used to working on a class novel over a period of weeks with some class readings, where the teacher read aloud, some independent reading and some reading in a guided reading context. The children kept reading journals, in which they recorded brief chapter notes or drawings, comments and questions (see Chapter 8 for more details).

Modelled by the teacher, the class were developing an ethos of discussion and were listening supportively to the ideas of others during extensive talk around the books read. The children were encouraged to reflect both on their growing understanding of the story and on *how* this had happened. Encouraging the children to be metacognitive – to think about how they had learnt as well as what they had learnt – is part of the process of creating reflective readers (Kelley and Clausen-Grace, 2007).

To encourage close attention to the text and deduction, and to teach visualisation as a skill that can enhance understanding, the children were asked to make a map of the compound after reading the first chapter. This involved them in careful rereading and deduction to work out where to place the hospital, the chapel and so on. This activity helped children 'see' the setting as well as read about it. The teacher was able to assess children's comprehension of the story so far and to help them make connections to map making /scale plans in geography and maths. Throughout their reading they noticed how the descriptions of the mountain environment and its weather gave richness to their studies of mountains in geography.

A compare and contrast activity was used to illuminate the relationship between the main character and his best friend. Children compared aspects of the characters and noted that over time the main character began to question what his father told him. This led to a dramatised conversation and an intense debate followed about tolerance, with the class drawing on their own lives for examples. The supportive and respectful ethos being developed, where talk and risk taking were encouraged, meant that one child felt able to reveal that his parents had divorced because of different beliefs. This aspect of the story touched on a deeply personal experience and enabled the child to examine it.

Freeze-frames, drama and hot-seating were used throughout to consider cause and effect within the story and to develop empathy, and the boy's decision whether or not to leave was explored in a conscience alley. Critical and alternative viewpoints were encouraged. The teacher had used drama conventions throughout the year and the children were familiar with them; they voiced the view that such activities meant they could 'get inside the characters', 'feel what they're feeling and say what they're thinking'. After the drama activities children sometimes completed a 'think, feel, say' grid from a chosen character's perspective.

The class also reflected on the changing emotions characters were feeling at different points in the story. Key points were noted on a board using post-it notes and groups were encouraged to arrange them on an emotions chart. This generated a great deal of discussion about the intensity of the emotions and how far up or down the happy/sad axis they should be placed. Finally, children recorded these on an emotional journey graph and searched for exactly the right word to convey the emotions (see Figure 5.1 for an example). In this activity, children were extending their vocabulary and vocabulary choices in a purposeful, contextualised context, not a paper exercise.

The teacher felt that the quality and amount of talk about the book increased 'phenomenally' over time and the children's comprehension improved as they explored the text orally, visually, aurally and kinaesthetically. This active, creative and collaborative approach had an impact on the readers' enthusiasm and enjoyment of the text. A measure of the children's engagement perhaps was that several of them went on to buy their own copy of the book.

There are many ways creative teachers of reading seek to ensure children's engagement. These include:

- creating a reading culture in their classrooms;
- selecting high-quality polysemic texts;
- encouraging talk around texts;
- offering creative opportunities for children to inhabit a book;

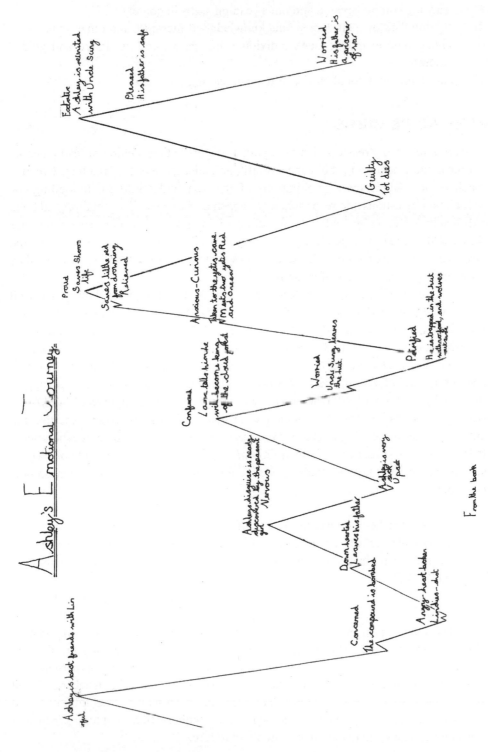

Figure 5.1 An emotions graph to reflect Ashley's journey

- reading aloud from engaging literature;
- not making every book they read aloud the focus of study;
- teaching comprehension and other reading skills in context;
- sharing their own enjoyment and knowledge of literature and other texts;
- giving time to independent, individual reading as well as shared and guided reading;
- supporting individual choice of diverse reading materials.

TEACHERS AS READERS

One omission from Pressley's list of important factors in the teaching of reading noted earlier is the teacher and the teacher's attitude and experience of reading. Creative teachers of reading share explorations of the text with children, modelling the speculation, questions and responses that happen as they read. They enthral and hook children into reading by reading books aloud, giving less able readers access to books they could not read independently. They also introduce children to new writers and new genres they may not try themselves and select books for extended study that they know have complex layers of meaning.

Studies of effective ways to teach literacy in the primary phase show that as well as knowledge of reading skills, teachers also need extensive knowledge of children's literature (Medwell *et al.*, 1998; Block *et al.*, 2002). Additionally, research in the US (Commeyras *et al.*, 2003; Dreher, 2003) and the UK (Cremin *et al.*, 2009b) has looked at links between teachers as readers, their knowledge of children's literature and the impact of this in their classrooms. The research and case studies suggest that teachers who read influence their pupils by modelling their love of books and reading and by being 'socially interactive' in sharing their knowledge, expertise and enthusiasm. However, the UKLA survey in 2006–7 reveals that many teachers seem to lack this knowledge of books (Cremin *et al.*, 2008a,b). Knowing about books would seem to be essential professional knowledge for primary teachers. As the researchers point out:

> Primary teachers, concerned to nurture positive attitudes and develop young readers' pleasure and engagement in texts, need to be able to make informed book recommendations and to introduce children to literature which sustains them as readers.
>
> (Cremin *et al.*, 2009c: 14)

The UKLA project *Teachers as Readers: Building Communities of Readers* (2007–8) aimed to support teachers as they enhanced children's reading for pleasure by matching texts to readers and readers to texts, widening children's experiences of literature (Cremin *et al.*, 2008c). Teachers can also network with other teachers, as well as use book review sites to see what is on offer and what works for children beyond a restricted range of very popular and well known authors. See Chapter 4 for further ideas on keeping up to date with children's literature.

RESPONDING TO READING

Children's personal and critical responses to a text are supported through the kinds of teaching outlined earlier. Formative assessment of a child's reading and their responses is an essential element of such teaching. This goes beyond just 'hearing a child read' and putting a tick or comment in a record book. It includes oral feedback and might also include self-assessment, peer assessment, such as reading partner comment books, and parents' comments and observations. Encouraging children to self-assess and compare this with teacher assessment provides areas for discussion; any gaps between the two can identify next steps. Assessment of reading should also publicly acknowledge and celebrate reading success and endeavour, be it via a Mexican wave, a 'happy teacher' postcard sent home, a certificate in assembly or a book award.

Involving children in reading assessment is valuable, as the following example demonstrates. Simon was a fluent reader in the sense that he was reading at an age appropriate level. His automatic word recognition skills were good and he seemed to enjoy reading, but he read aloud in a monotone. His teacher taped him reading aloud, played it back to him and asked him what he thought. He was quick to identify that '*I read in a boring voice*' and agreed a target with his teacher '*to read with expression and pace*'. His teacher ensured he had lots of opportunities to hear fluent expressive reading, including hearing her read aloud to the class, listening to story CDs, watching stories enacted on screen and matching him with a reading partner who modelled fluent reading. She gave him the chance to reread familiar texts to reduce some of the cognitive demand, build familiarity and deepen understanding of stories. She planned activities where he would have a purpose for using expressive reading in context, such as reading play scripts, taking part in choral poetry readings with actions, creating 'radio broadcasts' such as commentating on a playground football match, recording stories for younger children and so on. Simon often had an audience and having listened to his own recorded performances, he discussed his progress with his teacher. His improved oral reading was celebrated by his performance of an action poem in assembly, one which he performed with expression and passion.

Increasingly, children like Simon are being assessed against targets linked to specific learning goals/objectives, making the criteria for assessment clear and giving feedback against the target (Black *et al.*, 2003; Clarke, 2005). Such an approach aims to help a child see where they are in their learning and how to move forward. Specific feedback such as this is important, but teachers must guard against teaching to the target and criteria in such a way that they limit the range of possible ways of learning and demonstrating that learning. A child's target of 'I can recognise how characters are presented in different ways and show this using evidence from the book' could be taught and demonstrated in many ways: through discussion, role-playing characters and drawing or making puppets of the characters. It could also involve enacting a scene, through identifying 'show not tell' passages and talking about what they mean, and making character fact files and so forth. Teachers must also be alert to the potential danger that in focusing on one or two targets, they miss other significant evidence of learning. A child may demonstrate an understanding of simile in their reading even though that is not their target.

Teachers may use several reading assessments undertaken across the curriculum to consider where they would place a child in the cells of the assessment focus grids given for each year group in the new Assessing Pupil Progress (APP) in Reading materials (DCSF, 2008b). The APP process involves making periodic, teacher assessment judgements by matching the criteria for a given assessment focus to qualities noted in pupils' reading. These judgements are then refined by checking the criteria in the cells above and below. This can be used as a way of identifying targets for individual readers. The APP process aims to make teacher assessment more consistent and link directly to the National Curriculum leveling process. In creative classrooms, teachers will balance the focused nature of targets with a commitment to an engaging, playful and wide ranging exploration of texts.

FOSTERING CHILDREN'S INDEPENDENCE AS READERS

In order to develop as independent readers, children need:

■ to understand the pleasures and purposes of reading so they can see what is in it for them;
■ opportunities to read individually and independently, as well as in shared and group contexts;
■ access to quality materials;
■ opportunities to choose their own reading materials and explore their own preferences;
■ experiences to encourage them to widen their range and try new things.

Fostering attitudes of independence, self-agency and reading curiosity is crucial in the light of evidence that suggests that many children in England are not very interested in reading and spend little time on reading for pleasure. Clarkson and Betts (2008) found that 21 per cent of 9-year-old boys and 13 per cent of girls said they are not interested in books. For 11-year-olds the figures were 21 per cent and 14 per cent respectively. Additionally, only 30 per cent of boys and 45 per cent of girls reported that they read for enjoyment for more than 30 minutes each day (DfES, 2007b).

There are many programmes to foster recreational reading and these are often, but not always, incentive-based, such as reading a certain number of books to gain a reward. Such programmes have a role, but teachers will also want to ensure that the day-to-day reading experiences they offer children model the pleasures and positive purposes of reading. Successful school experiences help motivate children to read voluntarily (Allington and McGill-Franzen, 2003; Cremin *et al.*, 2009b).

Schools and teachers should offer blocks of time for sustained, independent silent reading. This can help create and enrich the habit of reading and offer space for imaginative engagement and the sharing of pleasure in reading. Research shows just fifteen minutes a day of independent *recreational* reading significantly improves children's reading abilities (Smith and Joyner, 1990; Taylor *et al.*, 1990). Creative teachers of reading also ensure children have access to a wide range of quality reading materials and include reading materials from popular culture. Evidence shows that low income children have consistently less access to reading materials (Nueman and Celano, 2001). Creative readers of teaching ensure they combat this. As well as offering a wide range of reading materials in school, teachers arrange regular visits to the local library, send home book bags and Curiosity Kits (see Chapter 10), run after school clubs and book swaps.

Children need to select their own reading materials to develop their independence as readers with preferences. As well as a free choice of books provided by the school, creative teachers encourage children to read materials from their life outside school, be it books, comics, magazines, hobby texts, collectors' cards or instruction manuals. They include such texts in their teaching sessions to give them value and status and to engage interest. They also encourage children to share their choices with each other and suggest related items that might extend children's choices. They invite in a range of adults and older children to talk about their reading histories and preferences, and are likely to arrange author and poets' workshops to enthuse and stimulate readers. They also let children know that they have the right to dislike a book and not finish a book if they have given it a good chance, but don't find it engaging (Pennac, 2006).

FOSTERING IMAGINATIVE ENGAGEMENT: EXTENDED EXPLORATIONS

Creative teachers of reading find imaginative ways to journey inside a book on extended explorations. For example, several teachers in West Sussex, in using the book *Dragonology: The Complete Book of Dragons* by Dr Ernest Drake, shared their ideas and found a myriad of ways of firing children's imaginations and heightening engagement.

In one class, children received a letter telling them that their application to take the secret and ancient Society of Dragonologists Course 'Working with Dragons' had been accepted (see Figure 5.2). Each morning thereafter, the class repeated the oath of the Dragonologist Society and their teacher 'found' an old school report that showed the most famous dragonologist and the 'author' of the book, had attended school nearby (see Figure 5.3). The report gave them evidence about his interests and skills that led to some informed and engaging hot-seating.

On another occasion, the teacher created a nest of stones and rocks in the middle of the classroom. Inside were thirty dragon eggs waiting to hatch. Candles were burning and music playing as the children entered the classroom. The teacher spoke of the tangible sense of awe and wonder present. How long would it take for them to hatch? What care would a baby dragon need? The book might provide the answers.

Other children watched a video their teacher had filmed in advance. Face to camera, in documentary style and using formal language, she confessed to being a secret dragonologist and showed them sites in a nearby forest where she claimed there was evidence of dragon occupation. Thus a dead tree had been killed by the heat of the dragon's breath, broken branches showed the dragon's fight path, a large heap of brushwood was the remains of a dragon's nest and so on. Still on camera she told them that they would be visiting the forest the following week to undertake their own search for evidence. What other signs might their be? Would they recognise them?

S.A.S.D.

SASD
Wyvern Way
London

Dear Student,

I am delighted to inform you that your application to take the Secret and Ancient Society of Dragonologists course 'WORKING WITH DRAGONS' has been accepted.

You may now consider yourself a fully fledged Dragonology student. Upon signing the *Oath of Dragonology*, you are entitled to honorary junior membership of the SASD.

Yours in Dragonology,

Earnest Drake
(President)

■ **Figure 5.2** The invitation to join the Ancient Society of Dragonologists

 Celtic Preparatory School

Progress report on Earnest Drake Age 10 yrs 11 months Form 6H Term 18 48

SUBJECTS	REMARKS	Examination	Effort	Teacher initials
READING	A keen reader but spends too much time reading about dragons, fairy tales, myths and legends. Needs to widen his interests.	98%	B	MH
WRITING	Earnest is a very capable writer. I am pleased to hear he keeps a journal of the wild life he has observed. He must NOT use the margins of his exercise book to draw dragons	92%	A	MH
ARITHMETIC	Earnest could do better if he applied himself. He spends a great deal of time daydreaming rather than getting on with his sums.	63%	C	CP
HISTORY	Has a strong interest in history, but needs to be more critical in distinguishing facts from fiction. Must realise that myths are NOT facts.	56%	B	GF
GEOGRAPHY	V. good. Knows all principal rivers, mountain ranges, climates of Great Britain and Europe etc. One would think he was a great traveller.	95%	A	WK
NATURAL SCIENCES	Has an excellent knowledge of fauna and flora and exceptional field work skills for a boy of his age.	99%	A	AE
CONDUCT Good ATTENDANCE one absence			PUNCTUALITY	
Good				

GENERAL COMMENTS: Earnest has the ability to go far if he concentrates on practical, everyday knowledge rather than ancient myths and stories. HEADMASTER

■ **Figure 5.3** Ernest Drake's school report

A real purpose for reading was established in these classrooms, imaginations were fired and the motivation to read was high. For several weeks the children read books about dragons, found a wealth of stories and myths about dragons, role-played dragons, created a dragon's den in their classrooms, and produced live and exclusive TV news reports as well as newspaper articles. The writing that arose from this engaged reading was unsurprisingly of consistently high quality. The teachers' creative approach inspired intense levels of imaginative engagement.

CONCLUSION

If teachers wish children to become lifelong, committed readers then they must bring passion and excitement into the teaching of reading, and teach reading *creatively* as well as teaching *for creativity*. They need to share their own pleasure and engagement in reading and read aloud regularly from powerful books. By encouraging sharing and reflecting on books, modelling reading behaviours, providing time, access and choice of books, welcoming multimodal texts and building on children's reading lives, as well as using formative assessment, creative teachers build communities of readers. In such communities they will be providing imaginative ways into reading and creative activities to explore texts of all kinds.

FURTHER READING

Cremin, T., Mottram, M., Collins, F., Powell, S. and Safford, K. (2009b) Teachers as Readers: Building Communities of Readers, *Literacy*, 43(1): 11–19.

Ketch, A. (2005) Conversation: The Comprehension Connection, *The Reading Teacher*, 59(1): 8–13.

Lewis, M. and Tregenza, J. (2007a) Beyond Simple Comprehension, *English 4–11*, 30: 11–16.

Pressley, M. (2000) What Should Comprehension Instruction be the Instruction Of?, in M. Kamil, P.B. Mosentahl, P.D. Pearson and R. Barr (eds), *Handbook of Reading Research*, Volume 3, Hillsdale, NJ: Lawrence Erlbaum, pp. 545–61.

CHILDREN'S BOOKS

Ashley, B. (1999) *Johnnie's Blitz*, Puffin.

Burgess, M. and Brown, R. (2000) *The Birdman*, Andersen.

Foreman, M. (1989) *War Boy*, Pavilion.

Gaiman, N. and McKean, D. (2003) *The Wolves in the Walls*, Bloomsbury.

Gallaz, C., McEwan, I. (ed.) and Innocenti, R. (1985) *Rose Blanche*, Jonathon Cape.

Gleitzman, M. (2006) *Once*, Puffin.

Hughes, S. (2002) *The Lion and the Unicorn*, Bodley Head.

McCann, R. and Marshall, A. (2003) *Luba: The Angel of Bergen-Belsen*, Tricycle Press.

Magorian, M. (1998) *Goodnight Mr Tom*, Longman.

Morpurgo, M. (2006) *King of the Cloud Forest* (new edition), Egmont Books.

Peet, M. (2005) *Tamar*, Walker.

Steer, D.A. (2003) (ed.) *Dragonology: The Complete Book of Dragons*, Templar.

Tan, S. (2007) *The Arrival*, Hodder.

Thomson, C. (2001) *Falling Angels*, Hutchinson.

Westall, R. (2004) *Blitzcat*, Macmillan.

Williams, M. (2008) *My War Diary*, Walker.

CHAPTER 6

DEVELOPING WRITERS CREATIVELY – THE EARLY YEARS

INTRODUCTION

Young children need to be offered the time and space to use different forms of writing in imaginatively engaging contexts, in which their early attempts at mark making are recognised as acts of communication and their words and meanings valued. As Vygotsky (1978: 118) suggested, 'an intrinsic need should be aroused in them, and writing should be incorporated into a task that is necessary and relevant for life'. When writing to express themselves, to communicate information of personal significance, to reflect upon their lives and voice their views, children should be affectively and cognitively engaged as young authors, not as scribes. This chapter focuses on teaching early writing creatively; it focuses primarily on developing the compositional skills of young writers aged 5–7 years. It highlights in particular the role of improvisation in early writing, the importance of play and imaginative engagement, as well as the teacher's role as model writer. In addition, the importance of fostering young writers' authorial agency and independence is examined.

By the end of the Early Years Foundation Stage (DCSF, 2008a), it is expected that children will be able to write their own names and other things such as labels and captions, and begin to form simple sentences as well as attempt writing for various purposes, using features of different forms such as lists, stories and instructions. The PNS (DfES, 2006a) strands most relevant to fostering the creative voice of the young child, both on page and screen, include:

Creating and shaping texts
- Write independently and creatively for purpose, pleasure and learning.
- Use and adapt a range of forms, suited to different purposes and readers.
- Make stylistic choices including vocabulary, literary features and viewpoints or voice.
- Use structural and presentational features for meaning and impact.

(PNS, Strand 9)

Sentence structure and punctuation
■ Vary and adapt sentence structure for meaning and effect.
■ Use a range of punctuation correctly to support meaning and emphasis.
■ Convey meaning through grammatically accurate and correctly punctuated sentences.

(PNS, Strand 11)

In relation to these strands, the PNS framework states that by the end of the first three crucial years of schooling, children aged seven will be expected to:

■ Draw on knowledge and experience of texts in deciding and planning what to write.
■ Sustain form in narrative, including use of person and time.
■ Maintain consistency in non–narrative, including purpose and tense.
■ Make adventurous word and language choices appropriate to the style and purpose of the text.
■ Select from different presentational features to suit particular writing purposes.

(PNS, Strand 9, Year 2)

It also states that children will be expected to:

■ Write simple and compound sentences.
■ Compose sentences using tense consistently.
■ Use question marks and use commas to separate items in a list.

(PNS, Strand 11, Year 2)

PRINCIPLES

To develop creatively as writers, children need extensive experience of texts, tailored teaching of the appropriate skills, the opportunity to be imaginatively engaged in open-ended interactive contexts and the chance to make choices and write for real purposes. Key principles in early writing include: recognising and building on children's existing and often implicit knowledge about language, providing a print rich environment and offering opportunities to write in playful contexts. The combination of the teachers' invitation to engage and imagine, and the professional use of observation and fine tuned intervention can help move children's learning forward (Geekie *et al.*, 1999). The Early Years Foundation Stage (DCSF, 2008a) profiles such a play-based observation oriented approach to language and states that early mark making and writing should take place within meaningful and engaging activities, although it is a matter of debate whether all teachers in the early years of the primary school retain this strong emphasis on contextualising writing in play (Bromley, 2004).

It is clear, however, that children in the very early years make no distinction between drawing, painting, modelling or writing as means of recording and exploring their experiences and need to be offered opportunities to mark make in a range of playful contexts using 'what is to hand' (Kress, 1997). Teachers' knowledge of the range of literacy practices in which children engage in their homes is also essential to enable them to build on their diverse literacy resources and cultural capital, and to recognise the influence of the digital literacies that young children have access to at home, as well as the more traditional print literacies. Creative teachers encourage children to connect their own 'school of knowing' with the 'school of expressing' (Malaguzzi, 1998), making use of words, images, sounds as well as their own bodies to help them compose.

In supporting young emergent writers, teachers encourage children to make independent attempts at communicating and focus on their intentions as writers. Through experimenting and playing with a range of materials, they draw on their knowledge and experience of different literacy practices and begin to gain control over writing, expanding their theories of how the writing system works in the process. It is argued that there are three phases in a developmental writing curriculum before the conventional writing phase, including:

■ children engaging in role-play writing, in which they become aware of written symbols and experiment with marks on the page;
■ children learning that speech can be written down and that there is a constant in the written word;
■ children beginning to have a sense of both audience and sentence.

(Raison, 1997)

Developing positive attitudes to writing and children who are confident in their ability to 'write' independently is crucial. Nathan's titled drawing of a diplodocus, which this 5-year-old chose to create in golden time, reflects his personal fascination with dinosaurs and knowledge that the creature can be represented through word and image (see Figure 6.1). Teachers must seek to avoid developing learners who can cope with the technical demands of written language, but who derive little pleasure or satisfaction from engaging in such activities, and who have little sense of what the written word can offer them. Creative teachers, convinced of the importance of developing individual child writers, rather than just teaching the skills of writing, acknowledge that writing involves both the emotions and the intellect and plan accordingly. They seek to offer a motivating and creatively engaging curriculum in which writing for a range of purposes and audiences is commonplace and the skills of writing are both taught and applied. Such teachers ensure opportunities are provided for developing independence and autonomy as writers and that children have the chance to use written language for real. They try to balance the development of children's technical competence alongside their ability to express ideas and communicate confidently with voice and verve. The concept of voice 'like a fingerprint, reveals identity' (Andrews, 1989: 21) and comes to represent:

the concept of individuality, the uniqueness of the individual writer, who draws upon their own experience, knowledge, attitudes and engagement.

(Grainger et al., 2005: 196)

■ **Figure 6.1** A free choice composition of a diplodocus

In celebrating children's unusual ideas, noticing their playful use of spoken language, and affirming their growing independence as writers who have something to say and the means to convey this, teachers can help children construct positive dispositions towards creativity, individuality and difference in writing. While young writers need to learn about the different types of texts and spelling and punctuation conventions, for example, they also need to develop an understanding of the purpose and pleasure to be found in writing and the impact of their work on others. Recent research also highlights that automaticity in handwriting is important in facilitating composition and deserves increased attention as part of a creative approach to supporting young writers (Medwell *et al.*, 2007).

READING, WRITING AND LEARNING

Reading offers young learners' different models of language and if texts are actively inhabited, explored, read and discussed, children appropriate such language into their own repertoires. Speaking and listening, reading and writing are interdependent language modes and need to be taught as such, to enable each mode to enrich the others. When teachers immerse children in powerful literature and other texts, and explore these in playful contexts on extended learning journeys, then a range of purposeful reasons for writing emerge. In Chapter 7, Figure 7.1 shows an extended process of teaching writing, which involves teachers developing units of work and immersing children in a text type, familiarising them with the genre and working to generate, explore and capture ideas through engaging the learners creatively. Supported by teacher demonstrations, and shared guided work, children can then commit to paper or screen as writers with something to say and a desire to communicate.

Shared reading feeds and enriches shared writing. Teaching about language and organisational features of texts, aligned with opportunities to work on sustained pieces of parallel writing in guided group contexts, helps children become aware of the way in which authors choose to organise, structure and manipulate language to achieve effects. With support, children can transfer this knowledge and understanding into their own work (Corden, 2000). Shared writing encompasses teacher modelling as well as scribing the children's suggestions in joint composition. Guided writing, the next step towards independent writing, involves children leaning on the model created and more independently drafting, revising and editing their work. Guided writing allows teachers to offer small group focused support, whereas shared writing is whole class oriented. In both, teachers may choose to use a writing frame to help scaffold the children's writing. Frames are skeletal outlines that offer a series of prompts or starters, con- nectives and phrases suitable for particular text types (Wray and Lewis, 1997). They can be very valuable to help embed the structure of different text types, although they should be viewed as flexible templates according to the purpose and audience of the writing.

Potent literature has a marked influence upon young writers, particularly when teachers take the time to explore the whole text and focus on the dilemmas of the characters, the issues arising and the themes. In one class of 6–7-year-olds, the teacher, seeking to challenge traditional assumptions about wolves as the evil characters in children's stories, sought to read a range of texts, created several 'roles on the wall' (giant outlines of the various wolves) and through drama and role-play investigated the particular characteristics of individual wolves. Many tales were told and read, including *Little Red Riding Hood*, *The Three Little Pigs*, Pascal Biet's *A Cultivated Wolf*, Michael Morpurgo's *The Last Wolf*, Helen Creswell's *Sophie and the Sea Wolf* and Emily Gravett's *Wolves*. The main focus, however, was on *Little Wolf's Book of Badness* by Ian Whybrow, the first in a series of books that examine Little Wolf's adventures. In this one the young wolf travels to Cunning College for Brute Beasts where he is meant to become a big bad wolf. The book is comprised of his letters home to his parents. Work on the book involved turning the role-play area into Beastshire and the 'Frettnin Forest' and other work in role, as well as creating 'rules of badness' and examining Little Wolf's spelling problems. The book and the wider work around it involved the children actively and imaginatively, and this was demonstrated in their writing. In Figure 6.2, Philip's letter, written in role as Little Wolf, shows how this young author has leant upon some of the text's features, such as the letter format, the deliberate misspellings and the ink-stains. However, in addition Philip playfully adds new rules and makes good use of a number of punctua- tion conventions, such as parentheses and exclamation marks that are also used by Whybrow. These had not been discussed by the class, but so many of the children used brackets in their letters home that the teacher was prompted to focus on this punctuation feature, celebrating the skill of these young writers who had noticed and imitated this appropriately.

■ **Figure 6.2** Little Wolf's letter home from the Adventure Academy

Children play with the possibilities of texts that they encounter and make use of these in their compositions, often combining both text and image as Philip does in this context (Evans, 2004; UKLA/QCA, 2004, 2005). While the communicative practices to which they are apprenticed at home include many traditional forms, these exist side by side with new practices that blend different media and so in school, teachers need to recognise and build on children's cultural experiences, and the plethora of digital literacy practices (that may involve, for example, computer games, Wii, video/DVD and TV), as well as their more traditional experiences of books and writing materials (Marsh, 2004; Marsh *et al.*, 2005). The new PNS (DfES, 2006a) acknowledges this diverse range of communicative practices and expects children in the early primary years to create simple texts, on paper and screen, that combine words, images and sounds, and select from different presentational features to suit their particular writing purposes. In leaning on contemporary films or television programmes, for example, teachers can motivate and involve young writers, as well as make explicit links between visual texts and written outcomes, teaching understanding and the language of media structures to support writing. Such work can also involve discussing images and pictures in order to widen children's vocabularies. See Chapter 11 for a fuller discussion of this issue.

TALK AND PLAYFUL ENGAGEMENT

Speaking and listening contribute significantly to learning, so ensuring a wealth of opportunities exist for children to talk before, during and after they write offers real support to young writers. The relationship between talk and writing has been demonstrated in a number of studies, many of which focus on developing boys' writing (Frater, 2000; Essex Writing Project, 2003; Bearne and Grainger, 2004). These indicate the importance of talk, interaction and creative engagement in developing young writers' motivation, interest, commitment and achievement.

Play, which is essentially improvisational in nature, can give rise to many reasons for writing, as well as help generate the content of the communication. Young learners can use different resources such as sand and water, paint and modelling clay, their bodies as well as pencils and paper with which to represent their meaning making. When children engage playfully they imagine possibilities, manipulate materials and objects and talk, draw and create meaning. In playing around with such materials and ideas in action, children begin to ask questions as well as play with words, their intonation and possible meanings. In imaginatively motivating contexts children can develop their creative capacity to experiment with language, interpretation and meaning. Their visual and bodily play, and their playful exploration of multiple modes of communication, enrich this capacity. While the serious play of writing is framed by rules or conventions, these are purposefully employed and experimented with in the context of creatively engaging playful experiences:

> The roots of writing lie in the other forms of symbolising (drawing, modelling, play, drama) that children engage in before they come to the abstract symbolic system of writing.
>
> (Barrs, 1988: 114)

Through the imaginative use of talk and by bringing texts to life in a variety of playful ways, children try out, absorb and transform others' voices and begin to trust and stretch their own; this can enrich the voice of the child (Bakhtin, 1986). In the extended process of composition, children use talk opportunities to voice their own and others' views and feelings within the imaginative experience. In such contexts, talk is used to reconstruct events, share ideas and generate new insights. As tellers of tales, for example, they may initially imitate and lean on known tales, but will gradually move to innovate and invent their own tales, leaning on the narrative repertoire they have established through retelling tales and reading. In effect, they internalise the form and structure of known narratives and borrow elements of the memorable language too, widening their written vocabulary in the process. They may, for example, borrow the repetitive language patterns in traditional tales, appeal rhetorically to the reader or borrow and adapt story beginnings they have heard and used orally, as the following extracts from a class of 6–7-year-olds' tales indicate:

> He travelled over many tall mountains, through many long valleys and across many rivers until he reached the River of Hope and a very little river it was too.

> And then Moonkaia whispered 'It's me your brother'. Sunkia looked up at him and could hardly believe her eyes. Was it really him?

> The little man stamped his feet so hard, Stamp Stamp Stamp and he banged his fists, Bang Bang Bang and he shouted 'No, No No!'. Can you hear him shouting?

> Many golden suns and many silver moons ago there lived a tiny fairy who loved to dance. She so loved to dance so much that . . .

> In the time before men and women had begun to live on the earth, when the skies were always blue, there lived a strange creature who . . .

Children at play, Vygotsky argued, often travel further and in such contexts act as if they are 'a head taller than themselves' (1978: 103). Through playfully engaging with stories, information, physical resources and each other, motivated young thinkers often move almost seamlessly into writing and in the process are able to draw on the source and substance of their improvised and imaginatively motivating play.

TEACHERS AS WRITERS

It has been argued that teachers lack confidence in their own writing skills and their ability to inspire pupils to write creatively (Grainger *et al.*, 2005). As Freire argued:

> Teaching kids to read and write should be an artistic event. Instead, many teachers transform these experiences into a technical event, into something without emotions, without creativity – but with repetition. Many teachers work bureau-cratically when they should work artistically.
>
> Freire (1985: 79)

If children are to take part in the creative processes of exploring and experi-menting, and selecting and evaluating their ideas for writing, teachers need to work artistically, offering sustained opportunities for composing and engaging themselves as writers in the classroom. This involves teachers in interpreting the PNS imaginatively and learning through composing. It also involves modelling writing and demonstrating to children that their own teachers are writers, who use writing for diverse purposes in the real world. In one survey, 310 primary children's views of their teachers as writers were ascertained. Unlike the older primary children, many of the younger children believed their teachers were writers, however, most thought that what their teachers wrote was work related (Grainger *et al.*, 2004d). While a few did acknowledge personal forms and purposes such as letters, notes and shopping lists, 82 per cent of the children recorded only school-based writing. The kinds of writing they noted included, for example, comments, reports, the register, the learning objectives, home-work, 'sentences for me to copy', 'worksheets', and 'my bad spellings'. Many appeared to perceive that the purpose of all this writing was to evaluate their learning, for example, 'she writes how good we've been' or 'she writes our name on the board if we're in trouble', 'she marks our writing' and 'he writes whether he likes our work'. Clearly there may be some way to go to demonstrate to children that writing in various forms is a common feature of human life, and that adults write for a variety of purposes, both for themselves and others. As Frater (2001) observed, too much writing in school is undertaken for the purpose of learning to write and for practising writing skills; too little has real purpose and relevance to the writer and fosters their creativity.

Recent research has shown that there are significant advantages of teachers engaging as writers in the primary classroom (Grainger, 2005; Grainger *et al.*, 2005; Cremin, 2006, 2008). When teachers write alongside children, and learn about writing from an insider's perspective, this evidence suggests they recognise for themselves the significance of talk and creative engagement in writing, the influence of choice and the writers' relationship to the subject matter and that they perceive renewed value in identifying a clear audience and purpose in writing (Grainger, 2005). There are many ways teachers can take part as writers in school, including:

- sharing what they write at home – the forms, purposes and audiences;
- demonstrating spontaneous modelling – thinking aloud as they compose;
- using their drafts – for class evaluation and response;
- leading shared writing sessions – engaging in whole class composition;
- writing alongside children – working towards the same goals;
- being a genuine response partner – listening to and responding to others' writing as well as sharing their own;
- publishing alongside children and teaching assistants;
- writing independently in school – in their own writing journal/during writing workshop time.

In the early years, teachers need to commit real time to engaging authentically as writers and modelling different forms as well as writing alongside the young learners. Through sharing their own writing and modelling possible ways to express ideas, teachers can enhance children's creativity. For more advice on teachers as writers see Chapter 7.

RESPONDING TO WRITING

Writing in the early years is a highly social process and classrooms need to reflect this not only in the generation of ideas, but also in the evaluation and response to them.

Children need to be both encouraged and enabled to read and respond to their own and each others' writing as well as their teachers. Additionally, this will involve teachers in reading aloud children's developing work back to them, for as Barrs and Cork (2001) indicate, this can reveal the pattern and texture of the writing and heighten the child's awareness of what they are trying to communicate. To be fully aware of what one has written, the young writer needs to hear it and listen to it. Too often, rereading one's writing at the point of composition is an untaught skill; reading aloud the children's unfolding work is crucial and needs modelling, use and discussion. While the work may initially be at the level of the sentence, it is still important that children are taught to read aloud and later sub-vocalise as they compose, since such monitoring allows them to hear the tunes and rhythms of their work and increases their syntactic awareness. It can also help them make clearer what it is they are trying to say. Rereading writing is essential to the development of assured writers (Flower, 1994).

Teachers' positive responses to young children's early versions of communicating meaning are also crucial; their knowledge of the history of a child's text and its multiple origins can contribute to this response, but demands that teachers make full use of their awareness of the child's interests and social, cultural background (Pahl, 2007). One of the most effective forms of feedback is to provide a focused oral feedback that helps children recognise the next steps they need to take, and how they might take them and in the process to focus on success, celebrating learners' achievements during an extended learning journey as well as at the end of it. (See Chapter 7 for a possible response framework.) Each unit of work needs to include an assessable outcome, although this will not always be written, but in addition, time needs to be built into literacy activities for ongoing reflection, response and assessment, whether in evaluating the teacher's writing in shared writing time, or commenting on their own writing in guided writing time.

In sharing learning goals and deciding how far the writer has fulfilled their intentions, teachers need to focus on the content as well as the skills used to convey their message. Teachers can help young authors consider their work and begin the process of self-assessment and evaluation, which will be further extended later in the primary school. Teachers may also wish to assess children's progression as writers by examining a range of writing from different contexts, using the new Assessing Pupil Progress in Writing materials (DCSF, 2008b). These materials are a valuable support for periodic assessment, but it is worth noting, however, that only two of the eight assessment foci (AF), namely AF1 'Write imaginative, interesting and thoughtful texts' and AF2 'Produce texts which are appropriate to task, reader and purpose' refer to the content and potential impact of writing so this may once again orient teachers to responding to and profiling children's functional writing skills. If teachers focus on the surface features of language – the marks on the page, at the expense of responding to the deep structure of language – the meaning (Smith, 1982), then young writers will focus on the important minutiae at the expense of developing a sense of themselves as authors with something to say and the ability to shape this effectively. However, if children's writing has a range of audiences, perhaps through creating mothers' day cards, writing and sending postcards home from an imagined trip to the mountains,

■ **Figure 6.3** A sticky note left in the teacher's notebook

letters in the 'Friday mailbox' or making notes to the teacher in her 'book of surprises' then the response of the interested readers will be salient. See Figure 6.3 for a message left on a sticky note in one teacher's notebook; the 5-year-old author was determined to cheer up his teacher, who had been rather tired and cross all morning – his simple message 'be happy' indicates he knew the power of writing, which was reinforced by his teacher's gratifying response.

FOSTERING CHILDREN'S AUTONOMY AS WRITERS

In order to foster increased independence as writers, creative teachers encourage children to communicate through writing and mark making in many ways; through the use of a writing table with a range of resources, for example, and through offering choice in writing journals and writers' workshops. Modelling the use of the writing table and sharing examples of texts produced, as well as offering ways for children's writing to be posted, passed on or shared with their chosen audience is important. Audiences can take many forms and may include parents and grandparents, friends, book characters, the teacher, headteacher, visitors and even soft toys that become imaginary characters in the classroom. Teachers can also establish a class post box and routinely empty this, writing to children and receiving letters, notes and cards from them as well as encouraging children to communicate with one another. See Figure 6.4 for an example of 6-year-old Lucy's self-initiated letter to thank her parents for helping raise money for the class's skylarks appeal. Practice that focuses on identifying real reasons to write can ensure a better balance is created between the teaching of writing and the actual production and creative use of it.

In addition, many teachers establish writing journals or run writing workshops in which children make choices about what to write and then plan and follow this

■ **Figure 6.4** A letter posted in the school post box

through (see Chapter 7 for more detail on establishing writing journals). Opportunities also need to be seized for children to write for real in response to religious and secular events, school events, such as a trip or a school show, and in response to their interests. For example, in teaching instructional texts, teachers can invite children to identify areas of interest and expertise and then create useful instructions that the young writers could give to someone to use. In one class of 6–7-year-olds the instructional texts produced included, for example, how to change a baby's nappy, how to ride a bicycle, how to look after various small animals, how to cheer mummy up, how to climb a tree, how to play snap and how to get your own breakfast. In offering content choice in this context, helping the children connect to their lives and identify a clear audience for their writing, the teacher gave real purpose and relevance to the work and supported the development of the children's autonomy as writers. There are a range of activities that can support choice and create real reasons for writing, including the following.

Activities to support choice and reasons for writing

■ *A writing table/area*: This can offer a wealth of resources, cards, post-its, paper of different sizes and colours, envelopes, notepads, notelets, labels, mini-books and writing/colouring implements. See Figure 6.5 for 5-year-old Elliott's writing, triggered by the thunder he had heard in the night, he sat for ages at the writing table completing this piece of work in which he used exclamation marks for the first time!

■ *A post box*: Setting up a post box can encourage diverse communication across year groups or in class. Birthday invites and thank you cards can also go through this postal system, emptied as 'the Friday post'.

■ *A class message board*: Owned by the children, this can display children's writing from home and might also include cut-outs brought in from magazines, comics, junk mail, catalogues and environmental print.

■ *A graffiti wall*: Created as a brick wall with paper bricks, children can write messages, poems, sayings, or information for others.

■ *Co-creating displays*: Children are invited to co-create displays and label items or make interactive wall displays.

■ *Registers*: Children's registers are created for free choice/golden time activities and signing in expected.

■ *The teacher's Notebook of Surprises/Reminders*: Teachers keep a precious note-book in which children can write reminders, messages, notes, information. This may prompt replies.

■ *A class diary*: A class diary is modelled over a week and tiny paper folded diaries for one weekend are offered and added to the writing table.

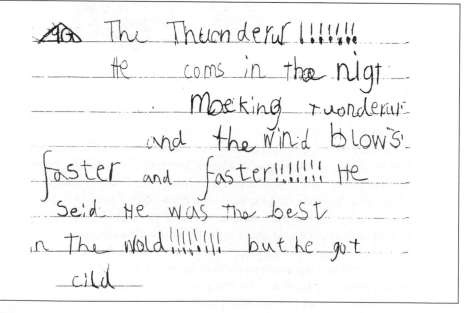

■ **Figure 6.5** 'The Thunderur'

■ *Mini-newspapers*: Through creating instant newspapers to take home, children choose the content and highlight personal, school and/or fantasy news.

■ *Letters/information to parents*: Children are encouraged to write to their parents about events in school, issues they care about and/or as information updates.

■ *Playing with notices*: The class are invited to collect, copy and display notices from their environment. For example: 'Keep off the grass', 'Do not feed the animals', 'Danger' and 'Men at Work'. They can then experiment with replacing some of the words.

FOSTERING IMAGINATIVE ENGAGEMENT: WRITING IN ROLE

When children write in role in extended drama sessions in which they are other people in another place and time with life to be lived and problems to be solved, their writing retains a sense of this other person and often has a stronger sense of voice and verve (McNaughton, 1997; Grainger, 2004). This is in part because dramatic improvisation is focused on the divergence of ideas through play: verbal, physical and mental play with ideas and options; it represents a rich and supportive resource for young writers. The opportunity to generate, explore and share options through improvisation appears to expand the flow of ideas available and thus supports the development of children's ideational fluency, helping them make unusual associations and connections and select particularly evocative language as they compose. As they are improvising in drama, children are thinking, feeling, visualising and creating multiple possibilities, and in their related writing they are often able to make this thinking visible. Their imaginative engagement in the tense scenarios of classroom drama appears to help them form and transform experience and effectively communicate their own and each others' ideas in writing.

Research findings indicate that the adoption of multiple role perspectives in extended classroom drama can contribute to the quality of writing (Cremin *et al.*, 2006b). For example, in one class of 6–7-year-olds, during a cross curricular exploration about the sea, the teacher used several books to trigger extended dramas, including for example Kathy Henderson's *The Little Boat*, Elisabeth's Beresford's *The Smallest Whale* and David Weisner's *Flotsam*. In these dramas the class travelled to distant lands, lived underwater as water sprites, rescued a beached whale and met and became many people and water creatures. During their drama based on *Flotsam*, a wordless picture book in which a boy finds an underwater camera, the film in which reveals an extraordinary world under the ocean, the class were shrunk via the use of fairy dust (sea salt) and a magic spell to enable them to travel inside the camera. Their under the sea adventures involved meeting mer-folk whose homes were being destroyed by human pollution and sheltering from real children who sought to plunder the contents of rock pools where the miniature class were hiding. They returned to the real world, were enlarged again and brainstormed the possible actions they could take to stop children ruining sea life in pools and adults polluting the ocean. Letters were written, posters designed and news items broadcast. Many of the children chose to write in role from a perspective of someone they had been in the drama; Gabriella wrote in role as a starfish to herself in class and Ethan wrote as the Mer-king affirming the agreements made. Their different perspectives demonstrate the importance of allowing children to choose.

Dear friends,

Thank you for visiting our land. We are depending on you to stop the troubles. Please do not let us down or forget us. All the families of the kingdom of Neptune are hoping you will win. Adults can be difficult to change. Good luck.

The Mer-king

PS. Come and visit us again to tell us the good news.

Dear Gabriella,

I liked meeting you under the sea. I hope you will be able to get rid of the oil that sits above us like a black cloud. I HATE it. I am glad I was able to help hide you in the anemones. Children often mess up the rock pools and steal my friends. It is scary when their fingers come down to grab you. You must tell them to stop it. NOW!

with love from your friend,

Sammy the starfish.

The different views expressed by these two children, the length of their written communication and the speed with which they were created, suggest that writing in role during a drama may be particularly accessible to children because of the immediacy of the imagined context that positions them in more significant roles, often as experts or at least as adults. When children write in role, this can help them use their vividly imagined details of the setting, characters or events they have constructed in action. Teachers can encourage writing in role in a number of different drama contexts, including the following:

- ■ *Extended drama sessions*: Improvisational classroom drama involves travelling to other worlds, countries and times and perhaps writing and drawing while present in these places. This may involve, for example, sending postcards home, or letters to the characters met as well as retelling the adventures experienced as news reports.
- ■ *Drama in literacy time*: Drama conventions can be used as part of shared writing to prompt in role work and develop an understanding of characters and plot.
- ■ *Imaginary friends*: Such characters, in the form of a stuffed bear, doll or mannequin may be found hiding in the classroom bearing a message or request. Over time children write to them and receive replies.
- ■ *The role-play area*: Teachers need to model the use of the literacy materials in the role-play area. This may prompt children to write in the Captain's log, record problems in the repairs book and draw the aliens met for example.

■ *Table-top role-play*: Children draw on a covered table top and create their own world with objects and small world play toys. This may involve oral storytelling and writing in role.

■ *Puppets shows*: Making paper bag or cloth puppets can encourage groups of children to gather a group of puppets, make a play to show to the class and create programmes as theatre managers.

■ *Story cauldron*: Create a story cauldron, in which one child dresses as a witch/wizard and the class add story features, such as characters, settings, possible problems, different beginnings and so on. Children stir the cauldron to make their own/class/group stories that they can retell as fairies or goblins.

■ *Fictional story boxes*: Shoe boxes lined and thematically decorated with small toys and objects inside can prompt small world story creation and may prompt in role writing. For example, dinosaur world, space, under the sea, the world of the fairies, Bob the Builder's yard.

■ *Story sacks*: Sacks that include a core text and small puppets, toys or objects which connect to the tale. These can encourage play, retelling from the point of view of one of the characters and the production of new stories and sequels.

CONCLUSION

When children are given space, time and appropriate resources to engage playfully and imaginatively, and are allowed to attend to what interests them and bring their own unique life experiences into the classroom, then their motivation increases and writing is undertaken as part of a meaningful creative endeavour, not as a separate task or an activity to practise. Writing that emerges in such contexts has stronger sense of the writer's voice and rings with authenticity and conviction. Through engagement in creative contexts, and through instruction and support in shared and guided writing, as well as though focused feedback and response, children make progress as writers – writers who have something to say and the means and desire to convey their message effectively and creatively.

FURTHER READING

Armstrong, M. (2006) *Children Writing Stories*, Berkshire and New York: Open University Press.

Grainger, T., Goouch, K. and Lambirth, A. (2005) *Creativity and Writing: Developing Voice and Verve in the Classroom*, London: Routledge.

Marsh, J., Brooks, G., Hughes, J., Ritchie, L., Roberts, S. and Wright, K. (2005) *Digital Beginnings: Young Children's Use of Popular Culture, Media and New Technologies*, Sheffield: University of Sheffield.

Pahl, K. (2007) Creativity in Events and Practices: A Lens for Understanding Children's Multimodal Texts, *Literacy*, 41(2): 81–7.

CHILDREN'S BOOKS

Beresford, E. (1996) *The Smallest Whale*, O Brien.

Biet, P. (1999) *A Cultivated Wolf*, Siphano.

Creswell, H. and Cockroft, J. (1997) *Sophie and the Sea Wolf*, Hodder.
Gravett, E. (2006) *Wolves*, Macmillan.
Henderson, K. (1997) *The Little Boat*, Walker.
Morpurgo, M. and Foreman, M. (2002) *The Last Wolf*, Corgi.
Weisner, D. (2006) *Flotsam*, Houghton Mifflin.
Whybrow, I. (1996) *Little Wolf's Book of Badness*, Collins.

CHAPTER 7

DEVELOPING WRITERS CREATIVELY – THE LATER YEARS

INTRODUCTION

In response to widespread criticism that the teaching of writing has focused too heavily on technical skills in recent years, the new PNS framework notes that 'particular attention has been paid to the development of independent creative writers able to make informed choices about form, audience and purpose' (DfES, 2006a: 15). Such writers use their knowledge of language form and feature, but crucially also have something to say that is worth saying and the voice and verve to express themselves effectively. This chapter focuses on teaching writing creatively to 7–11-year-olds; primarily examining the artistic process of composing, it also explores the teaching of grammar and punctuation in meaningful contexts. The PNS strands of writing, on page and screen, most relevant to fostering the creative voice of the child writer include:

Creating and shaping texts
- Write independently and creatively for purpose, pleasure and learning.
- Use and adapt a range of forms, suited to different purposes and readers.
- Make stylistic choices including vocabulary, literary features and viewpoints or voice.
- Use structural and presentational features for meaning and impact.

(PNS, Strand 9)

Text structure and organisation
- Organise ideas into coherent structure including layout sections and paragraphs.
- Write cohesive paragraphs linking sentences within and between them.

(PNS, Strand 10)

Sentence structure and punctuation
- Vary and adapt sentence structure for meaning and effect.
- Use a range of punctuation correctly to support meaning and emphasis.

■ Convey meaning through grammatically accurate and correctly punctuated sentences.

(PNS, Strand 11)

PRINCIPLES

Writing involves both crafting and creating, although in the last decade teaching writing to 7–11-year-olds has tended to profile the crafting elements, and has involved analysing and practising discrete linguistic features at the expense of creating, composing and completing whole texts (Frater, 2000, 2004). Children need to experience a balance between the technical aspects of writing and the compositional and content elements, as well as between writing as a finished product and writing as a process. Learning to write does not simply involve combining different skills – it involves the consolidation of experiences and the gradual development of a more informed understanding about written communication. Such knowledge, experience and understanding will constantly be reshaped across life as writers make choices and encounter different and more demanding text types in new communicative contexts.

In this new media age, the nature of writing continues to change, and writing is now seen by many as an act of creative design, in which meaning is created not just in words, but also through the visual layout (Sharples, 1999). In their writing, children reflect their rich and diverse experience of reading multimodal texts; texts that make use of sound, image, colour and a variety of visuals as well as words. In schooling, however, despite work to suggest alternative ways forward (UKLA/QCA 2004, 2005), current forms of assessment do not acknowledge the multimodal nature of writing. In recognising the diverse voices and multimodal forms on which children draw, their own 'funds of knowledge' (Moll *et al.*, 1992), teachers can help young writers connect the literacies of home and school and make more use of their text experiences and inner affective existences. This increases the relevance of writing and motivates their involvement in the extended compositional process. In addition, research suggests that when children are allowed to use their own resources and combine print, visual and digital modes, they demonstrate considerable imagination and creativity in the process (Pahl, 2007; Walsh, 2007). See Chapter 11 for an exploration of teaching visual and digital texts creatively.

Whatever the chosen modes and media, writers and designers need to be able to make choices about:

■ the purpose and readership of the text;
■ the most appropriate form of the text;
■ the level of formality demanded;
■ the amount of explicit detail needed;
■ the form and organisation of the material;
■ the technical features of syntax, vocabulary and punctuation suited to the particular text.

(Bearne, 2007: 88)

This list makes clear that while skills and techniques matter and must be taught, they are only part of a complex picture; they benefit from being contextualised in meaningful literacy experiences that motivate and engage young people and enable them to use their knowledge of texts from outside school. In extended learning journeys, reading and response, as well as conversation and dramatic improvisation, contribute to interim drafts and final pieces of writing. This extended process of teaching literacy, developed initially in the UKLA/PNS Project *Raising Boys' Achievements in Writing* (Bearne *et al.*, 2004), has been endorsed by the renewed Strategy (DfES, 2006a). Figure 7.1 shows a more detailed version of this process, which enables children to become immersed in a text type, familiarise themselves with the genre and work creatively to generate, capture and explore ideas. They can then select from among these, developed for example through discussion and drama, and, supported by teacher demonstration, can commit to paper or screen as they work towards the creation of a final assessed outcome. This may be a multimodal outcome or may be presented just in words. Examples of extended learning journeys are shared in Chapters 8–11, and planning them is discussed in Chapter 12.

READING, WRITING AND LEARNING

Writing involves exploring, generating, capturing and organising ideas in order to offer information to others through explanations, descriptions, persuasive and discursive arguments, as well as through more poetic and aesthetic forms. Narrative and poetry in particular, are valuable tools for preserving the past, reflecting on ideas and experience, and opening up conversations with others.

In terms of the process of writing, researchers in the field of composition studies suggest it encompasses *planning*, in which the imagination plays a central role and ideas are captured and selected, *translating* in which the chosen ideas are shaped into actual text, and drafting and *evaluating*, which involves revising and changing the piece (Flower and Hayes, 1980). Through the compositional process, writers develop, reshape and realise their ideas and meanings (Calkins, 1991; Graves, 1994). This model of writers as problem solvers, constantly juggling constraints has parallels with conceptions of the creative thinking process (Guildford, 1973; Sternberg, 1999). Both involve dynamic stages, identifying or clarifying a challenge, generating possible responses and moving between divergent and convergent thinking in search of a solution. Although the act of composing is essentially a cognitive one, becoming literate depends on both social conventions and the relationship between meaning, form, social context and culture. Thus written composition and indeed becoming literate depend on both social conventions and individual problem solving.

The transcriptional process involves paying attention to the spelling, grammar and punctuation of a piece of writing, as well as the presentation. Although both composition and transcription are important, children, parents and teachers may view the transcriptional elements of the process as more important than the compositional components. However, the value of transcription varies according to the purpose and audience of the writing; for example, writing to invite governors to a play requires more care and editorial attention than making a personal list of Christmas presents. In all

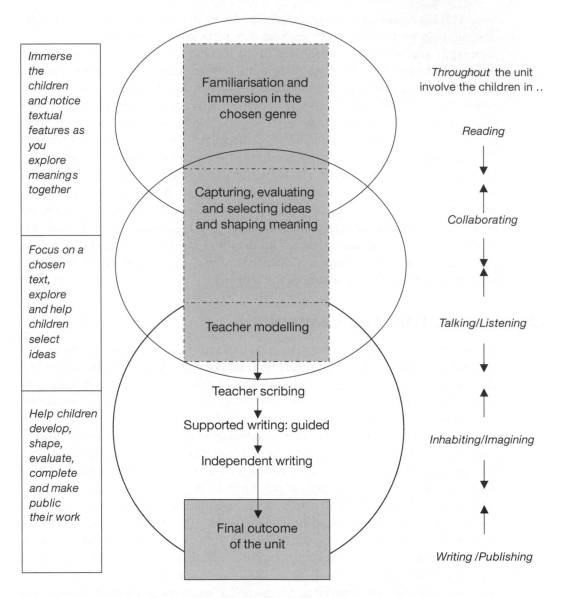

Immerse the children and notice textual features as you explore meanings together

Familiarisation and immersion in the chosen genre

Capturing, evaluating and selecting ideas and shaping meaning

Focus on a chosen text, explore and help children select ideas

Teacher modelling

Teacher scribing

Supported writing: guided

Independent writing

Help children develop, shape, evaluate, complete and make public their work

Final outcome of the unit

Throughout the unit involve the children in ..

Reading

Collaborating

Talking/Listening

Inhabiting/Imagining

Writing /Publishing

■ **Figure 7.1** The extended process of teaching writing

writing contexts, having something to say, understanding the demands of the form and being able to monitor, evaluate and revise what is being written are important elements. Awareness of the purpose and audience of the communication is also highly significant.

It is widely recognised that writers collect ideas from the texts of their lives and their experience of many different textual forms and that they draw upon this repertoire in their writing. Books and films, as well as television and computer programmes, can make a real contribution to children's involvement, response and eventual writing (Marsh and Millard, 2003). Research indicates that the three kinds of literary texts that make the most impact upon 7–11-year-olds writers are emotionally powerful texts, traditional tales and stories containing 'poeticised speech' (Barrs and Cork, 2001). Reading and studying such texts in extended units of work and enabling children to connect to and engage with them, as well as appreciate the writers' craft, can enable them to lean on and learn from literature. Indeed reflective reading and focused investigation of all types of texts is integral to the development of young writers. Creative teachers identify different texts for different classes each year, although they may return to 'failsafe' favourites that they know evoke a rich and creative response. These might include, for example, the challenging story of *Coraline* by Neil Gaiman, Anthony Browne's *Voices in the Park*, Michael Rosen's *The Sad Book*, Elizabeth Laird's *Secret Friends* or Gary Crew's *The Mystery of Eilean Mor*.

TEACHING GRAMMAR AND PUNCTUATION IN CONTEXT

Focusing on the language features of texts and noticing and naming these can be tedious and ineffective if children are not actively engaged in exploring issues related to the text's meaning. In the context of such playful engagement, however, attention can usefully be paid to a text's constructedness. For example, in working towards expanding children's knowledge and use of speech punctuation, role-play could be used to bring characters from a novel to life, generating dialogue from a recently read scene. The children's motivated engagement will feed the resultant shared writing and will increase the number of children participating in the whole class dialogue. The main focus of the initial piece of shared writing is likely to be the content of the conversation, the appropriacy of the characters' words and their effect on each other. In rereading and redrafting this writing together, the class could focus on the efficacy of the dialogue, the content, composition and effect of the conversation on the readers. Later, following a mini-lesson on speech punctuation and the children's examination of its use in their own reading books, the scribed argument could be re-voiced in role to support the selection, placement and punctuation of speech verbs and adverbs.

In one class of 9–10-year-olds, during an exploration of the characters in *Clive and the Missing Finger* by Sarah Garland, Marcus, aged 9, improvised various possible conversations in the context of the text (see Figure 7.2). In this dialogue the father is trying to persuade his daughter Dorrie to remove her make up, which is in his eyes excessive. The class had improvised the ensuing row in role, in pairs, small groups, half and half and as 32:1 with their teacher in role as Dad. They developed this row and others in shared and guided writing contexts and were expected for their final assessed piece of work in the unit to effectively convey the tension of the argument in no more than a page. They were expected to use language appropriate to the text and the characters and to make use of speech punctuation, speech verbs (in all four placements) and adverbs. These were then performed to the class. Freeze-frames were employed to show the consequences of the row, which was also requested to be evidenced in their writing. In this example, in Figure 7.2, Dorrie is described storming off upstairs, just as Marcus' partner Nadia had been seen flouncing off in role as Dorrie in their freeze-frame. In this work, talk, drama and the children's creative engagement, motivated and contextualised their learning about punctuation and enabled Marcus and

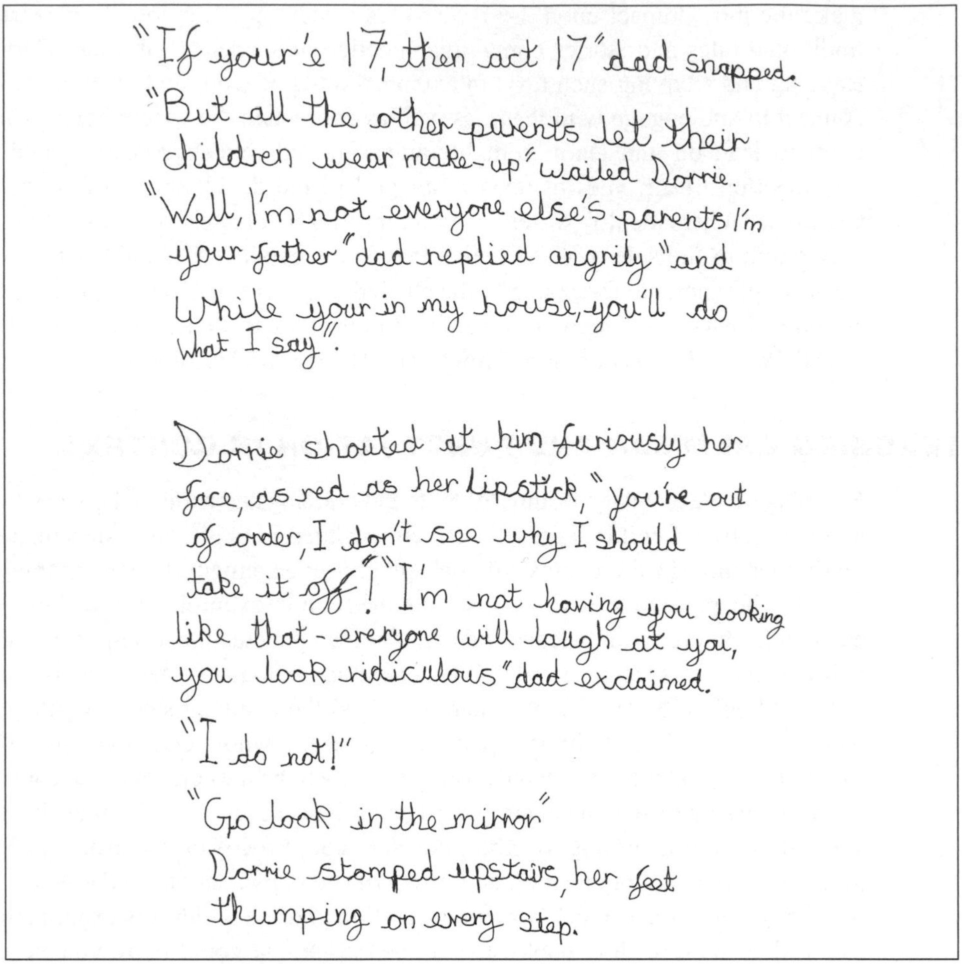

"If your'e 17, then act 17" dad snapped.
"But all the other parents let their children wear make-up" wailed Dorrie.
"Well, I'm not everyone else's parents I'm your father" dad replied angrily "and While your in my house, you'll do what I say".

Dorrie shouted at him furiously her face, as red as her lipstick, "You're out of order, I don't see why I should take it off!" "I'm not having you looking like that - everyone will laugh at you, you look ridiculous" dad exclaimed.

"I do not!"

"Go look in the mirror"
Dorrie stomped upstairs, her feet thumping on every step.

■ **Figure 7.2** A conversation in role

his peers to consider its effect on the reader, demonstrating that on the journey from reading to writing, talk, creative engagement, reflection and response each play a crucial role.

Effective teachers of literacy contextualise their teaching of spelling, punctuation and other sentence and word level work, and this has an impact on children's written composition (Medwell *et al.*, 1998; Wray and Lewis, 2001). Furthermore, in classrooms that promote curiosity about language and an interest in words and their etymology, children become increasingly independent as spellers and develop a positive view of their capacity to spell accurately. Taught to appreciate the problem solving nature of spelling and to take risks, they learn to proofread their writing for themselves and their readers. Research suggests that exercises out of context do little to help children learn spellings, but a focus on language patterns, the use of roots and suffixes as well as mnemonics and 'rules' set within an integrated study of whole texts does support young writers (O'Sullivan and Thomas, 2000). Teaching punctuation in the context of use is also important, since such teaching highlights the significance of punctuation as a tool for indexing meaning (Hall and Robinson, 1996). Paying attention to punctuation within shared reading and examining its use in children's personal reading books can also help, as can teacher demonstrations of the difference punctuation makes to reading aloud.

TALK AND PLAYFUL ENGAGEMENT

The relationship between talk and writing has been demonstrated repeatedly, showing that both underachievers and high achievers benefit from opportunities to talk before, during and after writing (Bearne, 2002; Andrews, 2008). Through talk at the initial stages of the writing process, children can generate and share ideas, experiment with options, and capture, shape and consider what it is they might want to say. This offers them a rich resource when they come to commit their ideas to paper or screen. Furthermore, through developing confidence in playful and creative oral contexts, children learn to take risks with ideas, words and images, which supports their fluency with ideas and enables them to make more divergent connections. Improvisation and playful engagement play a largely unrecognised role in the compositional process, yet they are at the heart of developing creativity in writing.

Children also need opportunities to talk over their writing during the compositional process, to reflect upon and refine their thinking, developing a metalanguage to talk about writing (Bereiter and Scardamalia, 1987). Working together as readers of each others' writing, they can explore ways of using language to clarify each others' ideas and offer secretarial support. In discussing their writing, it is important, however, that children retain ownership and control, talking about their intentions as authors and what they were trying to achieve. This focus on the evolving text, its emerging meaning and the reader's needs and responses is crucial to break through to the 'what next' stage of writing (Sharples, 1999). Working with response partners, children can talk through their intentions, celebrate their successes, reinforce what they have learnt and identify aspects that need attention. Such conversations require modelling and a structure of support and focused reflection to be successful (see Figure 7.4).

Once completed, the opportunity to make writing public and share it orally or through written publications becomes important; children need to hear their voices and experience feedback and responses from their intended audience. Far too much writing in school remains unpublished and, as Frater (2001) asserts, is undertaken merely for the circular purpose of learning to write, rather than really communicating and developing the voice of the child. However, when children engage creatively in a community of writers and connect affectively with the subject matter, as well as publish their work, their voices ring off the page with conviction and commitment.

In addition to talking before, during and after writing, children can write collaboratively; writing with a partner makes more explicit the social nature of writing. As some 8-year-olds commented: 'I love it when we write together because Sally's really good at ideas and I am good at punctuation and "wow" words – together we make a good team' and 'I much prefer writing with a friend – its SO much easier and my writing SO much better'. Working together in this way can ease the challenge of writing, as well as create new demands, and can heighten the motivation to polish and craft work. Collaborative writing is particularly conducive to developing children's creativity in writing and the computer is a useful tool to support this (Vass, 2004).

TEACHERS AS WRITERS

In order to teach writing creatively, teachers need to model the writing process and share the pleasures and challenges of composing. Research suggests that some, concerned about their ability to model specific literary features spontaneously and in public, prepare writing at home prior to sharing it, apparently spontaneously, in school (Luce-Kapler *et al.*, 2001; Grainger *et al.*, 2005). However, children deserve to be apprenticed to real writers, who demonstrate that writing is a problem solving activity (Bereiter and Scardamalia, 1987), a process of thinking and evaluating involving an internal dialogue. Modelling writing authentically involves teachers showing children what strategies they as writers use when confronted with a difficult spelling, or the need to write quickly for example. It also involves talking about their blank spots, false starts and uncertainties, how meaning evolves and understanding develops as authors exercise choices and write their way forwards.

As Chapter 6 suggested, children benefit when their teachers are involved as writers, modelling writing for real and writing alongside them in the classroom. Such 'insider engagement' fosters new understandings about the process of writing and challenges teachers to create a pedagogy that recognises the importance of having a purpose in writing, making personal choices as a writer and author, and the value of rereading at the point of composition. Teachers need to model this process, demonstrating that rereading writing and listening to one's voice is a critical ongoing skill, not one to be left to the end of the composition (Grainger, 2005). Modelling rereading and reviewing one's writing needs to be introduced gradually and reinforced throughout the primary years. In the process, writers can usefully consider the following prompts:

■ What am I trying to say?
■ How does it sound so far?
■ Why did I choose . . . , how else could I say this?
■ What do I want to say/do next?
■ How could I express . . . ?
■ What will my reader be thinking/ feeling as they read this?

Through engaging as writers and using writing to explore and evaluate possibilities, teachers can come to appreciate the complex, challenging and creative process of generating and shaping ideas, as Kathy metaphorically considers in the extract from her story *The Blank Page* (see Figure 7.3) (Cremin, 2006). In this teacher's story, the main character, Lucy, staring at a blank page, meets a mythical character Peter who invites her to join him on an adventure. In the process Lucy begins to trust herself and lets her intuition and imagination run free. Later she finds she has a story to tell. In a recent research project, 'Writing is Primary', the teachers noticed that the children, observant of their teachers' practices, settled more quickly when their teachers were

> *Lucy slowed down and seemed to lose her assertiveness. She wished she was back in her safe and predictable world and shifted uncomfortably from side to side, feeling unsure and insecure.*
>
> *"Trust yourself Lucy. Feel your instincts. Relax, release your imagination."*
>
> *"But I don't know what might happen" Lucy muttered.*
>
> *"Exactly" nodded the boy with a knowing smile, "you'll have to wait and see – that's the exciting thing!"*

■ **Figure 7.3** An extract from Kathy's short story *The Blank Page*

writing alongside them (Goouch *et al.*, 2009). The teachers also began to appreciate the persistence needed, the role of talk and the significant influence of life experience and other texts (Cremin, 2008). In tune with Pennac (2006), they spoke of the 'right to write' about what they chose and in a form that suited their chosen purpose; few appreciated having the subject or form imposed upon them. They realised, perhaps for the first time, the significance of fostering authorial agency, independence and choice in the development of young writers. Their insights, the opportunities for informed 'insider' instruction and the positive influences upon the children's attitudes to writing that emerged from this research, suggest that being a writing teacher – a teacher who writes and a writer who teaches, is a potent creative and instructional tool in a primary professional's repertoire.

RESPONDING TO WRITING

During the writing process, formative assessment will be accompanied by response, spoken or written, involving teachers and children identifying the value in young authors' writing. Teachers' evaluative responses have tended, in recent years, to be related to specific teaching and learning objectives or individual children's writing targets. However, while tailored feedback is important at times, there is a danger that responding only to a child's use of similes or connectives for example, or their ability to use complex sentences or 'wow' words, limits the teachers' response to the skill-set required or the techniques just taught. This is unlikely to help young writers appreciate how they influenced the reader's response and may not connect to the purpose of the endeavour – the actual communicative intent of the writing.

To develop children's ability to influence and shape readers' reactions to their texts, teachers need to foreground meaning in their responses, to read as readers first and as teachers second. This can be modelled through introducing children to responding to writing with EASE (see Figure 7.4). This involves readers/response partners:

Engagement: internalising the message

What thoughts, feelings, visual impressions come into your mind as you read?

Appreciation: considering the writers' achievements

How did the writer make you engage in this way?

Suggestion: considering specific ways to develop the writing

What can you suggest to improve the writing as present?

Extension: considering possible strategies and ideas to extend the writing

What can you suggest to extend the writing, what more is needed or would enrich?

(Goouch *et al.*, 2009)

■ **Figure 7.4** Responding to writing with EASE

- ■ Revisiting the author's intention – asking what they were trying to achieve.
- ■ Letting the author read their writing aloud or reading it to them.
- ■ Responding – orally or in writing with EASE.

This response framework, developed from the work of D'Arcy (1999), can be used by teachers in responding to children's work and by children in responding to their teacher's modelled writing. It can also be used to support children as response partners responding to each others' writing and to help children comment on and appreciate the work of professional writers. EASE operates as a potentially writer-oriented meaning focused evaluation framework. It profiles the engagement of the reader and seeks to recognise and identify the author's skills that created this engagement (D'Arcy, 1999). Additionally, the reader is invited to suggest possible strategies for developing and extending the writing. Using EASE, teachers avoid making a one-sided commentary or critique of children's writing, seeking rather to prompt a genuine dialogue between reader and writer, which should help children to discuss and critique their authorial choices in order to assess the value of their ideas. As children learn to reflect independently and critically on their own writing, their ability to develop a critical distance from their work and judiciously evaluate, edit and improve it is extremely important.

Another critical element of reflection, introduced in Chapter 6, is re-reading at the point of composition. Re-reading children's unfolding writing aloud to them and encouraging them to read it to themselves, enables young authors to listen to their own voices, get a feel for their writing and develop a more self-evaluative and critical ear. In reviewing their emergent writing at the point of composition, writers become readers and then writers again. This can help them edit, reshape and reflect upon the sounds, tunes and visuals of their words and meanings.

Teachers seeking to foster children's creativity will want to select, present and publish not only children's final writing/design products, but also their unfolding work, as well as the mediation and development of this. This may involve displaying annotations and various children's EASE commentaries on the work at different stages; these can help children reflect upon their own compositional journeys and enrich learning through reflection. Another strategy that can usefully help learners consider their writing journeys is for them to create compositional collages. Using materials from magazines and their own notes, children show the journey of a piece of writing and consider the myriad of influences upon this composition. Showing the ideas, texts and memories, for example, which may have influenced it, the EASE comments upon it and the author's redrafting in order to improve it.

In addition to ongoing formative assessment, teachers may also wish to undertake periodic assessments using the Assessing Pupil Progress in Writing materials (DCSF, 2008b), although as noted in Chapter 6, there is a tendency for these to be disproportionately focused on the construction of the writing and the skill-set demonstrated, at the relative expense of the meaning and the message. However, combined with use of the EASE Framework, such periodic assessment can be extremely useful.

FOSTERING CHILDREN'S AUTONOMY AS WRITERS

While children deserve to be introduced to different writing genres, they also deserve to assert their own agency as writers and authors. In underperforming schools, children have 'little notion of themselves as writers in control of the process, rather writing is seen as performing, the content, audience and purpose of which has been determined externally rather than internally' (Ofsted, 2002: 146). The backwash of assessment, too, tends to reduce children's choice in writing, although the new PNS (DfES, 2006a) laudably includes end of year objectives for all primary children relating to their ability to make decisions and choices about form, content, audience and purpose in writing. Fostering children's autonomy can increase young writers' personal involvement and investment in the process and can enrich their creativity, For when adults exert less control during writing events, children express more interest and initiate more verbal interaction, producing less conventional texts than when adults use a highly controlling style (Fang *et al*., 2004).

Establishing writing journals, in which children can choose what to write about and what form this might take, can support their growing independence and help them develop a sense of their own voice as writers. In such journals, children tend to write for themselves and each other in ways that satisfy them and connect to their personal passions and interests. The time and resources given to these sessions enable children to draw on the media that best suit their intentions. Typically, teachers do not read children's writing journals unless invited to do so, although they are likely to encourage writers to discuss subject choices, write collaboratively and share their writing with each other. For more detail on establishing writing journals see Graham and Johnson (2003). In writing workshops, children can also select their purpose, form and audience, perhaps supported by an A–Z of forms and an ongoing list of writing ideas. In such contexts, children often choose to mix elements of their cultural capital with the cultural capital of the school, exploring their interplay and their sense of identity in the process. For example, Abbi aged nine had a list of possible journal writing ideas – she chose several of these to develop, dropped others and added new ideas over time. See Figure 7.5 for her entry on hair styles – this has clearly been influenced by the magazines she reads and was followed in the journal by pages of accessories such as shoes, handbags and jewellery similarly treated. Abbi's early list of possible options that she might choose to write about included:

- review of Plain White T's latest album;
- my brother's madness about rugby;
- birthday present list;
- who I want to be with on the school trip;
- my birthday sleepover;
- top hair styles;
- my grandma;
- script for *America's Top Model*;
- my beautiful cat.

■ **Figure 7.5** A writing journal entry on hair styles

Setting time aside regularly to add possibilities to such a list is important, as is encouraging children to lean on their lives, on contemporary culture, on their views and concerns, and on drama and literature. In this way a desire to write is evoked and their young voices are activated through playful engagement with ideas and possibilities. After taking part in open-ended activities, see below for suggestions, children can be invited to record provisional titles or ideas in their journal/workshop lists. Their selections, connections and decisions will make a significant difference to the degree of commitment, interest and perseverance that they demonstrate. In sharing their personal choice writing with one another, children reveal a sense of their emerging identities. Such 'inside out writing' encourages reflection upon the expressive and social nature of writing and fosters a growing sense of control and authorial agency. This can contribute significantly to the creativity expressed in their writing: their voice and verve.

Activities to support choice

■ *Share personal stories*: Commencing with a teacher anecdote and using story titles, the class engage in swapping and sharing life stories in a story buzz. Each child will be able to share their tale many times and listen to others. Writing based on these stories may follow.

■ *Focus on story worlds*: Children draw and create new narrative worlds and populate these with creatures or they may just wish to create monsters or people

■ **Figure 7.6** A Navomark creature evolving

with special powers through drawing. See Figure 7.6 for 8-year-old Joe's drawing of a Navomark creature evolving. He imagined this species exist in the stratosphere and protect the world from invasion.

■ *Create mood/emotions graphs*: The horizontal axis represents a period of time, the vertical axis the emotions, low to high. Children plot significant memories on the graph and label the emotions/events in the key.

■ *Create timelines of life*: Children complete these at home, prompting stories to be told. After orally retelling one or two self-selected incidents in school, a choice for writing can be made.

■ *Focus on families*: Prompted by literature, visitors or discussion, children share anecdotes, descriptions and insights about significant family members. Letters, character descriptions, poems or short stories may follow.

■ *Views and concerns*: Children share their views, concerns, complaints, and perspectives on issues of interest to them. The class notice board with newspaper/magazine clippings can help highlight issues, as can literature. Persuasive, discursive or journalistic writing may follow.

■ *DVD shorts*: Children bring in favourite DVDs and extracts are viewed, prompting discussion of preferences. Children share their enthusiasm for particular films and may collaboratively create play scripts or reviews.

■ *Focus on personal passions*: Children bring in/collect material related to their favourite pop group, hobby, sport and so forth. Pamphlets, poems, fact files, diagrams, letters or stories may follow.

FOSTERING IMAGINATIVE ENGAGEMENT: WRITING IN ROLE

Writing in role offers children fictional purposes and audiences that feel real in the context of the drama. The lived experience of drama becomes a natural writing frame that is charged with the emotions and experiences of the imagined world, promoting voice, choice, stance and passion in writing. Drama in literacy time is a valuable precursor to writing, supporting the generation and selection of ideas. In drama children compose multimodally and shape their ideas in action prior to committing these to paper or screen. In using drama as a bridge to writing in brief literacy hour encounters, teachers need to align different drama conventions to particular forms of writing in order to ensure that the drama offers opportunities for oral rehearsal of the desired text type. This motivates young writers and enables the imagined experience to operate as an effective prompt, contextualising the act of composing. See Chapter 3 for examples of this significant bridging function.

Exploring texts through process drama in extended units of literacy work can also contribute to children's writing. Classroom/process drama proceeds without a script, employs elements of both spontaneous play and theatre, and involves the teacher in weaving an artistic experience together and building a work in the process. In such drama, both teachers and children engage in active make-believe, adopting roles and interacting together to create fictional worlds of their own making (O'Neill, 1995).

Research suggests that creative teachers remain open to 'seize the moment/s' to write during process drama, allowing themselves to follow the learners' interests, rather than working towards a particular written genre (Cremin *et al.*, 2006b). They offer the learners considerable choice of the form and content of their writing, which often becomes a vital and connected part of the imagined experience. In contrast to using drama in literacy time in a 'genre specific' way, to prepare for a particular form of writing, 'seize the moment' drama and writing is less explicitly framed, teachers respond spontaneously and writing arises naturally in response to the dramatic situations encountered. Three threads appear to connect process drama and writing and foster creative and effective compositions, these are: the presence of tension, deep emotional engagement, and a strong sense of stance and purpose gained in part through role adoption (Cremin *et al.*, 2006b). Through adopting different viewpoints and examining new and more powerful positions in both drama and writing, young learners experience alternative ways of being and knowing. As a consequence, and in response to their engagement in the tense dramatic experience, when the moment to write is seized, the work produced frequently demonstrates a higher than usual degree of empathy, a stronger and more sustained authorial stance and an emotively engaged voice. Such writing often very effectively captures and maintains the readers' interest.

Using process drama on extended learning journeys across the curriculum can also promote high quality writing in role and writing alongside role. For example, in exploring issues about the rainforest, writing in role might include letters or diaries of aid workers, European news reports or personal writing as the Huaroni. Writing alongside role, after the drama, might include a TV documentary script or a magazine article discussing the situation. Choice is again critical, since the imposition of a single written task does not sit comfortably with the various viewpoints developed in extended classroom drama.

CONCLUSION

Writing takes time. Children's journeys towards writing in extended units of work involve considerable reading, talking, playful exploration and close examination of texts prior to writing and then teachers modelling and demonstrating the genre to support children in imitating, innovating and drafting their compositions. The process also involves children in rereading and responding to their own and each others' writing in guided writing and response partnership contexts and in editing, evaluating and publishing their work. In separate independent writing contexts, young writers exert their authorial agency, and leaning perhaps on their lives, the world of popular culture and the multimodal texts they encounter, make their own choices of content, form, purpose and audience in their writing journals and/or writing workshop time. This combination of teaching and learning, instruction and support, experience and opportunity, as well as the exploration of freedom and form has the potential to foster creativity in children's writing.

FURTHER READING

Cremin, T. (2006) Creativity, Uncertainty and Discomfort: Teachers as Writers, *Cambridge Journal of Education*, 36(3): 415–33.

Myhill, D. (2005) Writing Creatively, in A. Wilson (ed.), *Creativity in Primary Education*, Exeter: Learning Matters, pp. 58–69.

Vass, E. (2004) Friendship and Collaboration: Creative Writing in the Primary Classroom, *Journal of Computer Assisted Learning*, 18: 102–11.

Walsh, C.S. (2007) Creativity as Capital in the Literacy Classroom: Youth as Multimodal Designers, *Literacy*, 41(2): 79–85.

CHILDREN'S BOOKS

Browne, A. (1998) *Voices in the Park*, Walker.

Crew, G. and Geddes, J. (2005) *The Mystery of Eilean Mor*, Lothian.

Gaiman, N. (2003) *Coraline*, Bloomsbury.

Garland, S. (1994) *Clive and the Missing Finger*, A. & C. Black.

Laird, E. (1997) *Secret Friends*, Hodder.

Rosen, M. (2004) *The Sad Book*, Walker.

CHAPTER 8

EXPLORING FICTION TEXTS CREATIVELY

INTRODUCTION

Children's literature and fiction in particular is at the heart of the English curriculum. It has the potential to play a powerful role in children's creative development. Literature can inspire, inform and expand the horizons of young people, challenging their thinking and provoking creative responses in art, drama and dance as well as in written forms on paper and on screen. This chapter explores how to teach fiction texts creatively in literacy and shows how, through employing the eight key features of creative practice, children can make rich connections, interpretations and representations of meaning. At the primary phase, teachers use literature to teach literacy, teach through literature in cross curricular contexts, teach learners about literature and encourage independent reading of literature for pleasure.

FICTION TEXTS

It is widely recognised that narrative pervades human experience; in dreams and daydreams, anecdotes, jokes and arguments, it is a way of thinking about the world and shaping experience within it. As Hardy (1977: 12) famously argued, 'narrative is not to be regarded as an aesthetic invention used by artists to control, manipulate, and order experience, but as a primary act of mind transferred to art from life'. As a way of making meaning, narrative pervades all human learning and therefore deserves a high profile in the curriculum.

Fiction enables children to vicariously and safely experience a range of emotions and promotes understanding of the human condition. It illuminates human behaviour in different cultures and societies, and facilitates reflection upon universal themes of existence, such as love and hate, envy, greed, sacrifice, loss and compassion. The nurturing effect of literature and its potential to educate the feelings can be tapped into in school if fiction and poetry are valued as more than mere resources for teaching literacy (Cremin, 2007). When reflecting upon why they love stories, two avid 10-year-old readers replied: 'You can lose yourself in another world and just kind of live there' and 'I like being in a hot tub in my imagination'. Such a hot tub enriches children's creative capacity, offering ideas and possibilities and the opportunity to ponder, hypothesise and problem solve their way forwards.

Many young people find narrative fiction very appealing: it offers a strong motivation for reading and viewing, and in the past has been the preferred reading choice of both boys and girls (Whitehead, 1977; Hall and Coles; 1999). Today it remains popular and is among the top reading choices for children outside school, who report a preference for jokes, magazines, comics, fiction, TV books and magazines in that order (Clark and Foster, 2005). In this National Literacy Trust survey, only 5 per cent reported not reading fiction. The most popular types noted were adventure, comedy and horror/ghost stories. Story writing is also frequently cited as the most popular written genre (Myhill, 2001; Grainger *et al.*, 2002), perhaps because in this form children are able to take control of their own world making play and express their creativity more freely.

Narrative fiction appears in a wealth of formats and can be found in magazines, in short story collections, in comics, graphic novels, picture fiction, novels, television and films. Characters from popular culture such as Bob the Builder, Dennis the Menace and the Simpsons also belong to the world of fiction that children encounter and on which they draw in their writing. In the classroom, the range will need to encompass series fiction that is currently extremely popular with the young and prompts many children to get hooked and persist as readers. Quality examples include the *Charlie and Lola* stories by Lauren Child, the *Horrid Henry* tales by Francesca Simon, the *Mr Majeika* stories by Humphrey Carpenter, Michele Paver's *Wolf Brother* series, Helen Dunmore's *Ingo* series and Paul Stewart and Chris Riddell's collection entitled *The Edge Chronicles*.

The lessons children learn about reading are shaped, not only by the interactions around text offered by their teachers' pedagogic practice, but crucially by the texts they encounter (Meek, 1988). It is clear that if they learn to read in the company of talented authors and illustrators this positively influences their motivation, persistence and success. Likewise in the stories children compose, the influence of the books they have read, heard and studied is visible (Barrs and Cork, 2001). This is evident in 6-year-old Alex's ant story in which the 'Where is Spot?' principle of many young children's narratives is evident (Figure 8.1). In this tale, the poor ant nearly meets his demise when an ant-eater pops up out of the bushes. Fortunately, however, Alex's ant is saved when a lion chases the ant eater away.

TEACHERS' KNOWLEDGE OF CHILDREN'S LITERATURE

Recent research suggests that teachers are not always sufficiently well acquainted with authors and picture fiction creators to enable them to plan richly integrated and holistic literature-based teaching, nor foster reader development (Cremin *et al.*, 2008a,b). In this survey, 1,200 primary teachers from eleven local authorities in England were asked to list six 'good' children's writers. In their responses, 48 per cent of the

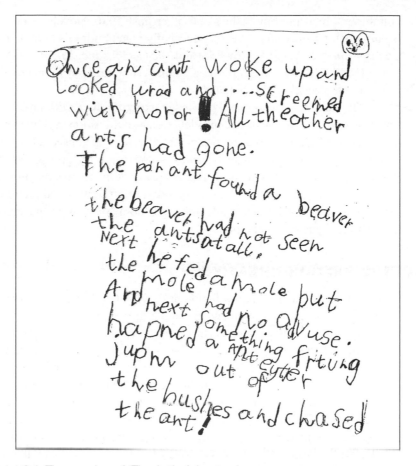

■ **Figure 8.1** The opening of 'The Ant's Adventure'

practitioners named six and 10 per cent named two, one or no authors at all. Roald Dahl gained the highest number of mentions (744). The next in order of mention were: Michael Morpurgo (343), Jacqueline Wilson (323), J.K. Rowling (300) and Anne Fine (252). The only other authors who received above a hundred mentions were: Dick King Smith (172), Janet and Allan Ahlberg (169), Enid Blyton (161), Shirley Hughes (128), C.S. Lewis (122), Philip Pullman (117), Mick Inkpen (106) and Martin Waddell (100). In terms of range and diversity relatively few writers of novels for older readers were included and there was little mention of writers from other cultures or even writers writing about other cultures.

The teachers' knowledge of poetry and picture fiction was also limited, with only 10 per cent of the teachers naming six picture fiction creators and 24 per cent naming none at all, and 10 per cent naming six poets and 22 per cent naming none (Cremin *et al.*, 2008b). There were very few mentions of named picture book makers who offer complex visual texts for older readers and almost no woman poets named. However, it is reassuring to note that these teachers read in their own lives; nearly three quarters reported reading a book within the last three months (Cremin *et al.*, 2008a). Popular fiction topped the list of their favourite reading (40 per cent), followed by autobiographies and biographies and other post 1980s novels (both 14 per cent). A smaller percentage (6.5 per cent) had recently read children's fiction, including novels such as *Harry Potter* (J.K. Rowling) and *The Curious Incident of the Dog in the Night-Time* (Mark Haddon). Such books are sometimes referred to as crossover fiction as they are also widely read by adults.

The lack of professional knowledge and assurance with children's fiction that this research reveals, the over-dependence on a small canon of writers and the minimal knowledge of global literature, has potentially serious consequences for all learners, particularly those from linguistic and cultural minority groups. Without a diverse knowledge of children's fiction, teachers are arguably not in a position to be effective, for as Graham (2000) observes, high quality fiction writers and picture book creators bring a second/third teacher into the classroom and foster the creativity of both teachers and younger learners.

TEACHING FICTION CREATIVELY

In recent years, the teaching of fiction has arguably suffered as a consequence of the twin pressures of prescription and accountability, and the over-use of text extracts to teach specific linguistic features. In 2003 and 2005 a group of professional authors, concerned at what they perceived to be an 'analysis paralysis' approach to fiction, which relied heavily on extracts, voiced the view to the Education Secretary that what was at stake was 'nothing less than the integrity of the novel, the story, the poem . . . valued for its own sake and on its own terms' (Powling, 2003: 3; Powling *et al.*, 2005). This group, which included Chris Powling, Bernard Ashley, Philip Pullman, Anne Fine and Jamila Gavin, were not alone in expressing their dissatisfaction; since the inception of the NLS (DfEE, 1998), concerns have been voiced about the ways in which children's literature has been positioned and may be used in the classroom (Dombey, 1998; Sedgwick, 2001).

However, many primary professionals realise that what they choose to read aloud, recommend, share and study, and how they explore literature in the classroom, is crucial if they wish to foster learner creativity. Such teachers seek to develop pedagogic practices that are open-ended and give space to the children's views, harnessing their curiosity through playful engagement with powerful fictions that have the potential to interest, involve and challenge the learners. In such work collaboration, interpretation and representations of multiple meanings are likely to be foregrounded (Lockwood, 2008).

Teachers who are readers themselves may be more likely to recognise literature as a rich source of possibility, a place for imaginative involvement and reflection, and may be less likely to treat it merely as a model for writing or a resource for cross curricular work. Those who read themselves and read children's literature widely are arguably better placed to make judgements about quality and appropriateness in selecting books and in matching books to individual readers. Such professionals have been called Reading Teachers: 'teachers who read and readers who teach' (Commeyras *et al.*, 2003). Research studies highlight an apparent continuity between Reading Teachers and children as readers. In summarising much of this work, Dreher observes:

> Teachers who are engaged readers are motivated to read, are both strategic and knowledgeable readers, and are socially interactive about what they read. These qualities show up in their classroom interactions and help create students who are in turn engaged readers.
>
> (Dreher, 2003: 338)

Such teachers model being readers and seek to share their reading lives and reading strategies in order to build genuinely reciprocal reading relationships that support young, engaged readers. This could involve teachers sharing their personal passions and preferences as readers and their feelings, questions and confusions about texts, as well as what and where they read and why. Research suggests creative professionals tend to adopt a humanitarian stance to education and build strong personal relationships with children (Craft, 2005). Reading Teachers certainly share their reading identities, interests and preferences with children, who in turn reflect upon their own reading histories and habits, their likes and dislikes. Reading Teachers focus on readers' rights and seek to build reciprocal relationships with young readers. (For more details see Cremin *et al.*, 2009b.)

There is strong evidence that picture fiction can make a rich contribution to children's creativity (Arizpe and Styles, 2003). Meek argued long ago that quality picture fiction books 'make reading for all a distinctive kind of imaginative looking' (1991: 119), and highlighted their potential for creatively engaging all readers. Authors such as Neil Gaiman and Shaun Tan, Emily Gravett, Anthony Browne and Gary Crew, for example, often experiment with the interplay between words and pictures and set up gaps between the literal and metaphorical interpretations of their narratives. As a consequence their demanding texts provoke multiple interpretations as well as discussion about the issues, themes and values expressed by the author/illustrator, as well as the language, characters and narrative structure used.

Complex novels can also prompt involvement, enabling children to sustain their engagement with longer texts and develop persistence. The talented work of Berlie Doherty, Philip Reeve, Marcus Sedgwick, Malorie Blackman and Kevin Crossley Holland, for example, often produces considerable discussion and debate. In addition, picture strip and cartoon style stories by Bob Graham and Marcia Williams, for example, as well as graphic novel partnerships such as that between Mariko and Jillian Tamaki, offer a rich expression of the potential of the imagination. Powerful fiction texts, whatever their format, leave space for the creativity of the reader to be brought into play. Creative teachers exploit these reverberating spaces and join learners in a range of problem finding – problem solving activities that seek to advance their understanding, their comprehension and their creativity. In order to get to know children's books, teachers clearly need to read widely (see Goodwin, 2008).

READING AND RESPONDING TO FICTION TEXTS

While the act of reading fiction is likely to be seen as a private affair, and children need to be able to make sense of texts for themselves, comprehension develops in large part through conversation and interaction around texts. Meaning emerges and is shaped and revised as readers engage with and respond to what they read, often in the company of others. Each reader brings him/herself to the text, their life experience, prior knowledge and understanding of the issues encountered, as well as cultural perspectives and insights. Meaning is thus created in the interaction between the author, the text and the reader. Benton and Fox (1985) argue that teachers should focus more on the creative act of reading and, in particular, on the expression of personal responses, as they believe this is where a deep delight in literature begins. Through discussing their responses children can make connections, interrogate their views about the world and learn about themselves in the process. In order to achieve this, however, teachers need to investigate the layers of meaning in a text and help children draw upon their prior knowledge. So while teachers' own responses are important, batteries of comprehension questions should be avoided and the children's questions, puzzlements and interpretations should lead the conversations.

In small guided groups, literature circles and in whole class contexts, children can take part as interested conversationalists, talking their way forward creatively and establishing new insights and understandings as well as developing a shared language for talking about texts in a reflective and evaluative manner. In group discussion and book talk, the reading comprehension strategies used by both children and their teacher are important. These need to be modelled and will often be framed as tentative statements or open questions to prompt discussion. They reflect the kinds of strategies effective readers employ to make sense of the text (see Figure 8.2).

Children's comprehension and understanding can be developed as they use this range of strategies in shared and guided reading, although all such discussion prompts need to focus on engagement and response first, leading to interpretation and consideration second. This will help to ensure that the pleasure principle is retained and reading fiction remains a problem-solving process. There are a number of other classroom practices that prompt exploration and engagement, for example drama can enable children to inhabit the narrative, experience the dramatic tension and examine the motivation of the characters. Art, music and dance can also encourage re-presentations of the themes and meanings identified and prompt children to reflect on each others' interpretations. Other open-ended fiction-based activities include literature circles and reading journals.

Literature circles seek to develop autonomous learners within a community of readers and involve children reading a text, mostly outside the session, and meeting regularly to discuss it, often with the support of an adult and/or reading journals (King, 2001; King and Briggs, 2005). Readers' expectations may be profiled and time is likely to be set aside to develop a sense of anticipation prior to reading the narrative. In addition, children will be involved in mulling over ideas together, identifying questions and confusions, and seeking clarification as they share their interpretations with one another. Literature circles aim to help children internalise the process of engaging in such exploratory talk and take the initiative in the choice of text as well as in leading the discussion. Initially, teachers may want to scaffold the children's learning by modelling the use of the reading strategies noted in Figure 8.2 in order to help them anticipate and reflect upon the text. However, in order to foster the ownership of learning and agency that are essential for creativity, it is essential that there is sufficient

Predicting/ hypothesising	I think what might happen is . . . although it might not because . . . . What if the character . . . ? I wonder what the character is thinking at this moment?
Picturing	When I read that I vividly saw a picture of . . . in my head – did anyone else see any moment/character very clearly?
Connecting/ comparing	This reminds me of . . . (other stories/films/TV or life experience) so it makes me feel . . .
Questioning	I wonder . . . why . . . what . . . .whether . . . if . . . .?
Engaging emotionally/ empathising	I'm not sure what I feel about this character, I used to think . . . but now I wonder if . . . .
Responding to issues	I wonder what the author/illustrator is trying to examine? I used to think he/she was exploring . . . but now I am less sure . . .
Evaluating	I like . . . but I'm less keen on . . . Exploring likes, dislikes, puzzles and patterns (Chambers, 1995)
Noticing language/ style/presentation	I noticed . . . were there words or phrases that anyone else noticed – what do you think made them leap out at you? I wonder why the author chose to present character X in this . . . way? The writing reminds me of . . . style – is anyone else reminded of another writer's work?

■ **Figure 8.2** Strategies for active reading

time, trust and space created for children to develop *their* ideas, and *their* questions and to probe each others' responses to these.

Reading journals can also support a focus on active interrogation and reflection upon texts. Creative professionals develop their own ways of developing journals with each class. Some may offer a bank of possible prompts at the back of the journal and invite children to record their responses following a literature circle discussion. Others may encourage children to annotate the text during reading, using post-it notes to highlight key phrases or short passages, puzzles or patterns. In this way reading journals can effectively integrate reading and writing and can support both literature circles and private reading. If a bank of prompts is offered, the reading strategies from Figure 8.2 could be listed and children could be encouraged to note their initial impressions and the questions or predictions that occur to them during reading. In addition, teachers may suggest children identify and copy memorable quotations or particularly pleasing words or phrases, as well as draw responses to the narrative, encouraging visualisation of particular characters or scenes at significant moments in the tale.

WRITING FICTION TEXTS: EXPERIMENTING WITH FORM AND FREEDOM

It is widely recognised that reading enriches writing and that literature offers a repertoire of possibilities for writers (Fox, 1993a,b; Barrs and Cork, 2001). Through open-ended explorations and focused discussions, children learn more about how texts are constructed; such deconstruction can lead to reconstruction in their own writing. At times this will be imitative, but at others, literature will be engaged with as a source of inspiration and ideas. As part of the extended process of composition, creative teachers map in opportunities to inhabit and explore texts through drama, discussion, storytelling, art, dance, music and performance. Such explorations encompass oral, kinaesthetic and visual approaches, and provoke children's intellectual and emotional engagement in the narrative, generating new ideas for writing. For example, through improvising with puppet characters from a story, children can collectively co-author new fictions, or through listening to oral stories and re-telling personal and traditional tales, they can learn a great deal about narrative structure and language features (Grainger *et al.*, 2005). Children's involvement with computer games has also been shown to influence their story writing (Bearne and Wolstencroft, 2007). Leaning on literature, life and a range of popular cultural resources supports young writers, although teachers will need to help them make their implicit knowledge about language more explicit.

In the contexts of their creative encounters with texts, children's attention can be drawn to the constructedness of text, so that their growing awareness of a writer's skill develops alongside their pleasure in the meanings conveyed. Young authors can develop the craft of writing in part through conscious use of the literary models that surround them. The Teaching Reading and Writing Links (TRAWL) project demonstrated that critical reading and investigation of texts is an integral part of the writing process, and children's metacognitive development and awareness of the reader can be enhanced through thoughtful teaching about the literary language of texts (Corden, 2001, 2003). The teaching on the TRAWL project, however, despite its emphasis on literary devices, was not at the expense of the meaning or purpose of text, and children were provided with opportunities to work on extended pieces of writing in which they could make use of their new knowledge and skills in context. As a consequence, their developing knowledge of text was coupled with an emerging understanding of authorship, and they became more aware of the way in which authors choose to manipulate language to achieve effects. Over time the knowledge and insights gained were transferred into their own writing (ibid.).

Specific response to text activities that allow children to interpret and reconstruct stories, as well as to increase their awareness of the author's craft, can pay dividends. Children can develop their explicit and implicit knowledge about language through a range of such affectively involving text activities that focus upon the key elements of fiction, character, language, setting, story structure and so forth. To help children develop a deeper understanding of these elements, teachers can use activities that enrich their repertoires of these elements. See Figure 8.3 for some of the many activities available to teachers that focus on narrative elements and foster the

Awareness of character

Role-play	Group sculpture
Speech/thought bubbles	Character ladder
Interior monologue	Emotions graph
Emotions map	Hot-seat

Awareness of structure

Story journeys	Bookzip
Stepping stones	Mural
Freeze-frames	Timelines
Story maps	Retelling

Awareness of language

No quote without comment	Puzzle possibility game
Reading journals	Dog's tail
Phrase/clause wall	Telling down
Forum theatre	Like, dislike, puzzle, pattern

Awareness of theme

Backbone summary	Share the essence
Thematic bracelets	Hint hunt
Contents focus	Sentence game
Sculpture and paragraph	Poster of the film

■ **Figure 8.3** Activities to focus on narrative elements

creativity of both readers and writers. For more details on these and other ideas see the series by Grainger *et al.* (2004a,b,c).

Such text-based activities need to be employed in the context of a text, for example in exploring Jez Alborough's book *Where's My Teddy?*, one teacher chose to focus on the two main characters, Eddie and the great big Bear. Both Eddie and the Bear have lost their teddies and find each others' in the wood. The class of 5- and 6-year-olds created freeze-frames of significant moments in the tale and then engaged in interior monologues, speaking out loud the thoughts of Eddie and the big Bear at the moments they had depicted. Once safely home, with their teacher in role as Eddie's mum, and the children in role as Eddie, they retold their stories about meeting the Bear and his giant-sized teddy and finding their own beloved teddy bear. Their teacher then re-read the book and focused on the end of the story, when both the big Bear and Eddie are in their own beds, 'huddling and cuddling their own little teds'. Through role-play in pairs, the children improvised their chosen character's conversation with their teddy and then added speech bubbles to a reproduced visual from the text to show this. The young writers eagerly selected the accompanying visual and rapidly recorded these conversations.

■ **Figure 8.4** Jenny's bedtime chat from *Where's My Teddy?*

Copyright © 1992 Jez Alborough, from *Where's My Teddy?* by Jez Alborough. Reproduced by permission of Walker Books Ltd, London SE11 5HJ

Jenny's conversation between Eddie and his beloved teddy (see Figure 8.4) suggests that the little teddy had rather enjoyed his adventure with the great big Bear, implying perhaps another story within the story. In fact, Jenny had a lengthy tale to tell about the cave in the mountains and the other animals the tiny teddy had seen when travelling with the great big Bear. In this exploration, several activities were woven together to help the class examine the feelings and motivation of the main characters, but this did not prevent Jenny from actively pondering on and creating another narrative from the perspective of a minor character, Eddie's teddy. Her story was shared and celebrated as a novel interpretation and later that week children were observed in the forest role-play area acting out the tiny teddy's adventures.

PROFILING FICTION IN EXTENDED LEARNING JOURNEYS

In profiling fiction across several weeks in the primary classroom there are a number of available options. Teachers might choose to focus on a particular form of fiction, such as myths or legends, for example and explore how oral and written storytellers convey their narratives. Or they might choose to lean on a theme such as friendship or bullying and draw together a wealth of texts to read and explore, considering how different authors, illustrators and poets examine the issue. Alternatively, teachers might choose to focus on one or two significant children's authors and read across a range of their works, reflecting upon their craft and style as writers. In each of these and other possible units of work, creative teachers are likely to draw upon narratives presented in a number of media, including perhaps: printed and graphic novels, oral tales shared by visiting storytellers, short stories in anthologies, narratives on radio, television and film.

If the focus is on a children's author then during the period of immersion and exploration of their fictional texts, children can be invited to search relevant websites (the author's own, publishers and other book sites) for additional information. It is also possible that radio or filmed interviews will be available to watch and supplementary materials found to help make connections between the writers and their work. Many authors respond to seriously written letters of enquiry and also visit schools to work alongside children.

The following account outlines a creative learning journey based on the autobiographical tales and short stories of some contemporary children's writers. The short story genre is a valuable resource for offering children models of writing narrative fiction and can help children make connections between reading and writing.

The route actually travelled across the unit will be shaped by the children's emerging needs and interests, and their response to the tales and the emergent themes. Letting the children lead during the journey will ensure that they take a degree of ownership and control of their learning, fostering their possibility thinking and creative engagement (Cremin *et al.*, 2006a). The learning intention/ long-term outcome of this unit is for each child to write and publish a short story, connected in some way to their own lives. Depending on the age of the class, adaptations will need to be made. The planning is mapped out with a junior aged class in mind and builds on the planning diagram in Chapter 7.

Initially, the teacher could work with the class to create a short story collection, perhaps borrowing from local libraries and inviting children to lend any from home as well as accessing short stories in magazines and websites. Kate Agnew's collection *A Family like Mine*, Kate Pettys's *Tales of Beauty and Cruelty* and Tony Bradman's *Skin Deep* are well worth reading, as are single author collections such as *The Rope* by Philippa Pearce, *A Fistful of Pearls* by Elizabeth Laird and *A Pack of Lies* by Geraldine McCaughrean. These and other texts could be added to the class collection for independent and/or guided reading. This unit focuses mainly on the work of David Almond, Beverley Naidoo, Allan Ahlberg and Michael Morpurgo, which should be extensively read aloud in order to find narratives of interest and relevance to the children and thus worthy of more focused exploration. Some of their collections, for example Morpurgo's *Singing for Mrs Pettigrew* and Naidoo's *Out of Bounds* draw upon their childhood experiences to recreate and re-envision narratives, while others such as Almond's *Counting Stars* and Ahlberg's *The Boyhood of Burglar Bill* are explicitly autobiographical.

Creative teachers will want to find tales within these collections that engage and excite them as adult readers, but might valuably start with Ahlberg's opening tale in *The Boyhood of Burglar Bill*, entitled 'One-arm man, three-legged dog'. This deliciously evokes his childhood, in which his love of football and a 'madman teacher' play a significant role. Commencing with this is likely to trigger personal connections and tale telling, which could be supported by the class drawing timelines of life and talking to their parents and carers about significant memories and events. In school,

My Nan

Her face lights up the stars
She reminds me of an old fashioned car.
that likes to take it slow
An old tiger like cat
that lies asleep in the rocking chair.
A loving person
that wouldn't leave me.
It was her time to go.

■ **Figure 8.5** A poem, 'My Nan'

pairs could swap selected stories in a story buzz and identify possible titles for their own and each others' tales, perhaps with reference to the variety of titles offered in the collections available. An emphasis on ambiguity, brevity, intrigue and/or subtlety may be foregrounded in this work on titles and another storybuzz with their titles might enable the children to revisit and reshape their chosen life stories by sharing them with different partners. In a story buzz, as the children move around the class pairing up, listening to and telling each other their tales, their narratives will not only be rehearsed and reshaped, but will be expanded on in response to their listeners' responses. In addition, revisiting Ahlberg's story or another of interest to the class to examine the craft of his writing more closely will pay dividends. This might include role-playing Mr Cork, the madman teacher in other imaginary situations to reveal more about him as a character. In one class of 7–8-year-olds engaged on a similar autobiographical journey, the teacher found several of the children writing other personal tales and poems about significant people in their lives in their writing journals at this time. Several shared their work with one another, for example, Shaun wrote about his Nan, see Figure 8.5.

Triggered in part by the personal storytelling focus, Shaun published this poem in a school anthology. A later focus on this journey could involve studying and discussing tales from *Singing for Mrs Pettigrew* and sharing Morpurgo's fascinating commentaries on each one. In these he explains his connections to the place, people and predicaments examined and recreated in the tale. By now the children may have chosen which of their stories they wish to retell, or which they want to lean upon to explore an issue connected to their lives, and they may have begun to map out their own tales on page or screen. Once their tales are nearly complete and response partners have made comments on each others' (see Chapter 7 for support for responding with EASE), the children could be invited to write their own commentaries mirroring Morpurgo's ruminations.

The class might also create their own compositional collages, using cut outs from magazines, visuals from the Internet as well as their own drawings and possibly photographs from home to indicate the many influences on their own narratives.

A focus on place in the short stories being read may be particularly helpful, perhaps enriched through the work of Beverley Naidoo, whose collection *Out of Bounds* is set during the apartheid years in South Africa or through examining David Almond's narratives in *Counting Stars*, which depict his formative years growing up in a large Catholic family in the UK. Shared and guided work throughout the unit will highlight the chosen teaching and learning objectives, which will be made relevant through the process of engagement and the creation of their own stories. The teaching will be both planned and responsive, allowing children to pursue their interests and personally chosen narratives, and offering them support and tailored instruction on the journey.

Finally, it will be important to celebrate the children's completed stories ensuring that copies of the class anthology are available, for example in print or on the school website, and readings of the tales in class and in assembly are encouraged. Reviews can also be sought from parents, peers and children in other classes or schools. Making public their work is important as it enables young writers to receive feedback from their readers and recognise themselves as authors, alongside the authors whose work they have read and studied. It might also be that the final collection could be sent to one of the authors or offered to local community centres, doctor's surgeries and libraries.

CONCLUSION

Creative teachers seek out fiction texts that require children to actively participate in making meaning – texts that trigger multiple questions, deep engagement and that build bridges of understanding. In exploring such texts, creative teachers employ a wide range of open-ended strategies that foster children's curiosity and develop their personal and creative responses, enriching their understanding of narrative and prompting related talk, reading and writing, inspired by the power of the powerful literature chosen for study. At the same time, creative teachers read aloud a wide range of other potent, affectively engaging texts.

FURTHER READING

Arizpe, E. and Styles, M. (2003) *Children Reading Pictures: Interpreting Visual Texts*, London: RoutledgeFalmer.

Barrs, M. and Cork, V. (2001) *The Reader in the Writer: The Influence of Literature upon Writing at KS2*, London: Centre for Literacy in Primary Education.

Cremin, T. (2007) Revisiting Reading for Pleasure: Diversity, Delight and Desire, in K. Goouch and A. Lambirth (eds), *Understanding Phonics and the Teaching of Reading*, Berkshire: McGraw-Hill, pp. 166–90.

Grainger, T., Goouch, K. and Lambirth, A. (2005) Artistic Voices: Literature, in *Creativity and Writing: Developing Voice and Verve in the Classroom*, London: Routledge, Chapter 5.

CHILDREN'S BOOKS

Agnew, K. (2003) (ed.) *A Family Like Mine*, Egmont.

Ahlberg, A. (2006) *The Boyhood of Burglar Bill*, Puffin.

Alborough, J. (1995) *Where's My Teddy?*, Walker.

Almond, D. (2000) *Counting Stars*, Hodder.

Bradman, T. (2004) (ed.) *Skin Deep: Stories that Cut to the Bone*, Puffin.

Laird, E. (2008) *A Fistful of Pearls*, Frances Lincoln.

McCaughrean, G. (1990) *A Pack of Lies*, Penguin.

Morpurgo, M. (2006) *Singing for Mrs Pettigrew*, Walker.

Naidoo, B. (2003) *Out of Bounds*, Puffin.

Pearce, P. (2000) *The Rope and Other Stories*, Puffin.

Petty, K. and Castle, C. (2005) *Tales of Beauty and Cruelty*, Orion.

EXPLORING POETIC TEXTS CREATIVELY

CHAPTER 9

INTRODUCTION

Poetry, a highly crafted kind of written language, offers a rich resource for teaching literacy creatively. Its particular structures and forms generate interest and its multi-modal nature incites physical movement from lips to fingertips. Poetry deserves to be read and responded to actively and imaginatively, prompting a desire to read more and discuss, perform, represent and write. In the PNS framework (DfES, 2006a), it is recommended as a literary genre for regular playful investigation across each year of the primary curriculum. As well as contributing to creativity, poetry can increase children's self-awareness, empathy and evaluation as key aspects of their learning. In this chapter the focus is on teaching poetry creatively and employing the eight strands of creative literacy practice to enable children to develop their creativity in reading, performing and writing poetic texts.

POETIC TEXTS

Outside the classroom, children's lives are packed with poetry. They engage in a world of rich language play, experimenting with and imbibing playground rhymes, songs, football chants, jingles, jokes and lyrics, often without recognising their essentially poetic nature. Their first experiences of poetry are often oral, for as Michael Rosen (1989) argues, poetry and fiction have their roots in everyday speech, and from their earliest years children meet poetry in word play, nursery rhyme, rhythm and song, taking particular pleasure in the playful and often subversive nature of poetic language (Grainger and Goouch, 1999).

There are multiple definitions of poetry, ranging from 'memorable speech' (Auden and Garret, 1935) to 'the right words in the right order' (Hughes, 1967), but as Zephaniah (2001) observes, while experts make it their business to tell readers what kind of poems they should like, individuals of all ages make their own decisions and develop their own preferences. Teachers need to introduce children to a wide range of forms and styles through reading aloud, shared and guided reading, and closer examinations of free verse and many different forms. These might include: shape poetry; list poetry; narrative poetry; rap; rhyming forms such as nursery rhymes and playground games; and short patterned poetry such as haiku, kennings and cinquains. Children can be encouraged to draw upon these and many other forms, as well as free verse, in their writing.

The presentation of poetry is important. Creative teachers celebrate the multimodality of poetry though drawing on a variety of resources enabling children to re-present poetry though art, drama, music and dance, for example, and offering children access to poets sharing their own work via the web-based *Poetry Archive*. Both the adult and the children's section of this online archive are well worth exploring with children and additionally, working with professional poets in school can be invaluable. The key features of poetry noted in the PNS (DfES, 2007c) progression in poetry materials include:

- sound effects – repetition, alliteration, onomatopoeia, rhythm and rhyme;
- visual effects – simile, personification, metaphor;
- selection of powerful vocabulary;
- surprising word combinations;
- use of repetitions and repeated patterns for effect.

Noticing, discussing and using the language features of various poetic forms is part of teaching and learning about poetry, but is not the *raison d'être*, for such features are harnessed to create meaning and achieve effects. Pleasure and engagement precede full understanding, so priority must be given to the meaning and message of poetic texts through creative approaches that foster the development of positive attitudes and dispositions towards this rich and varied art form.

TEACHERS' KNOWLEDGE OF POETIC TEXTS

It has been suggested that teachers' confidence in knowing and using children's literature and particularly poetry, may be limited (Arts Council England, 2003); this has been verified in a recent UKLA survey of 1,200 primary teachers (Cremin *et al.*, 2008a,b). When asked to name six children's poets, 58 per cent of the teachers named only two, one or no poets, 22 per cent named no poets at all and only 10 per cent named six poets. The highest number of mentions by far was for Michael Rosen (452) with five others gaining over a hundred mentions, namely: Allan Ahlberg, Roger McGough, Roald Dahl, Spike Milligan and Benjamin Zephaniah. After these, only three poets were mentioned more than fifty times: Edward Lear, Ted Hughes and A.A. Milne. Few women poets were mentioned and with the notable exception of Benjamin Zephaniah, black poets received very few mentions. The teachers lent towards those whose poetry might be seen as light-hearted or humorous (for example, Rosen, Dahl, Ahlberg or Milligan) or writers whose work might be seen as classic (for example, Rossetti, Browning, Blake, Wordsworth, Stevenson, Hughes, Milne). As Ofsted (2007: 13) noted, the majority of primary teachers are not English specialists and 'tend not to be keen or regular readers of poetry' so often rely upon poems presented in publishers' resources or those recalled from childhood. The poems named by title in the UKLA survey were mostly classics, which teachers probably studied in their own school days (for example, R.L. Stephenson's 'From a Railway Carriage' and W.H. Davies' 'Leisure'). This may suggest that teachers are focused more on poems than poets, and on using poetry to teach linguistic features at the expense of reading, responding to and enjoying poetry for its own sake.

Based on this data, it could be argued that primary practitioners' marked lack of knowledge of poets is restricting children's access to poetic voices in all their energetic and reflective diversity. It is questionable whether they are in a position to recommend, read from or share pleasure in the work of female poets, or poets from different cultures and they may not be knowledgeable enough about poetry to introduce children to a sufficiently wide selection to interest, engage and challenge them as readers. Perhaps not surprisingly, therefore, a recent survey has shown that many children are also unable to name a favourite book of poems or a favourite poet and some simply don't read poetry (Maynard *et al.*, 2007).

TEACHING POETRY CREATIVELY

In order to teach poetry creatively, teachers need to become acquainted with the widest possible range of writers, encompassing both older and newer voices such as Edward Lear, Spike Milligan, John Agard, Benjamin Zephaniah, James Berry, Gareth Owen, as well as Jackie Kay, Grace Nichols, Anton Fusek Peters, Tony Mitton and Claire Bevan. The work of writers from further afield, such as the Canadian Sheree Fitch and the American Shel Silverstein is also worth sharing, as is the poetry of popular novelists such as Berlie Doherty, Gillian Clarke and Kevin Crossley Holland. Any list, however, is invidious and incomplete, and a teachers' task is to keep up to date and to get to know both those whose work has immediate appeal and accessibility to primary aged learners and those whose writing is perhaps more layered and demanding. Borrowing books from the local library and inviting children to lend poetry anthologies from home can enrich classroom collections. Children can add to their repertoire through learning chosen poems by heart and creating an A–Z of Poets that they can add to over the year. They can also create friezes and displays of their favourite poems and explore poets' websites, as well as undertake surveys of their parents'/grandparents' favourite poems, songs and rhymes.

Through developing an open and creative ethos in the literacy classroom, teachers encourage experimentation with poetry in all its forms, building on the early sounds and savours found in nursery and playground rhymes. Such rhymes have much in common; they encompass repetition and rhythm, are easy to recall, highly adaptable, social and physical and are affectively engaging and fun. Children of all ages can brainstorm these, and will be reminded of them on the playground as they clap, skip, play two-ball games and take part in games and rhymes. On returning to the classroom they can revisit, read and share such rhymes, also examining examples such as Grace Hallworth's delicious collection *Down by the River*, an anthology of Caribbean playground rhymes and John Agard's *No Hickory, No Dickory, No Dock.* Identifying patterns and features of such rhymes and classifying them into collections of two ball poems, skipping games, counting rhymes and so forth will both build on and expand the class' repertoire and foster experimentation and performance. It may be that children know rhymes in other languages and if so these will be important to share, to nurture a variety of literacy experiences in a variety of languages' (Kenner, 2000: xi). Such explorations will involve both reading and responding to poetry and the opportunity to compose their own verse, individually and in groups. Talking about the poems and leaning on new knowledge about the forms encountered will be a central part of such creative explorations.

READING AND RESPONDING TO POETRY

Classroom approaches need to connect to and build on children's early oral experiences in which poetry is engaged with socially, physically and emotionally. If teachers use active approaches they can nurture children's affinity with rhythm, rhyme and beat, and capitalise upon their pleasurable engagement with language (Ofsted, 2007). Creative teachers seek to ensure poetry is voiced by the learners themselves; it is not enough for them to hear poetry read to them – they need to bring it to life by tasting the word textures, feeling the rhythms and discerning the colour, movement and drama in the text. Copies of poems need to be in the children's hands, and opportunities made available for them to release them from the page and read, chant, move and sing verse into existence. The marriage of poetry and music is centuries old, so percussion and song and even something as simple as a repeating ostináto of a line of the verse can help demarcate the rhythm and point up the meaning and tune. The physical embodiment of verse is also important and can trigger alternative ways of responding to poetry (Grainger, 1999). Children's performance readings and explorations may include dance and drama, and mime and movement, which can energise their engagement and provoke multiple interpretations of the sense and savour of the words. In choosing their own poems to perform, small groups can select one that connects to them and use multiple media to represent the poem to others.

Children can also use poetry as a form of play script with groups re-voicing verses, perhaps leaning on the conversational poetry of Kit Wright and Michael Rosen for example. Richard Edwards' collections, such as *The Midnight Party* and *Talk Poetry 2*, are helpfully marked for many voices and thus prompt collaborative play script-like readings of his verse. Using such poetry as play scripts can facilitate spontaneous readings as well as more thoughtfully prepared group or class presentations. Collaborating with others to bring the dead words on the page to life is a powerful form of reading and responding to poetry. In seeking to understand poetry in this way, children will be experimenting with language, interpretation and meaning in their small group discussions and in their shared readings and performances, as well as through experiencing the multimodal representations of others. Supported by their teacher's creative engagement and their own felt experience of the verse, new insights about a poem's meaning, rhythm and structure can emerge. In one class of 9–10-year-olds, small groups selected poems to perform. One group of girls chose 'Mary and Sarah' by Richard Edwards. During their exploration of it and in preparation for a performance of this play script-like poem, the group decided to write their own poem 'Boys and Girls' based loosely on Edwards' poem and performed that instead. (See Figure 9.1.)

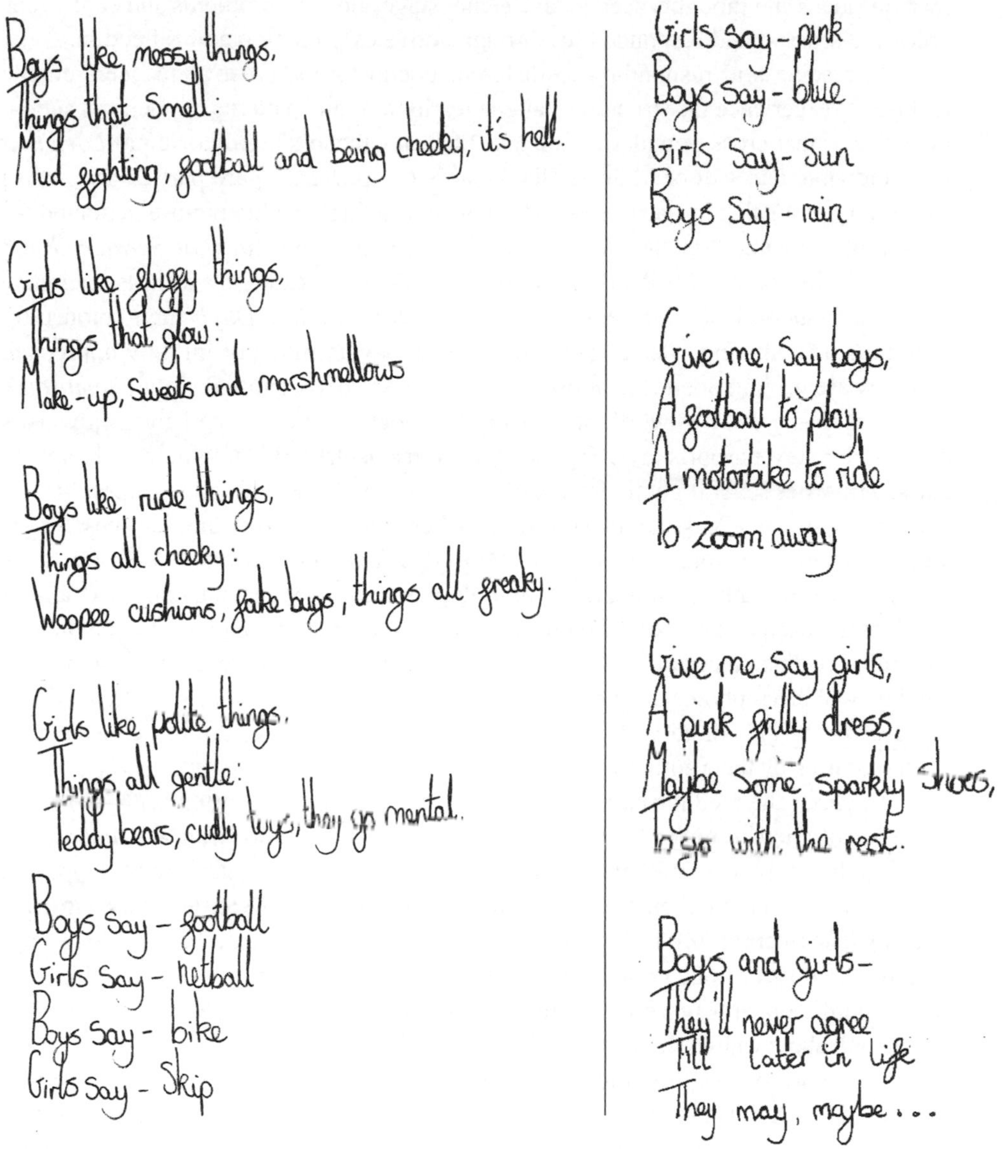

Boys like messy things,
Things that smell:
Mud fighting, football and being cheeky, it's hell.

Girls like sluggy things,
Things that glow:
Make-up, sweets and marshmallows

Boys like rude things,
Things all cheeky:
Woopee cushions, fake bugs, things all freaky.

Girls like polite things,
Things all gentle:
Teddy bears, cuddy toys, they go mental.

Boys Say - football
Girls Say - netball
Boys Say - bike
Girls Say - Skip

Girls say - pink
Boys Say - blue
Girls Say - sun
Boys Say - rain

Give me, Say boys,
A football to play,
A motorbike to ride
To Zoom away

Give me, say girls,
A pink frilly dress,
Maybe Some sparkly shoes,
To go with the rest.

Boys and girls -
They'll never agree
Till later in life
They may, maybe . . .

■ **Figure 9.1** A group poem 'Boys and Girls'

While research suggests that an emphasis on knowing and naming poetic form and feature tends to dominate primary practice (Hull, 2001; Wilson, 2005a), this is not inevitable. If meaning and purpose are foregrounded and opportunities for collaboration, exploration and engagement with poetic texts are offered, then children can learn about form and feature through active reading, response and writing, as the girls' group poem demonstrates (see Figure 9.1). In relation to reading, this avoids poems being subjected to analysis for the sake of naming literary techniques and reduces the tendency of teachers to ask 'recitation questions', which result in children offering predictable and convergent answers (Mroz *et al.*, 2000). Instead the children's own questions and thoughts need to take centre stage and their problems and confusions voiced, discussed and responded to, through active examination and reflection.

In reading and responding to different poetic forms, creative teachers enable children to experience the structures, language, rhythms and patterns of poetry in action. Poetic texts that cross boundaries, such as Sharon Creech's highly original *Love that Dog* and *Hate that Cat* or Malorie Blackman's *Cloud Busting* are particularly worth examining, as are the myriad of stories told in verse in high quality picture fiction books – examples include Jonathon Long and Korky Paul's *The Cat that Scratched* and Jeanne Willis and Korky Paul's dastardly *The Rascally Cake*, as well as Laurence Anholt's *Cinderboy* and Dr Seuss' *Hooray for Diffendooferr Day!* Such colourfully presented and enticing tales engage young readers who may not initially appreciate that they are reading poetry. In addition, Gary Crew's book entitled *Troy Thompson's Excellent Poetry Book* is worth purchasing for older children to read and enjoy. This post-modern text purports to be Troy's work from a poetry study unit in Miss Kranke's class. Troy tries several poetic forms, often parodying these and reflects upon his life in the process, while Miss Kranke responds rather hilariously from the sidelines. Single author poetry collections such as Tony Mitton's *Plum* and Jackie Kay's *Red, Cherry Red* are worth reading, and mixed anthologies can also be valuable in enabling children to hear the voices of different writers set alongside one another. Excellent new examples in this category include *The Ropes* edited by Sophie Hannah and John Hegley, which has photos and personal conversation, and *Inside Out: Children's Poets Discuss their Work* edited by Joarno Lawson, in which poems sit alongside fascinating commentaries by their authors.

In class, the meditative nature of one poem can be contrasted with the effervescence of another, not only through a teacher's detailed exposition, but also by the children themselves in small groups, making meaning together. They can be supported in such endeavours by their teachers' interventions in response to their puzzlements. In using Chambers (1993) reflective structure 'Like-Dislike-Puzzle-Pattern' to prompt children's conversations about poetry, one teacher in a class of 7–8-year-olds read John Agard's poem 'My Telly', from his anthology *I Din Do Nuttin*, several times to the class. It starts with the memorable lines 'My telly eats people especially on the news' and goes on to explore the kind of 'little people' that the TV devours. It closes with the line 'if you don't believe me look inside the belly of my telly'. The children chatted in pairs about their likes and dislikes about the poem, before sharing these and noting them on a copy of the verse. They then played the Puzzle Possibility Game, in which several children voiced their puzzles and others sought to offer possible responses to these. Many felt the poem was 'too simple' and 'boring' 'because it keeps on saying my telly this and my telly that'. Few grasped the meaning of the verse and most were puzzled by the telly eating people – those who read this literally thought it absurd.

As individual children's puzzles and questions about the poem were voiced and responded to, the issues of famine, death and the depressing nature of much news coverage was gradually foregrounded through the discussion. The anthology was seized and other books by John Agard were read, prompting further discussion about the presence of such a potent poem in a 'rather young looking' as one child observed, book of rhymes. Some weeks later, in a class assembly, one group chose to read this poem repeatedly while a series of PowerPoint™ images of people facing famine, downloaded from the Internet were displayed. One member of the group, Stephen, then read his poem 'Ethiopia', while a single visual image remained on the screen. The silence in the room was palpable:

Ethiopia

The face of the dying,
Feeling helpless,
Feeling weak,
His mother can do nothing
To help her struggling child,
The tattered cloth of the people's sorrow,
The horror of watching people fade away,
Humans begging for just one grain of wheat,
Flies on the sores of a dead child.

Stephen

Providing time to share poetry performances and reflect upon them, learners can come to understand more of the theme, structure, style and meanings of their chosen poem. In this instance, the children's journey of understanding, appreciation and later composition had been largely led by their interests and engagement, supported by their teacher and the initial choice of text. As this book argues, autonomy and ownership are key features of creative practice and contribute markedly to the children's creativity expressed here in oral and written words, performances and chosen images.

A wealth of other activities can help profile poetry and increase the opportunities children have to read and respond to it. Many of these can be woven into ongoing practice, although some will be more appropriate in extended units of work. They include activities such as identifying a poem of the week, a poetry reading slot when children share their favourites, a focus on pop songs and lyrics or playground rhythms and rhymes, creating poetry jigsaws and groups choosing and defending a favourite poet in an 'X Factor' type poetry competition.

WRITING POETRY: EXPERIMENTING WITH FORM AND FREEDOM

Poetry repays playful engagement and experimentation, not only in relation to reading, but also in relation to writing. A greater awareness of the power of pattern, repetition, literary language and creative energy inherent in poetry can be developed through open-ended group exploration. Poetry can also be creatively danced or sung into existence. Children may borrow a rhythm from a poem they have performed, write new lyrics to the tune of a well-known song, or choose to use the form of a known poem, imitating and leaning upon the rhythm, pattern or form already present. Such imitation will not necessarily lead to close replication and may, if children are offered opportunities to playfully engage with a variety of forms, lead to invention and innovation.

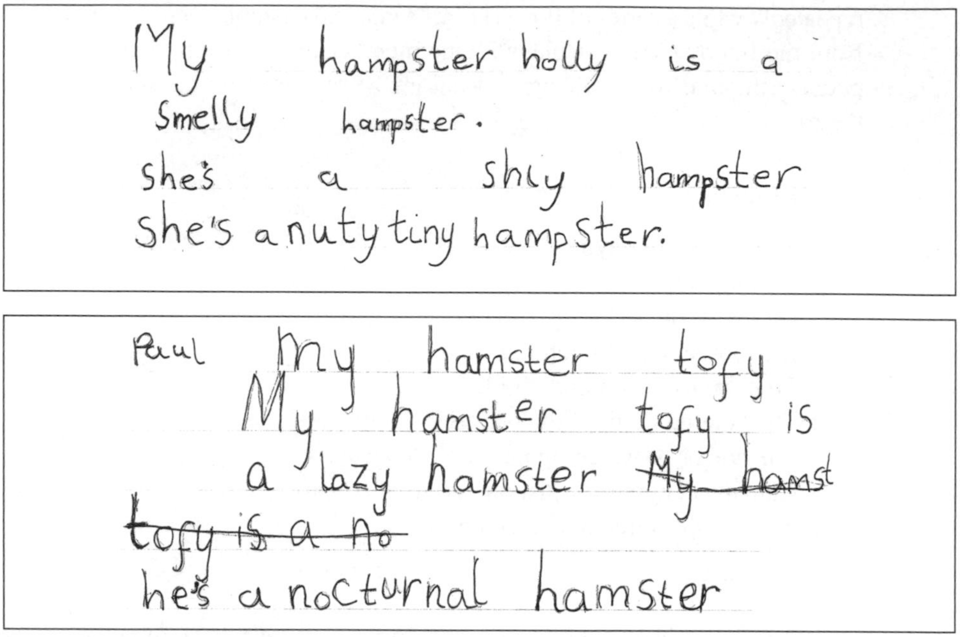

> My hampster holly is a smelly hampster.
> She's a shiy hampster
> She's a nuty tiny hampster.

> Paul My hamster tofy
> My hamster tofy is
> a lazy hamster My hamst
> tofy is a no
> he's a nocturnal hamster

■ **Figure 9.2** Two poems about hamsters

Using poems as models to imitate is too commonly employed by primary practitioners who tend, Ofsted (2007) observe, to require children to imitate a form without the opportunity to fully engage with it. The resultant writing may well be limited to 'knowledge telling', a limited re-description of an experience trapped by a chosen form, rather than 'knowledge transformation', transforming the experience through experimenting with the form or content to convey new meanings (Bereiter and Scardamalia, 1987). However, if children are offered the chance to engage with verse, feel its rhythms and connect to its content, then later leaning on sentence starters and the structure of this known verse can support them in composing and shaping their thoughts. For example, two 6-year-olds, Paul and Halcyon, had been reading and miming actions to 'My Cat Jack' by Patricia Casey with the rest of the class and later wrote poems about their hamsters. (See Figure 9.2.)

Finding a balance between form and freedom is part of the challenge of creative literacy teaching. While children deserve to be introduced to forms so they can craft their own versions, they also deserve to be recognised as authors and artists, and given the space and time to compose and shape their own work, finding their voices in the process. One 10-year-old, Anne Marie, leaning on Jack Ousbey's poem 'Gran Can You Rap?' cleverly borrowed the form and played with the content to create a poem about her teacher that was both apt and amusing (see Figure 9.3). This was self-initiated, in that her teacher had shared different poems about families and invited the children in groups to select one to reread and discuss. After a period of supported exploration, during which the class found other related poems, a class poem was composed and performed, and each child was finally invited to write their own poem about a member of their family. Anne Marie, asserting her authorial agency, however,

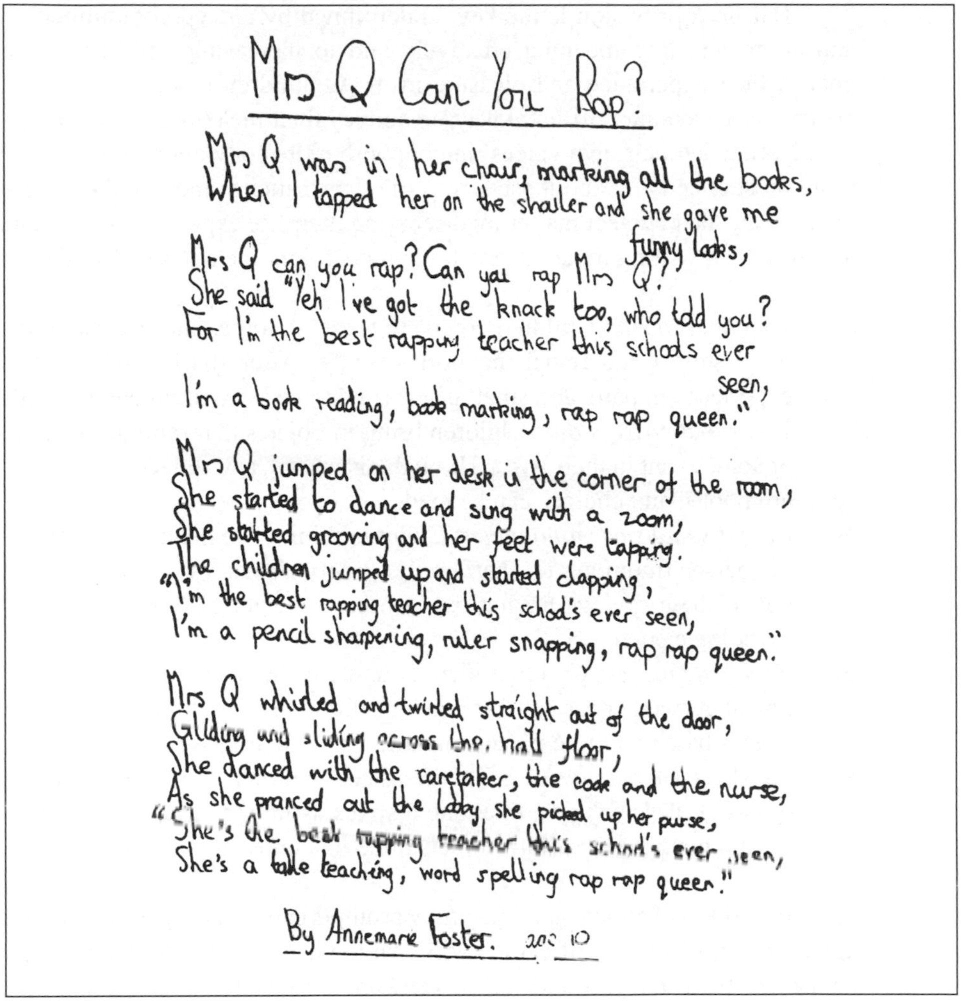

Mrs Q Can You Rap?

Mrs Q, was in her chair, marking all the books,
When I tapped her on the shoulder and she gave me funny looks,

Mrs Q can you rap? Can you rap Mrs Q?
She said "Yeh I've got the knack too, who told you?
For I'm the best rapping teacher this school's ever seen,
I'm a book reading, book marking, rap rap queen."

Mrs Q jumped on her desk in the corner of the room,
She started to dance and sing with a zoom,
She started grooving and her feet were tapping.
The children jumped up and started clapping,
"I'm the best rapping teacher this school's ever seen,
I'm a pencil sharpening, ruler snapping, rap rap queen."

Mrs Q whirled and twirled straight out of the door,
Gliding and sliding across the hall floor,
She danced with the caretaker, the cook and the nurse,
"As she pranced out the lobby she picked up her purse,
"She's the best rapping teacher this school's ever seen,
She's a table teaching, word spelling rap rap queen."

By Annemarie Foster. 2010

■ **Figure 9.3** 'Mrs Q Can You Rap?'

composed this engaging verse about her teacher instead and performed it with friends in assembly.

Creative practitioners support young learners in making their own choices for reading, writing and performing poetry from a wide repertoire of forms that they have heard, experienced and studied, and ensure they are not limited to reproducing particular forms or writing about particular prescribed subjects. While many writers recommend introducing children to forms and techniques for close imitation (Brownjohn, 1982, 1985; Pirrie, 1987), others suggest starting with the oral voice and life experiences of the child (Rosen, 1989). Both are valuable approaches, but if teachers focus too heavily on the analysis of poetic form and spend excessive time examining the techniques and literary language of poetry, then they risk separating the children's own experiences of poetry from the study of it – they may even risk creating a kind of 'schooled version of poetry'(Lambirth, 2002: 19).

Balanced provision is the key, underpinned by a deep commitment to making and communicating meaning creatively and to increasing children's repertoire of poetry, their experience and pleasure in it. As children read, write and experience poetry, they encounter different ways to convey their meanings more clearly and over time learn to let their own voices ring out with more conviction and energy. Children write most effectively about aspects of life that matter to them and can be supported in choosing their subject matter by discussing their life experiences and valuing these as a source of writing material. Starting points might include the following:

- *Timelines of life*: Children complete these at home, and use them in school to retell stories and revisit memories orally. After sharing some tales of lived experience in pairs and small groups, a choice for writing can be made.
- *Treasured possessions*: Children bring in objects that remind them of someone or some event in their lives. Through discussion and reflection, ideas for writing are pooled and choices can be made.
- *Conversations or monologues*: Children think of someone and list all the things the person (mum/my teacher/ brother/gran) often says. They then create poems out of these sayings having read Rosen's/Wright's/Ahlberg's conversational/ monologic poetry.
- *Favourite places*: Children identify some of their favourite places and seek to revisit, remember and reflect upon them through art or discussion. They can create poems based on these places, perhaps using their senses.
- *Passions and persuasions*: Children share their personal perspectives on a range of issues, their hobbies, likes and dislikes, irritations and fascinations, selecting from among these a subject to examine in a chosen poetic form.

In addition, fictional and imaginary prompts can support poetic writing, although again offering elements of choice will enable young writers to compose poems that connect to their thoughts and feelings and are not just attempts to mirror the form or demonstrate their knowledge of similes or metaphors for example. Starting points might include the following:

- *Magic shoes*: Decorate a pair of old shoes with glitter, wings, buttons, beads, and so on. Then use them as a starter, for example, 'In my magic shoes I can . . . fly to . . . walk over . . . dance with . . . see as far as . . . travel to . . . become . . .'
- *Borrow from the book blanket*: Spread the class library over the tables, children peruse in pairs collecting titles for a possible piece of poetry. Pairs choose, discuss and write individually or together, borrowing or adapting a title and generating ideas based on this.
- *Secrets*: Children write in role as a character in a tale and share imagined/real secrets. They could start with the line, 'It's a secret but I'm really . . .' or 'It's a secret, but although Mrs Cremin thinks I'm climbing the wall bars/sharpening my pencil/reading quietly, really I'm . . .'
- *Desires and wishes*: These can be shaped as whole verses or one liners; they might focus on literal desires for the world or themselves, but with work they

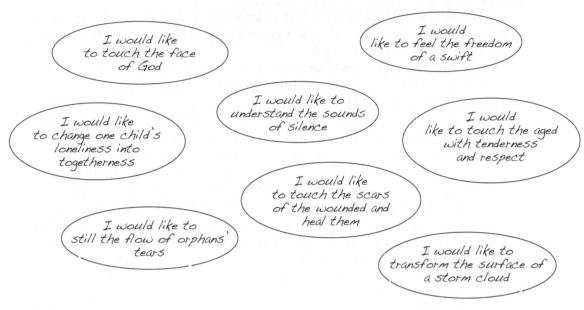

I would like
to touch the face
of God

I would
like to feel the freedom
of a swift

I would like to
understand the sounds
of silence

I would like
to change one child's
loneliness into
togetherness

I would
like to touch the aged
with tenderness
and respect

I would like
to touch the scars
of the wounded and
heal them

I would like to
still the flow of orphans'
tears

I would like to
transform the surface of
a storm cloud

■ **Figure 9.4** Children's poetic wishes

can be expanded to encompass imaginary poetic possibilities. (See Figure 9.4 for some wishes composed by 9–10-year-olds.)

Working as response partners can help young writers reshape their writing and examine its effect upon an audience (see Chapter 7 for support in responding to writing). Children's work will also be influenced by opportunities to celebrate and share work they have produced, and to make their work public in various ways, for example using art, ICT, music, voice, drama and dance to convey their meanings effectively.

PROFILING POETRY IN EXTENDED LEARNING JOURNEYS

Through playful exploration and thoughtful contemplation on focused learning journeys, children can widen their knowledge and enhance their understanding and pleasure in poetry as well as shape their own poetic voices. Creative professionals plan open-ended learning journeys involving periods of immersion in poetry and active exploration, representation and discussion, as well as time for composition and reflection. They also become fully involved as artists in the classroom, participating in such explorations with the children, experimenting with language, ideas and meanings, and modelling their own responses as well as composing poetry themselves. In the process they model being open to others' ideas and thoughts, as well as critically evaluative of their own emerging interpretations and personal poetic writing. As Hyland (2003: 10) observes, expressive approaches to poetry teaching, are 'likely to be most successful in the hands of teachers who themselves write creatively', since reflecting upon their own creative processes can help teachers teach writing from the inside out and bring their skills to class as vehicles for authentic learning (Spiro, 2007). When teachers write alongside children as well as share their work, this can offer significant support to young writers, and help adults appreciate the challenge and pleasure in poetic writing (see also Chapters 6 and 7).

Working towards a school arts festival, for example, children might be invited to read, write, research and select a themed collection of poetry, experimenting over time with their group's representations, using music, movement, images, drama or whatever they choose, and sharing these with a visiting poet or dancer as they build towards and shape their final performance and compose pieces for publication on the school's website. The sense of ownership offered by such an open, but purposeful, endeavour is likely to prompt a creative response as it allows time for detours, for aesthetic connections, the examination of alternatives and critical evaluation, as well as formative assessment and tailored teaching. In extended units of work of this nature, reflection, review, feedback and celebration can be given due space and time and the children can revise their work as they prepare for a full public sharing of it. In creating their own class or school anthologies over several weeks, for example, children can be involved in reading, composing and perfuming poems, as well as discussing selection and representation issues, layout, themes, images and much more besides.

Publication (and public review) of children's work is a significant part of the process of exploring poetry and may take many forms, including:

- a class/school poetry anthology – with contributions from teachers, TAs and other school staff;
- class, group or individual poetry posters with some of their own poems and some chosen verse;
- a poetry CD sold to parents with musical interludes or backing music;
- a poetry assembly with the words read while a looped PowerPoint™ runs with images and children's designs;
- a poetry festival within the school with groups/classes sharing their work;
- poems in the school newsletter;
- poetry around the school – like poems in the underground, poetry can be enlarged and printed and prominently displayed with accompanying children's artwork;
- laminated poetry cards of the children's poetic writing for guided reading;
- a cabaret evening of poetry with staff and children performing poems in various ways to their parents; and
- poetry on the school website – both printed text and filmed performances.

CONCLUSION

Poetry must be experienced before it can be analysed, and deserves to be engaged with playfully, actively and creatively as a multimodal art form. If teachers offer rich reading and response opportunities, introduce children to a wide range of poets and encourage them to suggest poems to be read and performed, then a positive climate towards the art form can be established. This will be enriched by ensuring there is time to investigate and explore chosen poems using multiple modes and media, which appropriately highlight the special nature of this intriguing game with words. Writing poetry will be an integral part of such extended explorations, not a separate activity, and one which draws upon the children's life experiences, interests and passions, as well as their experience of the work of many published poets, including each other and their teachers.

FURTHER READING

Dymoke, S. (2003) *Drafting and Assessing Poetry*, London: Paul Chapman.

Grainger, T. Goouch, K. and Lambirth, A. (2005) Artistic Voices: Poetry, in *Creativity and Writing: Developing Voice and Verve in the Classroom*, London: Routledge, Chapter 8.

Spiro, J. (2007) Teaching Poetry: Writing Poetry – Teaching as a Writer, *English in Education*, 41(3): 78–93.

Wilson, A. (2005a) The Best Forms in the Best Order? Current Poetry Writing Pedagogy at KS2, *English in Education*, 39(3): 19–31.

CHILDREN'S BOOKS

Agard, J. (1984) *I Din Do Nuttin*, Magnet.

Agard, J. and Nichols, G. (1991) *No Hickory, No Dickory, No Dock*, Young Puffin.

Andreae, G. and Wojtowucz, D. (1998) *Rumble in the Jungle*, Orchard.

Anholt, L. and Robbins, A. (1999) *Cinderboy*, Orchard.

Angelou, M. (1993) *Life Doesn't Frighten Me at All*, Stewart, Tabori & Chang.

Blackman, M. (2005) *Cloud Busting*, Corgi Yearling.

Bloom, V. (2007) *The Tribe*, Macmillan.

Brown, R. (1993) *The Midnight Party*, Cambridge.

Creech, S. (2001) *Love that Dog*, Bloomsbury.

Creech, S. (2008) *Hate that Cat*, Bloomsbury.

Crew, G. (2001) *Troy Thompson's Excellent Poetry Book*, Lothian.

Edwards, R. (1993) *The Midnight Party*, Cambridge.

Edwards, R. (1995) *Talk Poetry 2*, Cambridge.

Hallworth, G. and Binch, C. (1996) *Down by the River*, Mammoth.

Hannah, S. and Hegley, J. (eds) (2008) *The Ropes: Poems To Hold On To*, Diamond Twig.

Kay, J. (2007) *Red, Cherry Red*, Book and CD, Bloomsbury.

Lawson, J. (ed.) (2008) *Inside Out: Children's Poets Discuss their Work*, Walker.

Long, J. and Paul, K. (1994) *The Cat that Scratched*, Red Fox.

Mitton, T. (1998) *Plum*, Scholastic.

Morris, J. (ed.) (2007) *The Barefoot Book of Classic Poems*, Barefoot.

Nichols, G. (2004) *Paint Me a Poem: New Poems Inspired by Art in the Tate*, A. & C. Black.

Seuss, Dr (2001) *Hooray for Diffendooferr Day!*, Collins.

Willis, J. and Paul, K. (1994) *The Rascally Cake*, Puffin.

<table>
<tr><td>CHAPTER
10</td><td># EXPLORING NON-FICTION TEXTS CREATIVELY</td></tr>
</table>

INTRODUCTION

Creative teachers support their pupils in exploring a wide range of non-fiction texts, in print and multimedia forms, during literacy sessions and across the curriculum. They recognise the imaginative possibilities offered when children become interested in information they are listening to, reading and watching, and know that writing and presenting in role are powerful ways of helping children understand the content and forms of non-fiction texts. This chapter explores how to teach non-fiction texts creatively, providing opportunities for speaking, hearing, watching, drawing, reading and writing these texts for real purposes and real audiences. Creative teachers recognise the importance of engagement, motivation and playful interactions in children's encounters with information text, so that affective aspects of these texts are explored as well as factual elements. In addition, such teachers do not see textual genres as fixed and unalterable, so they recognise and encourage boundary crossing between genres when appropriate.

TEACHERS' KNOWLEDGE OF NON-FICTION TEXTS

One positive outcome from the introduction of the National Literacy Strategy framework in 1998 (DfEE, 1998) was the impact it had on ensuring exploring non-fiction texts became part of the literacy curriculum. Prior to this, the evidence shows that most primary teachers had little explicit knowledge of non-fiction texts and rarely used them in their teaching of English – concentrating mainly on narrative and poetic genres in teaching reading and writing (Wray and Lewis, 1997). Non-fiction texts were encountered across the curriculum, but were rarely used in these contexts for exploring the concept of reading and writing for authentic purposes and audiences, teaching contextualised literacy skills or for explicitly pointing out to children the literacy skills they were applying in using them. In spite of growing research interest and curriculum development work around non-fiction texts throughout the 1990s (Mallet, 1991;

Littlefair, 1992; Lewis and Wray, 1995), the importance of exploring the purposes and pleasures of non-fiction texts, the demands such texts posed and the ways in which teachers could support children in responding to, using and creating non-fiction texts, remained largely unconsidered in many classrooms.

The introduction of the NLS framework transformed this situation. It contained a wealth of objectives relating to non-fiction texts and widened teachers' knowledge of these, ensuring their inclusion in the curriculum. However, even though attention was paid to non-fiction texts in literacy sessions, initially this was often based around examining non-fiction text extracts or exploring texts created by educational publishers as teaching tools to demonstrate a set of criteria for a particular text type, rather than exploring authentic non-fiction texts created for real purposes and with real audiences in mind. Although by the turn of the century the presence of non-fiction texts was secure, they were arguably often divorced from learning about and using literacy in other areas of the curriculum. For example, learning how to use an index was more likely to have been taught through decontextualised exercises or standalone literacy sessions, rather than in the context of purposeful use in geography or science. The renewed PNS framework aims to address this latter problem by offering 'significant support on how the key aspects of learning in the teaching of literacy can be applied across the curriculum' (DfES, 2006a: 3).

Other concerns focused on the way the range of non-fiction text types (or genres) included in the original framework could be seen as fixed and rigid, leading, however unintentionally, to an inflexible view of the range of text types 'permitted'. The underlying theories (Rothery, 1985; Martin, 1989; Kress and Knapp, 1992; Lewis and Wray, 1995) argue that textual genres are created by the speakers'/authors' communicative purpose in creating a text, and thus textual genres can be infinitely varied as there are infinite reasons for creating texts. But this was not always fully understood by busy teachers who were guided solely by prescribed objectives. Mixed non-fiction texts, such as a tourist leaflet that contains elements of persuasion, report and instructions, were also seen as problematic in some classrooms where a narrow and fixed range of non-fiction text types was taught. Teaching in these classrooms was guided by a focus on technical details of the textual structures and language features of text types, rather than on *why* they were created, *who* would read/listen to them and *how* this impacts on form and language features. The renewed framework's (DfES, 2006a) planning units for non-fiction go some way to addressing this, by placing a much stronger emphasis on purpose and audience, and pointing out that many texts are 'mixed' texts.

It was also argued that the division of objectives into fiction and non-fiction implied that there were just two categories of texts ('made up' or 'true'), thus risking marginalising texts that straddle boundaries. Texts such as well researched historical fiction, parody texts (fictional versions of non-fiction texts) such as the many different non-fiction text parodies inserted into *The Jolly Postman* by Allan Ahlberg, or narrative non-fiction that mixes factual information with the imagined actions, thoughts, feeling of a real protagonist, do not fit into neat fiction /non-fiction boundaries. Significantly, the renewed framework no longer divides objectives into fiction or non-fiction. This encourages more exploration of boundary shifting texts, which are often highly motivating, imaginatively conceived and represent a rich resource for creative teachers and learners. Examples include *Archie's War* and *My War Diary* by Marcia Williams, *Auntie Dot's Atlas* by Eljay Yildirim, *Explor-a-Maze* by Robert Snedden, and Colin and Jacqui Hawkins' *Fairytale News*. The more holistic and encompassing stance towards non-fiction texts adopted in the renewed PNS framework also means that objectives such as 'Explore how different texts appeal to readers using varied sentence structures and descriptive language' (Year 3) can include creatively exploring the affective and aesthetic aspects of non-fiction texts as well as their efferent impact. All these new developments offer explicit support for teaching non-fiction creatively.

NON-FICTION TEXTS

'Non-fiction' is something of a portmanteau term – lots can be crammed into it. It covers a vast range of materials and continues to expand, as advances in technology offer access to new ways of creating and accessing non-fiction texts. At home and in school, a large proportion of the texts children encounter, see, hear, read and create are non-fiction. Many will be used to get things done in their everyday lives, such as replies to party invitations, text messages to communicate information, forms to fill in, lists to remember what to take to school, emails to friends and information books and ICT-based texts to find out some specific information. Adults and children watch, read and write non-fiction for pleasure and to enhance or share knowledge of something interesting and engage with hobby magazines, biographies, blogs, Wikipedia information books, reference books, documentaries, 'faction' series on television, video and DVDs and so on. Non-fiction texts are also used to persuade people, perhaps to buy things, believe a case, visit places, donate to charity, or put their names to a campaign. Visuals, text and sound can be used separately or combined and a wide variety of design and forms are experienced in books, newspapers, comics and magazines, as well as in leaflets, manuals, maps and diagrams for example. Texts are increasingly multimodal and ICT-based as well as paper-based. Children starting school in the twenty-first century are likely to be familiar with television, DVDs, computers, Internet, email, mobile phones, talking books and so on. As Bearne and Wolstencroft (2007: 78) speculate 'It may be that that there will soon be different ways of describing the mass of non-fiction encountered every day'. In the meantime, creative teachers exploit this rich variety held within the term 'non-fiction' and do not confine themselves to a limited or fixed range of texts, forms and modalities.

The renewed PNS framework (DfES, 2006a) concentrates on six important, but not exclusive, genres of non-fiction texts. Creative teachers of non-fiction include and expand on this list. The six text types mentioned are:

■ discussion texts;
■ explanatory texts;
■ instructional texts;
■ persuasion texts;
■ non-chronological reports;
■ recounts.

Summaries of the purpose, form, language features and 'knowledge for writers' for each of these text types can be found on the standards website. However, the following rubric to the charts and the non-fiction planning units offered there, clearly makes the points about the importance of purpose and audience and the need for flexibility already outlined.

Non-fiction texts are wide ranging and occur in many forms in everyday life. The following tables and supporting guidance select the most common forms of non-fiction. Many non-fiction texts in real life blur the boundaries between text types and their features. The most common language features are listed for each text type, but variants of all text types occur, especially when they are used in combination. The features listed are *often* but *not always* present.

(DfES, 2006b)

TEACHING NON-FICTION TEXTS CREATIVELY

The pedagogical principles outlined in the chapters on developing creatively engaged readers and writers apply just as much to non-fiction texts as they do to fiction texts. Creative teaching of non-fiction texts involves building a supportive, creative ethos in which talk and reflection around non-fiction texts, active and interactive approaches to using and creating texts, collaboration, co-operation and risk taking are encouraged. Creative teaching of non-fiction texts involves many of the same text-based activities that teachers might employ to encourage children to enjoy and be knowledgeable about fiction texts. Including, for example, reading aloud from engaging non-fiction texts, sharing enthusiasms and views on non-fiction texts, encouraging children to discuss non-fiction books, comment on them in their reading journals, pointing out non-fiction series and authors and allowing children opportunities to choose their own non-fiction reading materials.

Creative teachers of non-fiction understand that engagement and motivation are critical to learning (Fredricks *et al.*, 2004). These dispositions shape the breadth and depth of a learning experience. When children or adults are interested and committed to something, or can see its relevance, they are more likely to explore it deeply and persist with it even if it becomes challenging, and some non-fiction texts can be challenging if worthwhile information is to be both found and understood. The best non-fiction texts touch something within the reader. Potent, affectively involving non-fiction texts can bring a child into an experience and provide the starting point for engaged reading and creating their own texts.

Selecting meaningful non-fiction experiences and materials that reflect authentic purposes, make links to life and offer opportunities to adopt affective as well as efferent stances towards the experience, supports the creative teaching of non-fiction. Teachers should select information texts with the same care they reserve for fiction texts and should look out for a wide variety of attractive and appealing texts and ICT-based texts that invite children to become involved. This can be done in many ways. For example, through the fascination of detailed drawing, amazing photographs, 3D cross-sections and diagrams, through information presented in a variety of ways – newspaper formats, fact files, realia documents, a quality written text, – through a strong authorial/personal voice and through the use of multimodal forms. Teachers should also look for content likely to engage children's interests, reflect their lives and hobbies, broaden their horizons, link to topics being studied across the curriculum and give interesting, quirky or humorous insights into well worn subjects. These should include non-fiction texts from popular culture, such as card collections, sticker books, football programmes, catalogues and so on.

READING AND RESPONDING TO NON-FICTION TEXTS

Reading non-fiction texts can present particular challenges for the young reader. There may be technical or topic specific vocabulary, many complex sentences, the use of the passive voice and more formal registers than those used in narrative texts. Teachers can scaffold children's reading of such texts by:

■ helping children see a genuine purpose for engaging with the text;
■ helping them activate any prior knowledge they have on or around the topic;
■ preparing them for the kind of vocabulary they might meet;
■ giving them experience in hearing and using formal registers;
■ modelling active reading of the text and the strategies they use;
■ supporting children in understanding the text;
■ ensuring that any response to the text involves the reader in remodelling the information.

In particular, teachers will want to help children make the text their own, and avoid them merely recalling or parroting the information in an unchanged form. In supporting them in understanding the information, teachers often offer a range of grids and frames or other ways of interacting with the text, such as text marking or text sequencing to help children actively engage with the text and deepen understanding. In addition, creative teachers offer real reasons for reading. For example, in one class of 6–7-year-olds, the children were set the genuine task of deciding which plants they wished to purchase from a local garden centre in order to plant up hanging baskets for the school courtyard. They knew that only certain plants would be suitable and had to find out which plants would be best. Their teacher supported them in several ways. First, she led a discussion on what they knew already about hanging baskets and summarised the emergent criteria – they couldn't be too tall or too wide; they should be colourful and eye catching; they should smell nice; they could have interesting leaves as well as flowers. From this scribed list, the class jointly created a research grid (see Figure 10.1) with the following headings:

In creating this grid, the teacher used the children's criteria to introduce the more technical vocabulary they would encounter when they came to look in gardening reference books, and gave it back to them in written form to help them recognise the words when they encountered them in print. Involving the children in making the grid, rather than simply giving them one prepared earlier, created a real sense of ownership. The teacher then modelled how to use information books to complete a row on the grid. As she modelled using an index, locating the page and scanning the text, she talked

Name of flower	Height	Spread	Flowers	Colour	Leaves	Perfume

Figure 10.1 The children's research grid

about what she was doing and why in order to make this accessible to the children. The children then undertook research in pairs. Throughout their research, the grid reminded the children what they needed to know and prompted them to continue. The grid acted as a scaffold for the children, helping them move from joint action with an experienced teacher towards independent action.

The children used a variety of study skills during their research. They used these because they needed to use them and this kind of purposeful, contextualised teaching and using of information gathering skills helped keep them motivated even when the task was difficult. Persistence and resilience in the face of difficulty are key to creativity (Claxton, 2002) and were actively fostered in this project. Most of the children were willing to try several different techniques if their first attempt to find an answer failed. The subsequent sharing of suggestions, class discussion and selection, visit to the garden centre to buy the plants, planting up the baskets and returning to information books for advice on aftercare, gave these children powerful reasons to read and write non-fiction texts. They experienced pleasure and pride in their hanging baskets and could see, smell and touch the results of their successful non-fiction reading.

Reading non-fiction can also be creatively enhanced by linking it to reading fiction. This can help children understand that facts are not neutral, and can heighten the children's emotional engagement in and understanding of both the fiction and non-fiction texts being studied (Soalt, 2005), thus opening up new creative possibilities. See Chapter 3 for an example exploring pollution and the environment. A wealth of historical novels and texts linked to other learning areas exist – seeking these out and exploiting useful synergies between fiction and non-fiction representation of issues can be extremely valuable. Picture books such as *Encounter* by Jane Yolen (an alternative perspective on Columbus), *The Paperbag Prince* by Colin Thompson (exploring envir-onmental issues) and *Memorial* by Gary Crew and Shaun Tan (examining society's debt to those killed in war) and many more, offer creative teachers considerable scope for extended explorations.

One group of gifted and talented 10–11-year-olds were reading Michael Morpurgo's *Private Peaceful*, which tells the life story of a village boy and his family leading up to the First World War and his experiences there. They were also exploring the non-fiction ICT text *Fields of Glory*, the true story of Britain's first black, non-commissioned officer from his early life as a Barnardo's boy, to his time as a professional footballer, his war service and death in action. This is told through a variety of non-fiction genres – letters, diary entries, newspaper articles, film clips and so on.

Their teacher linked these two texts to an authentic non-fiction text in the children's own lives – one which many of them passed every day, often barely noticing it and rarely reading it. She took them to visit the village war memorial with its list of names from World War I and II. Reading the names, the children were struck for the first time by the realisation that the experiences, factual and fictional, they were reading and watching, probably happened to families who lived in the village. This had a powerful emotional impact on the group. It increased their level of engagement and motivation, and they undertook further research into the histories behind the names on the memorial. They gave a talk about this research in assembly, leading up to the sale of Remembrance Day poppies.

Throughout this cross curricular work they used a range of research skills, interrogated primary sources, including interviewing older people in the village, made notes and wrote brief biographies based on what they discovered. They also used drama and role-play to explore different scenes in the novel, which was enhanced and deepened by their exploration of the non-fiction texts. This in turn fed into their under-standing of the real experiences that must have taken place in homes in the village. For example, Charlie and Tommo's letters home make little mention of the horrors of the war. Discussing the reasons for this helped the children reflect on and enact the scene from the novel when Charlie explains to Tommo, why, when he was home on leave, he avoided mentioning the horrors of the trenches to his wife and mother. Afterwards, children wrote their reflections on 'Why we stayed silent'. These were both factual and empathetic, as the following example by Simon demonstrates:

> Soldiers in the trenches often didn't let their families know how bad it was. They didn't want their families to worry. They also felt that men should not complain. The public was protected from knowing too much. There was very little film or photographs for them to see at the time. Letters were censored so the soldiers knew they had to be careful what they wrote. It must have been very hard not saying anything when you were back with your family on leave. Many soldiers took years to recover from the war. They still did not talk about it. Mrs Edwards said her father never talked about the war. He often jumped at loud noises and sometimes he cried but he tried to hide it.

In the two examples outlined, the final response to non-fiction reading was action; hanging baskets were planted, children did an assembly presentation and sold Remembrance Poppies. However, responding to non-fiction texts can take many forms. It can be visual, three-dimensional, oral, drama /role-play, musical, written or any combination of these. Some of the many possibilities that creative teachers have developed include the following:

■ After reading about Viking houses, children drew and labelled a diagram showing the structure and materials used.

■ After reading about the location of towns, examining maps and visiting local bridges, children made a three-dimensional topographical model showing their town's position on the crossing point of a river and the roads that converged at that point

■ After receiving a letter from the headteacher asking for ways to spend £500 on playground equipment, each class researched playground games and equipment, decided on their 'bid' and prepared an oral/visual presentation to give to the school council (who made the final decision).

■ After gathering information about the earth in space, a class created a music/movement presentation showing the movement of the planets. They designed costumes to reflect the nature of each planet.

■ At the end of a unit of work on pirates, a class of children had a pirate day when they dressed up, spoke in pirate language, made hard tack biscuits, and role-played various aspects of pirate life. Some children acted as roving reporters taking photographs, videoing and interviewing 'pirates'. They shared this at parents' evening.

WRITING NON-FICTION TEXTS: EXPERIMENTING WITH FORM AND FREEDOM

Non-fiction writing is a complex business involving both compositional and transcriptional skills. The compositional aspects may be particularly challenging for children. It is tempting for them, when faced with apparently authoritative texts and maybe with several sources of information, to copy or cut and paste chunks of the originals. In order to help them overcome this problem, teachers need to ensure that children engage in an extended process of teaching and learning about writing (see Chapter 7 for a diagram of this process) and during this have:

■ had plenty of experience of the kind of texts they are producing;
■ read and understood the information;
■ engaged creatively in order to examine the information;
■ found ways to gather together what they want to say;
■ made this information their own, perhaps in collaboration with others, so they can 'speak' on the topic with confidence and if appropriate a personal voice;
■ been supported in exploring the best way to communicate the information, perhaps through teacher modelling or shared composition;
■ shaped, revised and published their own work.

■ **Figure 10.2** An advert for an ice cream machine

Additionally, as Bearne and Wolstencroft pointed out, 'Since young people have a wide experience of designed non-fiction texts, they want to use their knowledge of layout and presentation in their classroom work' (2007: 79). This adds a further layer of compositional /transcriptional demands in deciding what to include, what should be text and what should be visual, and in what medium to do this, on paper or on screen.

The decisions about what information to include and how to present it should depend on the purpose and audience of the communication. Thinking about this helps children see which textual and visual features can help them get their message across in the most effective way. For example, in advertising her invented ice cream machine 10-year-old Lara was prompted to make multiple decisions about presentation, colour and impact. Another class voted on the success of the children's adverts, prompting a fuller discussion of the significance, quality and placement of both visual features and words.

Scaffolds for non-fiction writing, planning and information gathering

A range of graphic and planning frames can be helpful in supporting children to gather information and to organise how to present it (for examples, see Wray and Lewis, 2001). While children should be encouraged to regard such frames as flexible and changeable, frames and graphic organisers help children capture information and initial thoughts

Activity/item	In a Victorian house c.1870	In a modern house
Clothes		
Heating		
Lighting		
Cooking		

■ **Figure 10.3** Example of a compare and contrast grid

and select those appropriate to the final outcome. So an 'argument for/argument against' grid or an 'argument/counter argument' grid would be helpful in preparing to write a discussion or take part in a debate, while a 'compare and contrast grid' would be helpful if children were, for example, comparing change over time, or the characteristics of several items (see Figure 10.3). The non fiction writing fliers available on the teaching materials section of the PNS website give many practical suggestions for graphic organisers and planning grids for the six listed non-fiction text types.

As well as non-fiction writing in these forms, creative teachers also encourage children to write mixed genre texts, use genres from modern life, use parodies of genres and sometimes challenge expectations by using an unusual genre to get a message across. These forms of writing encourage risk taking and a playful approach, which help develop creativity. Genre exchange and parody texts help children focus on form in a playful context. Such experiences also often make children reconsider the information they have gathered in the light of this new context. In genre exchange, children gather information and then present it in a form unlikely to have been current at the time (for example, a Roman newspaper) or in a form not usually used for presenting the kind of information given (for example, work on class rules and respect for individuals undertaken in PSHE could be written up as A Recipe for a Happy and Harmonious Classroom, rather than the more usual Our Class Rules). Parody texts involve placing unlikely or fictional content within a well recognised non-fiction form such as an instruction manual, a field guide and fostering alternative creations and playful exploration of both forms.

For example, a class of 8–9-year-olds read *How Dogs Really Work* by Alan Snow. This parody text looks like a technical manual and is a combination of non-chronological report and explanation text. The children enjoyed the humour and the

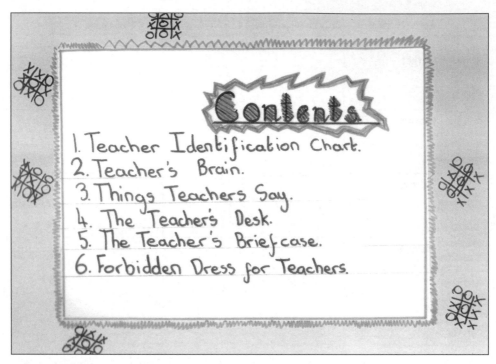

Figure 10.4 The Contents to *The True Guide to Teachers*

detailed 'technical' illustrations. Following their reading of the text they discussed the form of the book and what made it work. This led them to discuss the formal register and apparently technical language and illustrations. They then went on to create, in groups, their own *How X Really Works* or a *True Guide to X*. The challenge was to make the books look convincing as non-fiction texts. Together groups decided on the pages to include and allocated a page per child. They roughed out their ideas and held editorial group meetings to share and critique these. Finally, they completed their pages and added non-fiction book features such as contents, index and blurb. The pages were bound together into books, which became immensely popular reading resources in the book corner. In addition, each group prepared a talk on their specialist subject and role-played talking as an 'expert'. Along with all the fun, the children learnt a considerable amount about the structures and language features of non-chronological reports and explanations. (See Figure 10.4 for an extract from one group's *The True Guide to Teachers*.) This example demonstrates the importance of the children knowing and owning both the purpose (to entertain, describe and explain) and the audience (the teacher and the rest of the class). This helped give a genuine focus for their writing as well as shape the final form of their inventive texts.

Creative teachers of writing look out for real reasons for children to write and create non-fiction multimodal texts. These might include:

■ setting up genuine enterprise initiatives so children make posters, sales information sheets, letters to sponsors, launch information and so on;

■ writing a letter to the class that demands research and a response, for example from the local wild life trust asking them to advise on where to site bird boxes in the school grounds;

■ creating documentaries on a topic being studied in another curriculum area, write the voice over and perform it;

■ creating non-fiction book making opportunities – from books for younger children to fanzines and hobby magazines;

■ engaging the class in setting up a mini-museum in school and opening this to the community;

■ undertaking an extended drama in which a tourist shop for a place is established;

■ getting involved in genuine community-based campaigns or national initiatives such as recycling or responding to national calls to look after rare butterflies (see Figure 10.5 for an example of 6-year-old Natalie's contribution to the class butterfly book, created for The Wildlife Trust);

■ creating advertising leaflets for a local venue or a place visited on a school trip;

■ contributing to the school handbook or making their own prospectus.

The peacock butterfly has a wing span of 6cm and you would often find them in your garden It likes buddlea and It has a alarming hissing noise to defend themselves.

■ **Figure 10.5** A page from the class butterfly book

PROFILING NON-FICTION TEXTS IN EXTENDED LEARNING JOURNEYS

Creative teaching around non-fiction texts takes place in both literacy sessions and across the curriculum. The two contexts are often combined to provide an extended creative journey where children learn from first hand experiences, use non-fiction skills in context and read and write for real purposes. Teachers can model creative involvement and guide the experience by taking an active role on such extended journeys.

For example, working with a class of 8–9-year-olds, a teacher planned an extended thematic unit on World War II. In both history and literacy sessions, the children undertook some research on evacuation using information books and newsreel film cuttings and interviewing local people about their memories of evacuation. To make the experience more real to them the teacher also planned an extended role-play. The children had made cardboard suitcases in design and technology and brought clothes from home and a toy to pack. The class was taken to the school hall, labelled and made to sit in rows. In role – and in costume – their teacher played a WRVS volunteer and was thus able to organise the evacuees.

The children all walked in a crocodile to the local station and took a train journey. Some mothers waved them off and 'cried'. Unbeknown to them, the children were taken to a rather drab community hall and a group of adults (parents from another class, role-playing host families) came in to select the child/children they wanted. Many of the adults had dressed in period costume. The atmosphere changed as children were taken away, friends separated and just a few remained. Some 'late' host families turned up. Soon only two children were left, unallocated and wanted

Afterwards the children discussed their experiences and feelings. They reflected on what they had learnt and how it added to the research and reading they had already undertaken on evacuation. They wrote 'faction' accounts of evacuation drawing on their journey and their research. These were read to their writing partners who commented on factual accuracy and atmosphere. Throughout the unit, the teacher continued to weave role-play and factual investigation together. For example, ration cards were issued one day and a special wartime school lunch was served. A bomb shelter was created in the classroom, sirens sounded and bomb raid sound effects were played as the children sheltered in it. The teacher led community singing to keep their spirits up. Using books about the war, note taking and research skills were taught in the context of guided reading sessions, and children selected their own areas for further research. They recorded some of these as war time radio broadcasts using the call sound 'London calling, London calling'. This example shows how creative teachers undertake extended explorations and weave seamlessly together learning about a period and learning about non-fiction texts, through involving the children in playful and imaginatively engaging experiences that fostered their curiosity and provided 'real' purposes for reading, researching and text production.

CONCLUSION

Young people and adults continue to need to read and write non-fiction texts as these help organise both life and work. For some readers and writers they offer pleasure and satisfaction too. Increasingly, non-fiction texts are multimodal and ICT-based. The need for teachers to support children as they read and write non-fiction texts on paper and on screen is now well accepted in primary schools. However, the recognition that purpose and audience shape their encounters with non-fiction texts and that the necessary skills are best taught in the context of needing to use them, is perhaps less well established. Creative teachers of non-fiction lead the way in promoting this recognition and ensuring that children's experiences with non-fiction texts in school become as rich and engaging as their encounters with narrative and poetic texts.

FURTHER READING

Bearne, E. and Wolstencroft, H. (2007) *Visual Approaches to Teaching Writing*, London: Sage.
Ellis, S. and Safford, K. (2005) *Animating Literacy*, London: CLPE.
Soalt, J. (2005) Bringing Together Fictional and Informational Texts to Improve Comprehension, *The Reading Teacher*, 58(7): 680–3.
Wray, D. and Lewis, M. (2001) Developing Non-Fiction Writing: Beyond Writing Frames, in J. Evans (ed.), *The Writing Classroom: Aspects of Writing and the Primary Child*, London: David Fulton.

CHILDREN'S BOOKS

Ahlberg, A. (1986) *The Jolly Postman or Other People's Letters*, Heinemann.
Crew, G. and Tan, S. (1999) *Memorial*, Thomas Lothian.
Hawkins, C. and Hawkins, J. (2004) *Fairytale News*, Walker.
Morpurgo, M. (2004) *Private Peaceful*, Harper Collins.
Powell, J. (2005) *Fields of Glory: The Diary of Walter Tull*, Longman Digitexts.
Snedden, R. (1997) *Explor-a-Maze*, Templar.
Snow, A. (1995) *How Dogs Really Work*, Collins.
Thompson, T. (1992) *The Paperbag Prince*, Red Fox.
Williams, M. (2007) *Archie's War*, Walker.
Williams, M. (2008) *My War Diary*, Walker.
Yilirim, E. (1997) *Auntie Dot's Atlas*, Collins.
Yolen, J. and Shannon, P. (1992) *Encounter*, Harcourt Brace Jovanovich.

EXPLORING VISUAL AND DIGITAL TEXTS CREATIVELY

INTRODUCTION

Visual texts make an important contribution to our lives. Images, on paper and on screen, inform, direct, amuse, entertain and help us relax or pass the time. Not only is it clear that multimodal texts form part of the everyday experience of both teachers and children, the renewed PNS (DfES, 2006a) also now recognises reading and writing on paper and on screen. In terms of paper-based texts, words are now almost always accompanied by photographs, diagrams or drawings and print is often enhanced by a variety of font sizes and shapes. For children, particularly, there is a wealth of complex and challenging picture books as well as detailed information books where the images carry as much meaning as the words. These developments have been made possible by the use of digital technology, which has enhanced production and colour processes. But equally, digital technology has had an immense impact on screen texts: computer games, the Internet, television and film. A wide range of multi-modal texts exist, including drama, and this chapter explores teaching with such texts creatively. It considers examples of reading and composing multimodal screen texts and demonstrates the importance of teachers making use of the eight elements of creative literacy practice.

VISUAL TEXTS

The increase in the use of images and the screen means that many everyday texts are now multimodal, accompanying words with moving or still images, sound and colour. Teaching, too, is enhanced by the availability of different technologies that make discussions of the role of image, sound, colour and variations in typography much more possible through different media:

- the computer – Internet information and PowerPoint™ presentations;
- paper-based texts – picture books, magazines, novels, information books;
- sound and visual media – radio, television, videos and DVDs.

This increase in accessibility makes certain demands on teachers. Teaching about multimodal texts means rather more than concentrating on the words; it involves being explicit about the contributions to meaning made by different combinations of modes. These include:

- gesture and/or movement;
- images – moving and still, diagrammatic or representational;
- sound: spoken words, sound effects and music;
- writing or print, including typographical elements of font type, size and shape.

TEACHING VISUAL TEXTS CREATIVELY

There is ample evidence of even very young children's experience of media and digital technologies (Rideout *et al.*, 2003; Marsh *et al.*, 2005; Bearne *et al.*, 2007). In the street, home and school they are surrounded by texts that merge pictures, words and sound. They expect to read images as well as print, become attuned to the design of texts (Kress and van Leeuwen, 1996), increasingly use computers in seeking information and composing their own texts and are capable of handling the demands of the technology from the earliest years.

As the range of available texts grows and a more integrated approach to the curriculum becomes increasingly important, visual literacy is certainly an area that needs attention in school. The term has evolved from different theoretical sources including aesthetics, art history, cultural studies, education, linguistics, media studies and semiotics, and has a complex theoretical history. In a very useful document, Bamford defines visual literacy as the ability to construct and interpret meaning from visual images. She suggests that it involves:

> developing the set of skills needed to be able to interpret the content of visual images, examine the social impact of those images and discuss purpose, audience and ownership. It includes the ability to visualise internally, communicate visually and read and interpret visual images.
>
> (Bamford, 2008)

This definition offers clear similarities with the development of print literacy. There are parallels between elements of different kinds of written texts, with different organisational features and stylistic aspects, and visual texts. Both can be engaged with, enjoyed, critically appreciated and analysed. Like written texts, multimodal texts have structures that can be discussed, explained, modelled and taught. But just as it is stultifying to teach narrative or poetry by starting with structure and style, so it is with visual texts. There is a balance to be struck between learning about conventions and having the chance to develop individual creative responses through making connections between what is known and what can be imagined (Wilson, 2005a). The key lies in meaning.

Children's experience of visual texts gives them a good grounding for their appreciation and response. Films and other screen texts are ideal vehicles for involving all pupils and for developing their collaborative creativity; not only do children have experience and expertise in reading visual texts, everyone views them together, generating curiosity, problem solving and collaboration as they make sense of what they see together. Screen texts offer teachers a perfect opportunity to adopt a more flexible and creative approach to language, interpretation and meaning. In this way, viewing and making visual texts can contribute to a classroom atmosphere of openness, and the development of an environment that encourages children to offer their own views, ask their own questions and play with ideas and possibilities. Within the new framework (DfES, 2006a), teachers can seize opportunities to pay more attention to screen texts in extended units of work. This may involve comparing the presentation of a narrative as a novel and as a film, for example exploring the different ways in which meanings are conveyed in both Ted Hughes' book *The Iron Man* and the film *The Iron Giant*. Additionally, teachers can creatively explore a chosen film as a core text and enable the children to develop their literacy skills in the process.

It is worth remembering, however, that films are texts in themselves, which can be read, studied and enjoyed for their own worth, not only as vehicles for developing reading and writing.

TEACHERS' KNOWLEDGE OF VISUAL AND DIGITAL TEXTS

While there is considerable evidence of children's affinity with multimodal texts, and the capacity of young people to respond flexibly to new technologies as they emerge has been well documented (Mackey, 2002), there is much less evidence of teachers' experience of screen texts and confidence in using digital technology. The QCA national discussion *English 21* revealed some ignorance among teachers about the types of digital texts that children know about (QCA, 2005c). Additionally, surveys carried out into pre-service teachers' and teachers' experience of digital technologies and texts (Robinson and Mackey, 2006) suggest some gaps between teachers' and children's knowledge and experience. There is evidence, however, that younger teachers have experience and assurance both with the texts and the technology (Graham, 2008), and there has been significant commitment by the British Film Institute to develop teachers' expertise (Marsh and Bearne, 2008). But questions still remain about how much challenge children are given in classrooms in relation to their home experience of screen texts, because of teachers' lack of experience or confidence (Bearne *et al.*, 2007). Yet adults do know quite a lot about screen texts, particularly film and television; for a variety of reasons, teachers' own experience and competence can be ignored in classrooms (Honan, 2008), even though these qualities are potentially rich resources alongside the children's experience and expertise.

In seeking to teach creatively and develop children's creativity, teachers may need to consider their own views, experiences and attitudes towards visual and digital texts, and also find ways to recognise and build upon the children's strengths. One teacher observed 'a significant gap between my students' struggle with print texts at school compared with their fluent out-of-school digital literacy practices' (Walsh, 2007: 74). As a consequence, he sought to offer a more creative curriculum that took into account the multimodality of his students' out-of-school experiences and practices.

As a teacher he took a risk, moved out of his own comfort zone and went well beyond print-based work. He began to set tasks and projects that involved the young people in integrating images, written text, sound, music and animation. Immediately, his students' motivation, commitment, creativity and attainment flourished (ibid.). While his work was with older learners, such an approach that recognises the learners' expertise is more than possible with younger learners as research demonstrates (Marsh, 2005; Watts, 2007).

Teachers can also seek out support for such work in school. Recommended resources include the British Film Institute's teaching guide for using film and television with 3–11-year-olds *Look Again!* (BFI/DfES, 2003), as well as their teaching guide and DVD for younger learners *Starting Stories* and *Story Shorts I* and *II* for teachers working with older primary children. Additionally, for practical examples of schools engaged in projects that combine film and other visual texts and animate literacy, see Ellis and Safford (2005). Teachers can also contact local independent cinemas to explore possible collaborative projects or partnerships.

READING AND RESPONDING TO VISUAL TEXTS

One primary teacher, working within the requirements of routine literacy sessions set out to use film creatively, to encourage close reading of the text and multiple responses (Watts, 2007). Drawing on Woods' (2001) definition of 'creative reading' and Craft's (2000) conception of possibility thinking, she developed a teaching unit where her class of 6–7-year-olds learned how to read film and designed storyboards for their own films. After the project was over she interviewed the children about whether teaching them about reading film had made any difference to their watching films at home. On child Rosie commented 'Yeah, it has made you um actually understand more about how a character is feeling – and his actions and how it makes it look more exciting or magical' (Watts, 2007: 106). Her teacher observed that the children had:

> learned to identify and use cues for character development; to use colour as silent signs to create mood or convey feeling. Ultimately they had learned the craft of the meaning maker and in doing so had improved their ability to understand through inference, deduce meanings, use context, interpret ideas and respond to them.
>
> (Ibid.: 108)

All of these elements contribute to children becoming creative readers; readers who ask questions of texts, use available evidence and each other to make multiple interpretations and personal connections and who imagine, appreciate and understand the texts they read on several levels.

As the UKLA *Reading on Screen* project discovered (Bearne *et al.*, 2007), many children not only use sophisticated screen reading processes, but can also explain how they go about reading screen texts. Listening to the voices of two 10-year-olds, Peter and Poppy, reveals how these experienced readers vary their strategies according to whether they are reading on paper or on screen:

When asked where they started to read a book, comic or magazine, Poppy said: 'With books you start at the first page, start reading at top and stop if it gets boring. With magazines: you flick through and look for a good picture and read about it.'

Peter said he starts reading comics at the same place as a book but maybe flick to the end. He uses a more strategic process with magazines: flick through, look for football, game cheats, check for games I'm playing at the moment.

With computer game reading, Peter looks for important buttons on the keyboard at the start of the game and Poppy looks for the main symbols. During a game Peter explained: 'if it's a racing game, you keep your eyes on the car ... if it's a fighting game, then keep your eyes on the other person.' Poppy concentrated on the main character.

(Bearne *et al.*, 2007: 15)

While children's comments on their approaches to reading on screen are illuminating, there is still a need for teachers themselves get to grips with reading moving image texts. After a British Film Institute project designed to develop Leading Teachers' confidence in using film in the classroom, the teachers involved were asked to reflect on the project. Two comments suggest the importance of developing teachers' assurance in including moving image texts as part of the reading repertoire:

For me personally, understanding that word 'text' [has been a key outcome] – I can think much more widely now and I can think of film as text and can show teachers that there's another way to do it, to motivate children.

I think it's opened our eyes really. A light went on in my head when I thought you could read a film like you read a book and get the inference and deduction out of there, so it's been a huge change for me and I really enjoy doing the training when I see that same reaction in people.

(Marsh and Bearne, 2008: 18)

These leading teachers found similarities between reading written narratives and reading multimodal narrative texts. To do either means being able to:

■ understand the narrative, even if it involves flashbacks or fantasy episodes;
■ notice how colour and motif (in sound or in images) are used to help the reader/viewer keep the thread of the story;
■ comment on how sound, music, colour, viewpoint/camera angle and focus contribute to creating atmosphere or establishing setting;
■ read facial expression, gesture and posture;
■ discuss the use of perspective and camera angle or point of view in communicating with the reader/audience.

All of these features: story structure, setting, characterisation and author's intention or theme, are familiar from reading books with children. Any of them can become the focus for viewing a film as a whole class and for teaching film creatively.

WRITING VISUAL TEXTS: EXPERIMENTING WITH FORM AND FREEDOM

As the earlier explanation of multimodality might suggest, there is an inherent problem with using the word 'writing' for the multimodal texts that children compose. When children make visual texts they are combining modes – whether in picture books, information texts, moving images or in PowerPoint™ presentations. Of course, these may well include writing at some stage, in preparation or production of the texts, but the power of the text will not rely on the written word alone. Presentational software allows for a range of composing activities – poetry, information and persuasive texts and narrative.

While there are parallels between writing and composing multimodal texts, elements of movement, sound, colour and design have to be taken into account. Composing multimodal texts includes:

Deciding on mode and content for specific purpose(s) and audience(s)
■ Choosing which mode(s) will best communicate meaning for specific purposes (deciding on words rather than images or gesture/music rather than words).
■ Using perspective, colour, sound and language to engage and hold a reader's/viewer's attention.
■ Selecting appropriate content to express ideas and opinions.

Structuring texts
■ Paying conscious attention to the design and layout of texts, organising texts using pages, sections, frames, paragraphs, screens, sound sequences.
■ Structuring longer texts with visual, verbal and sound cohesive devices.
■ Using background detail to create mood and setting.

Using technical features for effect
■ Handling the technical aspects and conventions of different kinds of multimodal texts, including line, colour, perspective, sound, camera angles, movement, gesture, facial expression and language.
■ Choosing language, punctuation, font, typography and presentational techniques to create effects and clarify meaning.

Further to these text elements, there is the need to reflect on and evaluate both the process and the product:

■ explaining choices of modes(s) and expressive devices including words;
■ improving the composition: reshaping, redesigning and redrafting for purpose and readers'/viewers' needs;
■ commenting on the success of a composition in fulfilling the original design aims.

The following account shows how some of these elements were used by a class of 10–12-year-olds in a special school. Composing visual texts can be liberating for children for whom literacy is difficult, in part at least because as noted earlier children

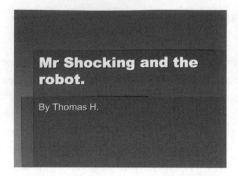

Mr Shocking and the robot.

By Thomas H.

Mr Shocking goes to the basketball court with a robot.

The robot and Mr Shocking arrive.

Mr shocking cheats by using the robot.

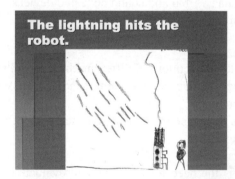

The lightning hits the robot.

The robot chases Mr Shocking.

■ **Figure 11.1** Thomas's story *Mr Shocking and the Robot*

have extensive experience of such texts to draw upon. Thomas, whose work is shown in Figure 11.1, is 12 years old, has specific learning difficulties and is on the autistic spectrum. His teacher planned a narrative unit for the class using PowerPoint™ and after watching the Nick Park Wallace and Gromit animation *The Wrong Trousers* (the final section of this chapter outlines an extended unit of work using this film). After storyboarding the movie, the children's drawings were scanned into PowerPoint™ screens and, supported by teaching assistants and their teacher, they made use of the

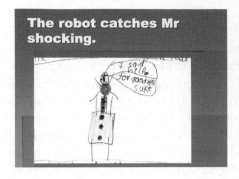

The robot catches Mr shocking.

And throws him in the air.

Mr Shocking lands on the floor.

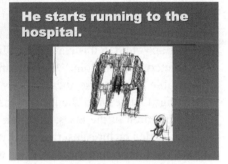

He starts running to the hospital.

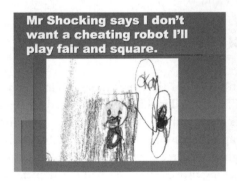

Mr Shocking says I don't want a cheating robot I'll play fair and square.

The end

■ **Figure 11.1** *continued . . .*

effects of transitions, animations and sound. Unfortunately, because of the different affordances of books and screens (UKLA/QCA, 2004, 2005) these features cannot be shown in printed form. However, even without the sound and other visual effects, Thomas's story is still engaging and reflects his sense of humour. It also shows how he draws on his experience of other texts.

Thomas's tale tells of Mr Shocking who uses the powers of a robot to cheat in basketball. However, when lightning hits the robot, reminiscent of the Frankenstein story, perhaps, the robot turns against Mr Shocking and the story ends with him realising that it is not worth cheating if you end up in hospital. The text combines still images and words on each screen but Thomas also uses speech bubbles and sound effects that add to the appeal of the tale. When Mr Shocking is being chased by the robot, in one screen he yells 'Help'. It seems that no-one answers because in the following screen he shouts exasperatedly, 'I said help! for goodness sake.' The robot is evidently enjoying itself, saying as it throws Mr Shocking in the air 'This is great basketball' and then, when it has used Mr Shocking as a ball and scored, it calls out 'two points'. Thomas maintains colour and detail throughout as cohesive devices, with three coloured buttons on the front of the robot and Mr Shocking's red shirt, yellow head and moustache. In the final screen, Thomas introduces a character in blue, perhaps a nurse at the hospital who agrees that it would be wise not to cheat in future. This young designer goes beyond 'combinational creativity' and demonstrates 'exploratory creativity' (Boden, 2001); he playfully makes use of a myriad of other texts, but also explores possibilities and ideas that are unique to him.

Each child in this class, all with significant problems with literacy and learning, completed a PowerPoint™ presentation. Thomas and his classmates would not have been able to compose these stories in writing alone. It is obvious from Thomas' drawings that he has difficulties in manipulating pens and pencils, as have some of the other children in the class, but their stories were typed, saved and developed, their storyboarded pictures inserted and then, through the use of the interactive whiteboard, shared with the rest of the class. This would have been much more arduous, and perhaps not even possible for some, in terms of maintaining effort and narrative flow, without the appeal, stimulus and facilities of digital technology. Such is the potential of this medium for creative teaching and learning.

PROFILING VISUAL TEXTS IN EXTENDED LEARNING JOURNEYS

As has already been suggested, many films follow the conventions of familiar narrative and the plan for an extended unit of work outlined in this section is based on *The Wrong Trousers*. The film, designed by Nick Park and the Aardman studio, lasts for thirty minutes and is about friends stumbling over a plot to carry out a robbery, thwarting the villain and restoring the stolen goods – a recognisable narrative structure. The outlined unit of worth follows the teaching process as described in Chapter 7 and the planning process as described in Chapter 12. This learning journey extends to between three and four weeks and can be used with any age group. As with any outline plan, however, creative teachers will want to select and adapt the ideas to suit specific classes and are likely to change elements of the plan as the work unfolds in response to the needs and interests of the learners. Initially, it will be important to identify an assessable outcome – this could be a multimodal mystery story presented either as a PowerPoint™ or as a digital film. Then key learning objectives for the age group need to be selected to fit with the genre of an adventure narrative.

The focus in the first half of the extended exploration will be on familiarising the children with the genre and capturing ideas. Thus the focus of the session is likely to be on setting, perspective, sound, characterisation and editing as the children build towards a storyboard that will be the basis of the multimodal outcome.

The class could view the film in sections, pausing at key moments to discuss what might happen next. At this stage, the idea is just to enjoy the film with the children, simply recording the stages of the narrative, identifying the key sections and noting them on the IWB or board. These sections might include the following, although with younger classes this might need to be simplified:

- *Establishing section*: A domestic setting with several characters/friends.
- *Development*: A new character is introduced who causes trouble/ disrupts the harmony.
- *Complication*: There is a mystery to be solved associated with the character.
- *Action*: The 'hero' discovers the plot and tracks down the villain.
- *Resolution*: There is a chase where the friends deal with the villain.
- *Conclusion*: Domestic peace is restored.

In order to generate and capture ideas the class could be asked to freeze-frame an episode from each section; the teacher could usefully take digital images of these for later work and annotation, or alternatively, could take screen captures from the film's key incidents, for the same purpose. In analysing the setting, notes could be added to the appropriate sections on the saved IWB/flipchart notes.

In preparing for the visual outcome, the class will need to review the film and discuss selected episodes that illustrate how atmosphere and narrative tension are created. Discussion might focus on a specific aspect of the film, for example, setting, characterisation, perspective or the creation of atmosphere. The children will be preparing to compose a new episode that might be inserted during the 'action' part of the story. The episode will be a short storyboarded sequence where the hero follows the villain to a place not shown in the film. In preparation for the independent work, the teacher may need to model how to establish the setting for this episode. In order to ensure the children are encouraged to work independently, pairs could identify and draw a new setting for an additional episode, perhaps downloading pictures from the Internet as inspiration.

Work on perspective: During this first half of the extended unit, work on perspective could involve analysing camera angles to identify the director's point of view. This is best done by taking one section of the film that has suitable variation in perspective and camera angles. One excellent sequence is the part where Gromit leaves the house at night thinking that he has been replaced in Wallace's affections by the Penguin. Discussion on perspective can be guided by explaining that often, but not necessarily always:

- a long shot establishes setting or tells the action of the film;
- a mid shot is used to show relationships between characters as well as action;
- a close-up tells us about a character's thoughts or feelings;

- ■ perspective shot from below often indicates difficulty or threat for the main character;
- ■ perspective shot diagonally can mean confusion, fear or disorientation;
- ■ perspective shot from above can mean superiority by another character or can create narrative tension.

As part of their independent group work, children could continue working in pairs to create an eight-frame storyboard of the new episode using different angles and perspectives for each frame. They might use the one discussed in class or think up their own to fit the setting they have designed.

Work on sound: This could involve the teacher in selecting a section of the film where the music/sound effects are particularly evocative and, having covered the screen, inviting the children to note what they think is happening as they listen. As it is difficult to find language to describe atmosphere created by music, they might be given pre-prepared envelopes of words to choose from. With older pupils these might include words such as: 'haunting, intriguing, melancholy, tense, mysterious . . .' They will need time to discuss these with their partners before feeding back to the whole class. After noting their descriptions they should then view the section of the film that they have just listened to and discuss the differences and similarities between their guesses and the film itself. The children could then, in their independent work, add notes to their storyboards about what sounds they want to use to create atmosphere or share something about characters.

Work on characterisation: This might involve the teacher again selecting parts of the film for the children to concentrate on the characters and discuss how the film director makes the audience know that some characters are 'good' and some 'villains'. The emphasis should be on how facial expression, posture and gesture indicate characteristics and feelings, for example, raised eyebrows, hands on hips to show anger, drooped body posture to suggest unhappiness. After the independent work, notes for the three main characters – Wallace, Gromit and the Penguin – could be recorded on the IWB/flipchart for all the main characters under the headings 'What the character says' and 'What the character does'. As a consolidation of reading character in film, a section of the film where the camera concentrates on the feelings of one of the characters can be selected and the children asked to discuss how the character is feeling and how they know this. They might also be asked to write a short diary/journal entry from the point of view of the character describing her/his feelings. This writing could be enhanced by using drama conventions such as interior monologue, hot-seating or role on the wall to explore the characters more fully. See Chapter 3 for ways to bridge between drama and writing. Alternatively, screen-captures of images of characters could be used for the children to attach speech or thought bubbles, prior to adding dialogue in speech bubbles to their own storyboards.

Work on editing: This is important as this process creates narrative drive in film. Sometimes it is slow and reflective, which gives some sense of how the characters are feeling;

sometimes it is fast and creates narrative tension. The power of editing can be shown by selecting a section of the film where the editing either develops character or narrative tension and reviewing it several times while the teacher models how choices about changes of shot help build up narrative tension or characterisation. Both the sequence in which Penguin is stealing the diamond and the final chase sequence are ideal for this. Afterwards the children can annotate their own storyboards to show length of shots.

At this point, after approximately two weeks, each pair should have an eight-frame storyboard, with a particular setting (annotated to explain details) of a new episode showing angles and perspective. During the ongoing sessions, they should have added notes about sound to create atmosphere or characterisation, given some indication of length of shots and attached speech bubbles. In the later sessions of this extended unit of work, the focus will be on shared composition of the multimodal text, to make a PowerPoint™ presentation or a digital film. If this has not been done this before it might be best for the teacher to model making a whole class presentation or film, involving the children in groups for each aspect, for example, writing dialogue, designing and drawing settings and so on. Alternatively, they could work in their pairs to create their own movies/PowerPoint™ presentations. Both presentations and films can have sound effects and dialogue added. The children might download images for settings and software designed for drawing, or draw their own screens based on the storyboards. Equally, they could act out the extra episodes, taking digital images of freeze-frames or use small world play figures or puppets.

At this point, time will need to be spent on:

■ designing, drawing/downloading settings and characters and making them larger or smaller according to the perspectives chosen in the storyboards;
■ drafting, trying out, editing and finalising dialogue;
■ deciding on sound for each screen/shot and recording/making it;
■ timing length of shots or transitions between screens;
■ putting it all together;
■ designing advertising for their film;
■ organising screenings or launch events;
■ showing it to other people;
■ evaluating the process and the films or presentations.

Reflecting on the work might include discussing their audiences' responses and the written reviews produced by other classes or parents. It might also involve asking the children why they chose to use close-ups, mid- or long-shots, or particular colours. They could also consider how they could improve their composition and what particularly satisfies them about their multimodal narratives. To support their own evaluative reflections, it is important for the teacher to comment on how they have used the technical devices they have learned about to make their own creative compositions.

CONCLUSION

The predominance of visual texts may make demands on teaching but at the same time does liberate a wealth of children's text experience that can be shared, enjoyed and creatively built upon in the classroom. There is clear evidence (Bearne *et al.*, 2004; Warrington *et al.*, 2006; Walsh, 2007) that reading visual texts, composing them and using them as a basis for writing can help children find their own voices. In terms of reading, there is also evidence of children developing a critical eye and becoming more discriminating and responsive readers of print texts as a result of viewing film (ibid.). Since it is likely that children will increasingly draw on screen texts for entertainment, information and enjoyment of narrative, the development of a critically analytical stance is essential. This will be made possible by the explicit discussion of how the different modes of communication and representation work together to make meaning. For this to happen, teachers themselves need to have confidence in their own knowledge of the structures and imaginative possibilities of digital texts and technologies. They also need to teach creatively, taking risks and being prepared to work with the full range of visual and digital texts that children encounter every day outside school.

FURTHER READING

Bearne, E. and Wolstencroft, H. (2005) Playing with Texts: The Contribution of Children's Knowledge of Computer Narratives to Their Story Writing, in J. Marsh and E. Millard (eds), *Popular Literacies Childhood and Schooling*, London: RoutledgeFalmer.

Bearne, E. and Wolstencroft, H. (2007) *Visual Approaches to Teaching Writing*, London: Sage.

Graham, L. (2008) Teachers are Digikids Too: The Digital Histories and Digital Lives of Young Teachers in English Primary Schools, *Literacy*, 42(1): 10–18.

Honan, E. (2008) Barriers to Teachers Using Digital Texts in Literacy Classrooms, *Literacy*, 42(1): 36–43.

CHILDREN'S BOOKS AND FILMS

Bird, B. (1999) (dir.) *The Iron Giant*, Warner Bros.

Hughes, T. (1968) *The Iron Man*, Faber & Faber.

Park, N. (1993) (dir.) *The Wrong Trousers*, Aardman animation.

CHAPTER 12

PLANNING TO TEACH ENGLISH CREATIVELY

INTRODUCTION

In the last decade teachers have assiduously planned for curriculum coverage, to ensure that each literacy objective and those in other areas of the curriculum are given due time and attention. Arguably, this view of the curriculum as planned, in response to the prescribed requirements, has dominated over the conception of the curriculum as lived/experienced. However, with the emergence of increased governmental support for creativity and in the light of the Rose Review of the Primary Curriculum (Rose, 2008), more creative approaches to the curriculum are being developed.

As teachers seek to restructure the curriculum with personal, learning and thinking skills at the core, the creative process and its outcomes are being revalued and planned for more explicitly in English. The PNS (DfES, 2006a) now emphasises planning extended units of work and includes experiential, enquiry-based and problem solving pedagogic approaches within its recommendations. It also encourages teachers to develop more flexible and open-ended practices and to teach English across the curriculum. This chapter, in focusing on planning to teach English creatively, explores the significance of building a creative environment and the principles and practice of planning for creative learning. It also explores examples of teachers working alongside creative practitioners from outside the school community, and highlights the importance of integrating the eight core elements of creative practice into the English curriculum experience.

BUILDING A CREATIVE ENVIRONMENT

It is difficult to draw a dividing line between a creative approach to English teaching and a creative ethos in the classroom; the teachers approach towards English teaching significantly influences the climate created. Educators' attitudes to reading, writing, speaking and listening are very influential, and are implicitly as well as explicitly shared. Their perceptions of what is important are reflected not only in the literal displays, role-play area, computers, writing table, message board, reading corners and so forth, but also in the climate created and the evocation of imaginative contexts for purposeful literacy learning.

In order to foster creativity children need to feel safe, valued and trusted, and able to take risks as readers, writers, speakers and listeners and not be critiqued for so doing. Research indicates strong links between creative learning and emotional security, and suggests that creativity is best fostered in inclusive environments that foster, for both teachers and children, a high degree of ownership and control over the agenda, as well as emotional relevance and collaboration (Jeffrey and Woods, 2003; Craft, 2005). Positive relationships are crucial in fostering creativity. It flourishes in situations where there are trusting teacher–learner relationships, when teachers not only respond to children's feelings and protect them from ridicule, but also tolerate mild or polite rebellion, and respect the generation of child initiated alternatives (Shayer and Adey, 2002). Individual creativity is affected by even very minor aspects of the immediate social environment (Amabile, 1988); the school ethos will affect the ethos created by teachers in their classrooms and thus the opportunities for creative teaching and learning in English and across the curriculum.

In classrooms with a secure ethos, children will be happy to ask and answer questions, confident enough to take sensible risks and get their risk taking rewarded. An ethos that encourages curiosity and profiles children's questions also encourages core elements of creativity, such as problem finding as well as problem solving, and the development of a speculative stance that expects and welcomes challenge. Teachers who show their own creativity tend to voice their exploratory thoughts and model tentative thinking in the classroom, revealing themselves as learners and as writers for example. Such teachers are likely to deal positively with uncertainty, to tolerate ambiguity and perceive failure as a learning opportunity (Halpin, 2003).

The new personal learning and thinking skills framework (QCA, 2008) recognises the complex relationship between children's creativity and their development as independent enquirers, effective participants, team workers, self-managers and reflective thinkers, all of which are influenced by the ethos and environment established by the teacher. Creative teachers not only seek to develop playful environments of possibility in which ideas are generated and privileged, but also help literacy learners share and review their ideas, subjecting them to serious scrutiny, so that action and reflection can lead to transformation and outcomes of value. They therefore profile judgement as well as playfulness, and encourage reflection in multiple modes.

PRINCIPLES OF EXTENDED LEARNING JOURNEYS

If teachers are to move from being presenters of content to becoming leaders of creative learning journeys, which are in essence extended explorations set within purposeful units of work, then thoughtful use will need to be made of the key elements of creative English practice documented in this book. On such journeys, literacy is both taught and applied in meaningful contexts that enrich children's creativity, enhance their lateral thinking, and develop their motivated and enthusiastic involvement in learning. The eight elements of creative English practice that need to wove through such learning journeys are, as noted in Chapter 1:

1   profiling meaning and purpose;
2   foregrounding potent affectively engaging texts;
3   fostering play and engagement;
4   harnessing curiosity and profiling agency;
5   encouraging collaboration and making connections;
6   integrating reflection, review, feedback and celebration;
7   taking time to travel and explore;
8   ensuring the creative involvement of the teacher.

In planning extended units of work, ranging from between a fortnight to half a term or more, all four language modes will be integrated and opportunities for learners to direct some of their own learning planned from the outset. This can help create an increasingly negotiated and co-participative English curriculum. Since creativity arises from interactions with ideas and others, and is supported by open-ended discussions, improvisations, structured simulations and playful encounters, these experiences need to be threaded through each learning journey and a wealth of opportunities for individual, pair and group work planned. In addition, formative assessment will be mapped into this flexible and creative approach in order to enable teachers to be responsive to learners' needs and offer tailored instruction and focused feedback.

In seeking to adopt a creative approach, teachers work to temper the planned with the lived and let the learners lead more frequently, creating a responsive English curriculum, which seeks to build coherently on unexpected contributions or enquiries, and ensures the appropriate knowledge and skills are developed in the process. At its simplest this might involve identifying children's key questions and puzzlements about a text and planning accordingly, or by inviting the class to vote on whether *Lady Daisy* by Dick King Smith or Berlie Doherty's *Street Child* or *My Granny was a Buffer Girl* will be read during the Victorian focus. However, many teachers will wish to involve the learners more extensively in planning and developing the unit of work, in shaping their journeys and in negotiating their own goals and expectations. This enhances their agency and enables them to take a degree of greater responsibility for their own learning, as Cochrane and Cockett (2007) demonstrate so effectively. In working to promote creativity through planning, QCA also recognise the significance of building in opportunities to enhance children's involvement and autonomy, suggesting teachers need to:

■   stimulate imaginations making significant connections;
■   be clear about freedom and constraints;
■   use a range of learning styles;
■   give clear purpose – relevance to the work;
■   provide opportunities for pupils to work together;
■   build in autonomy.

(QCA, 2005a,b)

PLANNING EXTENDED LEARNING JOURNEYS

Extended explorations may focus entirely upon English or may seek to combine teaching and learning across the creative arts, integrating the teaching of English, music, art, dance and drama for example. Alternatively, the core planning focus may be a cross curricular theme in which literacy is both taught and applied in a humanities or science learning journey for example, although even in this context the creative arts may well be involved. Whatever the particular combination of areas of learning sought, the following key steps will serve to help primary professionals identify a way forward when planning extended learning journeys.

Choose the focus, the duration and the text type/s to be explored

Teachers will want to decide whether to tie literacy work into cross curricular activities – if this is the case a 5–6 week plan may not be excessive, or two mini-units may be chosen, both of which might relate to the Victorians for example, but focus specifically on narrative for three weeks and recounts/ newspapers for the following two weeks. There is no hard and fast rule about length, but coherence is important, as is the need to allow time for the children to develop and complete an extended piece of work of which they can be proud. This relates to the second step in planning.

Identify an assessable outcome

Each extended unit of work needs to work towards a long-term outcome or product. This provides a clear aim for the children and enables the teacher to formatively assess their work as it develops over the weeks, knowing that the goal is, for example, to write a fairytale for inclusion in the class anthology, or to produce clear instructions on PowerPoint™ for another class to use in art and craft. There is no need for the outcome to be a written one in each case. The assessed piece may be focused on a performance of understanding, perhaps in the form of a documentary programme, poetry festival or storytelling event, or alternatively, teachers may work towards the production of an audio tape or DVD of short stories written and read by the children. Making public the assessed outcomes is important and a variety of these need to be included across a school year.

Collect and consider textual and other resources

Collecting a rich range of examples of the genre in focus and one or two that are likely to be examined in more detail is essential. For example, gathering together a range of traditional tales in picture books and anthologies, to be used in shared and guided time, as well as story tapes for children to read/listen to independently. A display of these may help to promote the genre and encourage the children to bring in their own examples to add to the loan collection. There is no need for these to be in the same media, for example films such as *Shrek* or *Aladdin* could be integrated into such a unit to compare screen-based and print-based versions, to explore the myriad of inter-textual references to other tales or to examine parody. Visual approaches to teaching literacy need to be integrated into the literacy curriculum and not left to chance. Much will depend upon the intended outcome and purpose of the unit and whether it is linked to cross curricular work, as in the case of the storytelling focus being linked to a geographical examination of different cultures for example.

While teachers will want to underpin the learning journey with potent, imaginatively engaging texts, they may also want to supplement these with opportunities to work with storytellers, poets, authors, journalists, dancers, musicians and actors for example, or with practitioners from a connected area of work, as well as members of the community whose expertise, stance and experience could enrich the children's travels.

Select appropriate strand objectives

Teachers will want to select relevant strand objectives from the PNS framework (DfES, 2006a) to be explored and attended to in order to achieve the final outcome. These will need to encompass a rich mix of objectives from several of the twelve literacy strands. On an extended learning journey, teachers will be involved in both supporting and challenging learning and seizing opportunities to integrate focused instruction when needed. Creative teachers do not ignore form and function, rules or language conventions, but actively seek to help children explore these in meaningful and engaging contexts. Open-ended approaches, involving all the learners in a stimulating process of exploration and experimentation, can be planned and developed from a learning objective and should embed learning about conventions and codes within them.

While opportunities for explicit instruction in context will be planned into the unit from the outset, they are likely also to be seized by teachers in response to children's interests and the evolving nature of the work, as well as in response to on-going formative assessment. Thus while some objectives will be profiled throughout, others may be identified for closer examination as the unit develops. In addition, areas of the personal, learning and thinking skills framework may be woven through a unit and cross curricular threads and objectives also identified.

Alternatively, teachers may wish to look back retrospectively at the end of the unit, or periodically through a unit, to see which literacy objectives and strands have been examined through the class's exploration. Such an approach has been found to enhance teachers' freedom, flexibility, creativity and professional autonomy (Bearne *et al.*, 2004) and is worth considering.

Plan the process of teaching English creatively

In planning a range of teaching and learning activities that explicitly build upon the eight elements of creative English practice, teachers will also want to map the journey towards the identified assessable outcome and may wish to link this to the framework for teaching in Chapter 7.

While initially focusing on familiarising the class with the genre and immersing them in the text type, time also needs to set aside to outline the challenge, purpose and relevance of the unit. Rather than presenting the work as 'a three week unit on haiku' for example, teachers could seek to site this element of the children's journey within a wider exploration, perhaps of Japanese cultural habits and traditions. They might then frame an invitation to the class to create a Japanese tea ceremony/festival for members of the community at which their poetry may be read, their Japanese dance and artwork shared and their calligraphy displayed.

Another unit on poetry might be framed by inviting the class to organise a week long poetry festival for the school community. After considerable discussion of possibilities, groups might be established to plan particular events at which their own and others poetry may be shared, read, viewed, performed and published. This could involve working with parents and professional poets or musicians, and the class working as poetry ambassadors; much will depend on the combination of ideas finally agreed upon. Constructing learning journeys in consultation with the children in this way can harness their curiosity, and enhance their agency and sense of ownership of their learning, enriching both their commitment and their creativity.

Throughout the unit, teachers will plan to foster the children's playful engagement, perhaps through appealing to their interests and passions, involving them in imaginative experiences, finding powerful texts that inspire and/or connecting the learning to their lives. In a poetry unit, classroom drama might be used to investigate the issues in a narrative poem, poetry boxes established with a wide range of poetic texts, including jokes, playground rhymes, lyrics and riddles, and the Poetry Archive explored to listen to poets reading their work and to identify favourites. Music, dance and art could all be woven into the journey, triggering different interpretations and work on inference and deduction, as well as supporting the production of poetic compositions and performances. The identified objectives will be woven through the unit as appropriate to the activities and their purposes, so that children's knowledge and understanding of poetry will be developed through their engagement and accompanying tailored instruction.

Across each unit, teachers will want to ensure there are a range of opportunities for children to work individually and together, in pairs, groups and as a whole class, sometimes on set activities and sometimes in self-directed ways that nurture their capacity to collaborate and participate with one another. In such contexts, children will be generating ideas for the poetry festival, for example, and for their own compositions and performances, and will be evaluating and refining these together. Teachers may also want to widen the remit beyond the classroom, perhaps through establishing poetry partners in a neighbouring school and enabling the children to email their poems to them for comments and feedback. These partners might also be invited to visit during the poetry festival.

Teachers, as well as framing the exploration, will sensitively and spontaneously shape the unfolding journey in response to the children's interests and needs, while retaining a sense of the overall goal, the learning intentions and curriculum requirements. They will also seek to inspire and engage the children through actively participating themselves as language artists and creative professionals, modelling the process of asking questions, making connections, and taking risks as well as trying alternatives as they discuss, perform and compose their own poems for example.

In this way they will be demonstrating many of the same creative attributes that they seek to foster in children, namely curiosity, perseverance, playfulness, resourcefulness and reflection.

Plan to review and celebrate

Throughout the extended learning journey, children will need time and space to play and explore, to speculate and question, and to critically review and evaluate their work. Time for this will need to be built in both during the unit and towards the end of the journey, to involve the children in generating and appraising their work, reflecting on the insights gained, the ideas shared and the accomplishments achieved. This should encourage the capacity to reflect critically and support them as they seek to craft their work to a high standard over time.

Teachers will also want to celebrate the children's achievements by making public their work in a variety of informal as well as more formal ways. This should trigger consideration of both the process and the product of their learning and profile reflection, evaluation and feedback. It will also be important to help the children assess the degree to which their ongoing work, their responses to texts, work in groups and the multimodal texts that they produce, are innovative or alternative and demonstrate their creativity.

Working in partnership to plan creative and critical events

The concept of critical events was coined by Woods (1994) to describe holistic projects, which include external specialists and have unusually ambitious long-term goals, such as the production of a radio programme, an opera, a film or a play perhaps. Such projects develop with community partners, seek to stimulate creative learning and encourage children to initiate activities and direct more of their own work. In many ways the extended learning journeys described in this chapter are small-scale versions of creative and critical events, although not all will encompass working with specialists from beyond the school. Teachers learn to expect the unexpected when engaging in critical and creative events and need to be prepared to respond spontaneously, reframing the curriculum as the events unfold.

> Critical events are in large measure intended, planned and controlled. But the plans contain within them seeds for growth and scope for opportunities. There are elements, therefore, that are largely unforeseen, and unpredictable new pastures that all, teachers and pupils alike are venturing into, with what consequences no one exactly knows.
>
> (Woods, 1994: 2)

Such opportunities to work on extended projects with external visitors and learning partners from outside school can significantly enrich children's learning experiences and make a real contribution to their literacy development (Ellis and Safford, 2005; Brice-Heath and Wolf, 2005; Pahl, 2007). This has been demonstrated in numerous studies, most recently in relation to a number of projects developed as part of the Creative Partnership initiative in England (Creative Partnerships, 2008). This initiative seeks to establish long-term sustainable partnerships between schools, organisations and individuals such as architects, theatre companies, museums, cinemas, film makers, installation artists, dancers, web-designers, authors, poets, storytellers and many more. Schools not involved in this work can still, however, work on extended creative events with external partners, and may choose to connect to English Heritage sites or a local gallery, library or museum for example. Historically, schools have often invited children's writers to work with them, most recently under the initiative Writing Together (Sprackland and Coe, 2005). This practice of working with artist partners and others from the business and cultural sector has expanded significantly in recent years, and the 2008–2011 pilot programme 'Find Your Talent', which seeks to create a universal cultural offer of five hours of quality arts and culture a week, takes this still further. Such programmes offer literacy learners the chance to work imaginatively with others both inside and outside the classroom and seek to foster their creativity.

Examples of creative and critical events

In one umbrella project entitled *Animating Literacy*, Creative Partnerships working with the Centre for Literacy in Primary Education, spawned several school-based projects in drama, the performing arts, multimedia and film making (Ellis and Safford, 2005). The projects involved primary teachers in interpreting and adapting the curriculum more creatively and working with various artists over time. For example, in one project short films were both devised and made by a class of 9–10-year-olds working with their teacher, a film director and videomakers/photographers. The teacher noted that the children all developed their speaking and listening skills through this work as well as their self-esteem and capacity to collaborate with others.

In another project, a class of 10–11-year-olds worked closely both with the Young Vic Theatre and English National Opera. The former were staging a production of David Almond's book *Skellig* and the youngsters became involved in this, watching it, interviewing the actors, producing their own scenes from it in the theatre and later performing on stage at the Young Vic as part of a Schools' Theatre festival. Their teacher successfully developed their curiosity and critical thinking skills through this work, this is evident both in their talk and in their writing. The success of this project may be due in part at least to the real world connections and relationships established and because the artists became role models extending the children's horizons in various ways. Although, as their teacher noted, there were real consequences for curriculum planning:

> Working with arts organisations rather than an individual arts partner in my classroom meant that planning over the year of *Animating Literacy* had to be flexible. We had to seize and make the most of opportunities that presented themselves. I was willing to adapt and change the topics children studied whenever there were opportunities for in-depth experiences.
>
> (Hickman, 2005: 87)

In another Creative Partnerships project an infant school worked with a resident artist and an architectural designer to create a reception area for the new school building. Oral language, visual literacies and strategic thinking were the focus of this research, which encompassed many themes and demonstrated, for example, the significance of constructing a creative vocabulary in the classroom and opportunities for learners to inhabit this discourse (Brice-Heath and Wolf, 2004). The artist's language seeped through into the children's everyday conversation and his desire to talk about great works of art and remain open to different interpretations, prompted the young children to look more closely, take risks in responding and apply these skills to their conversations about picture books. This not only supported them as readers, but also arguably gave them insights into other possible worlds as well as their own. Additionally, the evidence suggests it helped them develop a sense of the aesthetic and a language to comment upon and evaluate their own and others' creations.

Combining visual images and children's literature is also at the heart of the ongoing initiative 'Take One Picture' run by the National Gallery in London, which invites schools to participate and seeks to demonstrate the power of combining visual art forms and narrative/ poetry. In one school some 6–7-year-olds, in responding to Katsushiika Hokusai's 'Caught by the Ejiri Wind' arguably found their voices through the process of being physically, aesthetically and artistically engaged on their compositional journeys (Smith, 2007). The role of the body in enriching literacy learning is also evidenced in another collaborative project, in which three schools worked with a contemporary dance team and the Medway Arts and Literacy teams (Wells, 2008). The focus in this work was on folk tales from around the world and Madonna's *The Adventures of Abdi* was selected as the core text because of the aesthetic qualities of the illustrations and the fact that the Arabic culture offered rich potential for dance and music connected to the theme of journeys. The work led eventually to groups of children performing their final interpretations of parts of the narrative to their own school communities and creating multimedia presentations of the project for their school website. It demonstrated again that weaving critical events around dance, literacy and art and working with experts beyond the school can be highly effective in fostering children's creative learning in English.

Such opportunities to work with creative partners and members of the community does cost time and money, and demands flexibility on the part of all the professionals involved. It offers children the chance to work with talented colleagues from outside the school on holistic projects in which their literacy skills and understanding can be applied and developed in meaningful real world contexts, over which they have some control.

THE TEACHER AS A CREATIVE PRACTITIONER

However, while such partnership projects are increasingly common and are to be welcomed, they may, inadvertently, focus the profession on external experts, and underestimate the creative capacity of classroom teachers. The conception of teachers as artists also deserves attention, support and development (Jeffrey, 2005). The ability of teachers to operate as co-participators and creative practitioners, apprenticing learners and modelling possibilities is, Craft (2005) suggests, central to a creative approach to teaching and is one of the eight core elements of creative English practice articulated in this book. It represents a possible way to develop a balance between developing children's knowledge about language and creative language use and has the potential to offer increased job satisfaction to members of the profession, many of whom 'value the link between creative approaches and their own motivation and sense of pleasure in the job' (Barnes, 2003: 41).

As literacy educators, teachers are personally and professionally involved, both as individuals and as managers of the learning. They can also be involved as fellow artists in the classroom, as creative practitioners themselves. In this role, they are arguably more personally and affectively involved, thinking and feeling their way through situations, asking questions, taking risks, and profiling pedagogies and language practices that help them develop their own and the children's creativity in action. 'Young people's creative abilities are most likely to be developed in an atmosphere in which the teacher's creative abilities are properly engaged' (NACCCE, 1999: 90). Language arts activities in particular can help all members of the classroom community create environments of possibility, generating and evaluating alternative interpretations and insights, and expressing themselves creatively.

The challenge of developing teachers and children's imaginations is an exacting one; it depends in part upon adult involvement, with teachers and teaching assistants participating as writers, tale tellers, poetry performers, film makers and role-players for example. This will not evoke a profession of extroverts or performers in the flamboyant sense, but a creative profession actively involved in the artistic processes in which the children are also engaged. The consequences of such educator engagement are manifold, particularly the pedagogical consequences. For example, with reference to reading, teachers can share their identities as readers and their emotional response to texts, demonstrating that this is a normal and legitimate part of being a reader. Through storytelling, teachers can share the challenges and satisfactions of spinning tales into existence and enticing the audience to wonder, feel and respond. Modelling their oral artistry in this way may also encompass teachers' reflecting upon the process of remembering and retelling tales, and their growing awareness of story structure, characterisation, vocabulary choices and so forth. Additionally, as teachers in role, professionals will experience the energising open-endedness of classroom drama, and may seize the moment to write as the tension mounts and multiple perspectives are explored. Furthermore, through engaging as writers in the classroom, teachers can experience the reflective emergent nature of composing and identify insights from within the writing process, such as the emotional struggle, the role of incubation and experimentation, the importance of developing a listening ear and the value of authentic meaning-focused feedback (Cremin, 2008).

Teachers' involvement as language artists in their classrooms may help them avoid routinising textual encounters, enabling them to raise possibilities rather than confirm probabilities; to open doors rather than close them. Their creative engagement in literacy teaching and learning may also help them to exploit the potential spaces, problems and possibilities that literature and other texts offer; gaps in texts increase the degree of uncertainty, provoking questions and potential for creative engagement.

Widening teachers' experience of and engagement in the language arts and new technologies, can also prompt them to use strategies that unsettle the status quo or open up new avenues for investigation, interpretation and problem solving. Teaching literacy creatively, therefore, demands high levels of professional assurance and artistry, a degree of 'confident uncertainty' (Claxton, 2000) and the capacity to respond spontaneously, responsively and imaginatively.

CONCLUSION

In this era of personalisation, a creative approach to teaching English offers children a voice in the learning conversation and the chance to direct more of their own work, making choices and decisions in collaboration with others during purposeful and engaging learning journeys. Such an approach can help teachers respond to the dual pressures of prescription and accountability and the demands to teach creatively and teach for creativity. Adopting a creative approach can additionally help teachers construct a better balance between form and freedom, structure and innovation in their teaching. If teachers integrate the eight elements of teaching English creatively into their planning, and work to extend their engagement as language artists, they will be fostering children's creativity: enriching their capacity to question, pose problems, make connections, generate, innovate and imagine alternatives and reflect critically as readers and writers, speakers and listeners. Creative English teaching fosters creative English learning.

FURTHER READING

Boden, M. (2001) Creativity and Knowledge, in A. Craft, B. Jeffrey and M. Liebling (eds), *Creativity in Education*, London: Continuum, pp. 95–115.

Cochrane, P. and Cockett, M. (2007) *Building a Creative School: A Dynamic Approach to School Improvement*, Stoke-on-Trent: Trentham.

Cremin, T., Burnard, P. and Craft, A. (2006a) Pedagogy and Possibility Thinking in the Early Years, *International Journal of Thinking Skills and Creativity*, 1(2): 108–19.

Fisher, R. and Williams, M. (2004). *Unlocking Creativity: Teaching Across the Curriculum*, London: David Fulton.

CHILDREN'S BOOKS

Almond, D. (1998) *Skellig*, Hodder.

Doherty, B. (1995) *Street Child*, Collins.

Doherty, B. (2007) *My Granny was a Buffer Girl* (new edition), Catnip.

King Smith, D. (1993) *Lady Daisy*, Puffin.

Madonna with Dugina, O. and Digin, A. (illus.) (2004) *The Adventures of Abdi*, Puffin.

REFERENCES

Alexander, R. (2004) *Towards Dialogic Teaching: Rethinking Classroom Talk*, Cambridge: Dialogos.

Allington, R.L. and McGill-Franzen, A. (2003) The Impact of Summer Set Back on the Reading Achievement Gap, *Phi Delta Kappan*, 85(1): 68–75.

Almond, D. (2001) Writing for Children, Lecture given at NLS Writing and Creativity Conference, 4 June, London.

Amabile, T.M. (1988) A Model of Creativity and Innovation in Organisations, in B.M. Staw and L.L. Cunnings (eds) *Research in Organisational Behaviour*, Greenwich, CT: JA.

Andrews, R. (1989) Beyond 'Voice' in Poetry, *English in Education*, 23(3): 21–7.

Andrews, R. (2008) Shifting Writing Practice: Focusing on the Productive Skills to Improve Quality and Standards, in DCSF, *Getting Going: Generating, Shaping and Developing Ideas in Writing*, Nottingham: DCSF, pp. 4–21.

Arizpe, E. and Styles, M. (2003) *Children Reading Pictures: Interpreting Visual Texts*, London: Routledge Falmer.

Armstrong, M. (2006) *Children Writing Stories*, Berkshire and New York: Open University Press.

Arts Council England (2003) *From Looking Glass to Spy Glass: A Consultation Paper on Children's Literature*, London: Arts Council.

Auden, W.H. and Garrett, J. (1935) *The Poets' Tongue*, London: Bell.

Bakhtin, M. (1986) *Speech Genres and Other Late Essays* (trans. V.W. McGee), Austin, TX: University of Texas Press.

Bamford, A. (2008) The Visual Literacy White Paper, Adobe Systems Pty Ltd, Australia, available at www.adobe.com/uk/education/pdf/adobe_visual_literacy_paper.pdf (accessed 16 June 2008).

Barnes, J. (2003) Teacher's Emotions, Teacher's Creativity: A Discussion Paper, *Improving Schools*, 6(1): 39–43.

Barrs, M. (1988) Maps of Play, in M. Meek and C. Mills (eds), *Language and Literacy in the Primary School*, London: Falmer Press.

Barrs, M. and Cork, V. (2001) *The Reader in the Writer: The Influence of Literature upon Writing at KS2*, London: Centre for Literacy in Primary Education.

Bearne, E. (2002) *Making Progress in Writing*, London: Routledge.

Bearne, E. (2007) Writing at Key Stage 2, in T. Cremin and H. Dombey, *Handbook of Primary English in Initial Teacher Education*, Cambridge: UKLA/NATE/Canterbury Christ Church University, pp. 83–95.

Bearne, E. and Grainger, T. (2004) Raising Boys' Achievements in Writing, *Literacy*, 38(3): 153–9.

Bearne, E. and Wolstencroft, H. (2005) Playing with Texts: The Contribution of Children's Knowledge of Computer Narratives to Their Story Writing, in J. Marsh and E. Millard (eds), *Popular Literacies, Childhood and Schooling*, London: Routledge/Falmer.

Bearne, E. and Wolstencroft, H. (2007) *Visual Approaches to Teaching Writing*, London: Sage.

Bearne, E., Grainger, T. and Wolstencroft, H. (2004) *Raising Boys' Achievements in Writing*, Joint research project, Baldock: UKLA and the Primary National Strategy.

Bearne, E., Clark, C., Johnson, A., Manford, P., Mottram, M. and Wolstencroft, H. with Anderson, R., Gamble, N. and Overall, L. (2007) *Reading on Screen: Research Report*, Leicester: UKLA.

Beckett, S. (2006) An Exploration of How Children Respond to and Interpret Image and Word in Picture Books, unpublished MA dissertation, Canterbury Christ Church University.

Beetlestone, F. (1998) *Creative Children, Imaginative Teaching*, Buckingham: Open University Press.

Benton, M. (1984) Teaching Poetry: The Rhetoric and the Reality, *Oxford Review of Education*, 10(3): 319–28.

Benton, M. (2000) *Studies in the Spectator Role: Literature, Painting and Pedagogy*, London: Routledge Falmer.

Benton, M. and Fox, R. (1985) *Teaching Literature 9–14*, Oxford: Oxford University Press.

Bereiter, C. and Scardamalia, M. (1987) *The Psychology of Written Communication*, Hillsdale, NJ: Lawrence Erlbaum.

Black, P., Harrison, C., Lee, C., Marshall, B. and William, D. (2002) *Working Inside the Black Box: Assessment for Learning in the Classroom*, London: Department of Education and Professional Studies, King's College London.

Black, P., Harrison, C., Lee, C., Marshall, B., and Williams, D. (2003) *Assessment for Learning: Putting It Into Practice*, Milton Keynes: Open University Press.

Block, C., Oakar, M., and Hurt, N. (2002) The Expertise of Literacy Teachers: A Continuum from Preschool to Grade 5, *Reading Research Quarterly*, 37(2): 178–206.

Boden, M. (2001) Creativity and Knowledge, in A. Craft, B. Jeffrey and M. Liebling (eds), *Creativity in Education*, London: Continuum, pp. 95–115.

Bolton, G. (1998) *Acting in Classroom Drama: A Critical Analysis*, Stoke-on-Trent: Trentham Publishers.

Booth, D. (1994) *Reading, Writing and Role-playing Across the Curriculum*, Ontario: Pembroke.

Booth, D. (1996) *Story Drama: Reading, Writing and Role-playing Across the Curriculum*, Markham: Pembroke.

Bourdieu, P. (1977) *Outline of a Theory of Practice* (trans. by R. Nice), Cambridge: Cambridge University Press.

Bradley, L. and Bryant, P. (1983) Categorising Sounds and Learning to Read: A Causal Connection, *Nature*, 301: 419–21.

Brice-Heath, S. and Wolf, S. (2004) *Visual Learning in the Community School*, Kent: Creative Partnerships.

British Film Institute/DfES (2003) *Look Again! A Teaching Guide to Using Film and Television with Three to Eleven Year Olds*, London: BFI/DfES.

Britton, J. (1970) *Language and Learning*, London: Penguin.

Bromley, H. (2002) Meet the Simpsons, *The Primary English Magazine*, 7(4): 7–11.

Bromley, H. (2004) Play and Writing in Year 1, *The Primary English Magazine*, 10(1): 27–31.

Brownjohn, S. (1982) *What Rhymes with Secret?*, London: Hodder & Stoughton.

Brownjohn, S. (1984) *To Rhyme or Not to Rhyme?*, London: Hodder & Stoughton.

Bruner, J. (1966) *Towards a Theory of Instruction*, London: Oxford University Press.

Bruner, J. (1984) Language, Mind and Reading, in H. Goelman, A. Oberg and F. Smith (eds), *Awakening to Literacy*, London: Heinemann.

Bruner, J. (1986) *Actual Minds, Possible Worlds*, Cambridge, MA: Harvard University Press.

Bruner, J. (1996) *The Culture of Education*, Cambridge, MA: Harvard University Press.

Burgess, T., Fox, C. and Goody, J. (2002) *When the Hurly Burly's Done: What's Worth Fighting for in English in Education*, Sheffield: NATE.

REFERENCES ■ ■ ■ ■

Burnard, P., Craft, A. and Cremin, T. (2006) Documenting Possibility Thinking: A Journey of Collaborative Inquiry, *International Journal of Early Years Education*, 14(3): 243–62.

Burns, C. and Myhill, D. (2004) Interactive or Inactive? A Consideration of the Nature of Interaction in Whole Class Teaching, *Cambridge Journal of Education*, 34(1): 35–49.

Bus, A.G., Van Ijzendoorn, M.H. and Pellegrini, A.D. (1995) Joint Book Reading Makes for Success in Learning to Read: A Meta-analysis on Intergenerational Transmission of Literacy, *Review of Educational Research*, 65: 11–21.

Bussis, A.M., Chittenden, E.A., Amarel, M. and Klausner, E. (1985) *Inquiry into Meaning: An Investigation of Learning to Read*, Hillsdale, NJ: Lawrence Erlbaum Associates.

Calkins, L.M. (1991) *Living Between the Lines*, Portsmouth, NH: Heinemann.

Cambourne, B. (1988) *The Whole Story: Natural Learning and the Acquisition of Literacy in the Classroom*, Auckland, New Zealand: Ashton Scholastic.

Cambourne, B. (1995) Towards an Educationally Relevant Theory of Literacy Learning: Twenty Years of Inquiry, *The Reading Teacher*, 49(3): 182–90.

Carter, J. (1999) *Talking Books: Authors Talk about the Craft, Creativity and Process of Writing*, London: Routledge.

Carter, R. (2004) *Language and Creativity: The Art of Common Talk*, London: Routledge.

Centre for Literacy in Primary Education (CLPE) (2002) *Simply the Best: Books for 0 to 7 Years*, London: CLPE.

Chambers, A. (1993) *Tell Me: Children, Reading and Talk*, Stroud: Thimble Press.

Chambers, A. (1995) *Book Talk: Occasional Writing on Literature and Children*, Stroud: Thimble Press.

Chappell, K., Craft, A., Burnard, P. and Cremin, T. (2008) Question Posing and Question Responding: The Heart of Possibility Thinking in the Early Years, *Early Years: An International Journal of Research and Development*, 28(3): 267–83.

Clark, C. and Foster, A. (2005) *Children and Young People's Reading Habits and Preferences: The Who, What, Why, Where and When*, London: National Literacy Trust.

Clarke, S. (2005) *Formative Assessment in Action: Weaving the Elements Together*, London: Hodder & Stoughton.

Clarkson, R. and Betts, H. (2008) *Attitudes to Reading at Ages Nine and Eleven*, Research summary, Slough: National Foundation for Education Research.

Claxton, G. (2000) The Anatomy of Intuition, in T. Atkinson and G. Claxton (eds), *The Intuitive Practitioner*, Buckingham: Open University Press, pp. 32–52.

Claxton, G. (2002) *Building Learning Power: Helping Young People Become Better Learners*, Bristol: TLO.

Cliff-Hodges, G. (2005) Creativity in Education, *English in Education*, 35(3): 47–61.

Cochrane, P. and Cockett, M. (2007) *Building a Creative School: A Dynamic Approach to School Improvement*, Stoke-on-Trent: Trentham.

Commeyras, M., Bisplinghoff, B.S. and Olson, J. (2003) *Teachers as Readers: Perspectives on the Importance of Reading in Teachers' Classrooms and Lives*, Newark, DE: International Reading Association.

Cook, M. (2002) Bringing the Outside In: Using Playful Contexts to Maximize Young Writer's Capabilities, in S. Ellis and C. Mills (eds), *Connecting, Creating: New Practices in the Teaching of Writing*, Leicester: United Kingdom Reading Association, pp. 8–20.

Corden, R. (2000) *Literacy and Learning Through Talk Strategies for the Primary Classroom*, Birmingham: Open University Press.

Corden, R. (2001) Teaching Reading–Writing Links (TRAWL) Project, *Reading, Literacy and Language*, 35(1): 37–40.

Corden, R. (2003) Writing is More Than 'Exciting': Equipping Primary Children to Become Reflective Writers, *Reading Literacy and Language*, 37(1): 18–26.

Craft, A. (2000) *Creativity Across the Primary Curriculum: Framing and Developing Practice*, London: Routledge Falmer.

Craft, A. (2001) Little Creativity, in A. Craft., B. Jeffrey and M. Leibling (eds), *Creativity in Education*, London: Continuum, pp. 45–61.

Craft, A. (2005) *Creativity in Schools: Tensions and Dilemmas*, Oxford: Routledge Falmer.

Craft, A., Cremin, T., Chappell, K. and Burnard, P. (2007) Possibility Thinking and Creative Learning, in A. Craft, T. Cremin and P. Burnard (eds), *Creative Learning 3–11*, London: Trentham.

Creative Partnerships (2008), available at www.creative-partnerships.com/ (accessed 12 August 2008).

Cremin, T. (2006) Creativity, Uncertainty and Discomfort: Teachers as Writers, *Cambridge Journal of Education*, 36(3): 415–33.

Cremin, T. (2007) Revisiting Reading for Pleasure: Diversity, Delight and Desire, in K. Goouch and A. Lambirth (eds), *Teaching Phonics, Teaching Reading: Critical Perspectives*, Milton Keynes: Open University Press, pp. 166–90.

Cremin, T. (2008) Teachers as Writers: Insights from Inside the Writing Process, Paper presented at the BERA Conference, Edinburgh, 3–6 September.

Cremin, T. (2009) Creative Teachers and Creative Teaching, in A. Wilson (ed.), *Creativity in Primary Education*, Exeter: Learning Matters.

Cremin, T., Burnard, P. and Craft, A. (2006a) Pedagogy and Possibility Thinking in the Early Years, *International Journal of Thinking Skills and Creativity*, 1(2): 108–19.

Cremin, T., Bearne, E., Mottram, M. and Goodwin, P. (2008a) Primary Teachers as Readers, *English in Education*, 42(1): 1–23.

Cremin, T., Mottram, M., Bearne, E. and Goodwin, P. (2008b) Exploring Teachers' Knowledge of Children's Literature, *The Cambridge Journal of Education*, 38(4): 449–64.

Cremin, T., Mottram, M., Collins, F. and Powell., S. (2008c) *Building Communities of Readers*, Leicester: UKLA/PNS.

Cremin, T., McDonald, R., Blakemore, L. and Goff, E. (2009a) *Jumpstart! Drama*, London: David Fulton.

Cremin, T., Bearne, E., Mottram, M. and Goodwin, P. (2009c) Teachers as Readers in the 21st Century, in M. Styles and E. Arizpo, *Acts of Reading: Teachers, Texts and Childhood*, London: Trentham.

Cremin, T., Goouch, K., Blakemore, L., Goff, E. and Macdonald, R. (2006b) Connecting Drama and Writing: Seizing the Moment to Write, *Research in Drama in Education*, 11(3): 273–91.

Cremin, T., Mottram, M., Collins, F., Powell, S. and Safford, K. (2009b) Teachers as Readers: Building Communities of Readers, *Literacy*, 43(1): 11–19.

Crumpler, T. and Schneider, J. (2002) Writing with their Whole Being: A Cross Study Analysis of Children's Writing from Five Classrooms Using Process Drama, *Research in Drama Education*, 7(2): 61–79.

D'Arcy, P. (1999) *Two Contrasting Paradigms for the Teaching and Assessment of Writing*, Leicester: NATE.

DCMS (2006) *Government Response to Paul Roberts' Report on Nurturing Creativity in Young People*, London: DCMS.

DCSF (2008a) *Statutory Framework for the Early Years Foundation Stage: Setting the Standards for Learning, Development and Care for Children from Birth to Five*, London: DCSF.

DCSF (2008b) Assessing Pupil Progress, available at www.standards.dfes.gov.uk/primaryframe work/assessment/app/ (accessed 15 September 2008).

DfEE (1989) *English for Ages 5 to 16: The National Curriculum*, London: DfEE and the Welsh Office.

DfEE (1998) *The National Literacy Strategy Framework for Teaching*, London: DfEE.

DfEE (1999a) *All Our Futures: Creativity, Culture and Education – The Report of the National Advisory Committee on Creative and Cultural Education*, London: DfEE.

DfEE (1999b) *The National Curriculum: Handbook for Primary Teachers in England*, London: HMSO.

DfES (2003) *Excellence and Enjoyment*, London: HMSO.

DfES (2006a) *Primary National Strategy: Primary Framework for Literacy and Mathematics*, Nottingham: DfES Publications.

DfES (2006b) Primary Framework for Literacy, Guidance on Planning, available at www.standards.dfes.gov.uk/primaryframework/literacy (accessed 23 August 2008).

DfES (2007a) *Letters and Sounds*, London: DfES.

DfES (2007b) *Gender and Education: The Evidence on Pupils in England*, London: HMSO.

DfES (2007c) Progression in Poetry, available at www.standards.dfes.gov.uk (accessed 20 June 2007).

DfES/QCA (2003) *Speaking, Listening, Learning: Working with Children in Key Stages 1 and 2*, London: DfES.

Dombey, H. (1998) Changing Literacy in the Early Years of School, in B. Cox (ed.), *Literacy is not Enough*, Manchester: Manchester University Press and Book Trust, pp. 125–32.

Dreher, M. (2003) Motivating Teachers to Read, *The Reading Teacher*, 56(4): 338–40.

Dymoke, S. (2003) *Drafting and Assessing Poetry*, London: Paul Chapman.

Ellis, S. and Safford, K. (2005) *Animating Literacy*, London: CLPE.

English, E., Hargreaves, L. and Hislam, J. (2002) Pedagogical Dilemmas in the National Literacy Strategy: Primary Teachers' Perceptions, Reflections and Classroom Behaviour, *Cambridge Journal of Education*, 32(1): 9–26.

Essex County Council (2003) *Visually Speaking Using Multimedia Texts to Improve Boys Writing*, Chelmsford: The English Team, Essex Advisory and Inspection Service.

Evans, J. (ed.) (2005) *Popular Culture, New Media and Digital Literacy in Early Childhood*, London: Routledge Falmer.

Fang, Z., Fu, D. and Lemme, L. (2004) From Scripted Instruction to Teacher Empowerment: Supporting Literacy Teachers to Make Pedagogical Transitions, *Literacy*, 38(1): 58–64.

Find Your Talent (2008), available at www.teachernet.gov.uk/teachingandlearning/cultural learning/ (accessed 20 August 2008).

Fisher, R. and Williams, M. (2004) *Unlocking Creativity: Teaching Across the Curriculum*, London: David Fulton.

Fleming, M., Merrell, C. and Tymms, P. (2004) The Impact of Drama on Pupils' Language, Mathematics and Attitude in Two Primary Schools, *Research in Drama Education*, 9(2): 177–97.

Flower, L. (1994) *The Construction of Negotiated Meaning: A Social Cognitive Theory of Writing*, Carbondale: Southern Illinois University Press.

Flower, L. and Hayes, J.R. (1980) The Dynamics of Composing: Making Plans and Juggling Constraints, in L.W. Gregg and E.R. Steinberg (eds), *Cognitive Processes in Writing*, Hillsdale NJ: Lawrence Erlbaum Associates, pp. 31–50.

Flower, L. and Hayes, J.R. (1984) Images, Plans and Prose: The Representation of Meaning in Writing, *Written Communication*, 1: 120–60.

Fox, C. (1993a) *At the Very Edge of the Forest: The Influence of Literature on Storytelling by Children*, London: Cassell.

Fox, C. (1993b) Tellings and Retellings: Educational Implications of Children's Oral Stories, *Reading*, 27(1): 14–20.

Frater, G. (2000) Observed in Practice: English in the National Literacy Strategy – Some Reflections, *Reading*, 34(3): 107–12.

Frater, G. (2001) *Effective Practice in Writing at Key Stage 2: Essential Extras*, London: Basic Skills Agency.

Frater, G. (2004) Improving Dean's Writing: What Shall We Tell the Children, *Literacy*, 38 (2): 45–56.

Fredricks, J.A., Blumenfeld, P.C. and Paris, A.H. (2004) School Engagement: Potential of the Concept, State of the Evidence, *Review of Educational Research*, 74(1): 59–109.

Freire, P. (1985) Reading the World and Reading the Word: An Interview with Paulo Friere, *Language Arts*, 62(1): 15–21.

Fryer, M. (1996) *Creative Teaching and Learning*, London: Paul Chapman.

Galton, M., Hargreaves, D.L., Comber, C., Wall, D. and Pell, A. (1999) *Inside the Primary Classroom: 20 Years On*, London: Routledge.

Gardner, H. (1993) *Frames of Mind: The Theory of Multiple Intelligences*, London: Fontana Press.

Geekie, P., Cambourne, B. and Fitzsimmons, P. (1999) *Understanding Literacy Development*, Stoke-on-Trent: Trentham.

Goodwin, P. (2008) *Understanding Children's Books: A Guide for Education Professionals*, London: Sage.

Goouch, K., Cremin, T and Lambirth, A. (2009) Writing is Primary. Final report for the Esmée Fairburn Foundation, March.

Goswami, U. (1999) Causal Connections in Beginning Reading: The Importance of Rhyme, *Journal of Research in Reading*, 22: 217–40.

Graham, J. (2000) Creativity and Picture Books, *Reading*, 34(2): 61–7.

Graham, L. (2001) From Tyrannosaurus Rex to Pokemon: Autonomy in the Teaching of Writing, *Reading, Literacy and Language*, 35(1): 18–26.

Graham, L. (2008) Teachers arc Digikids Too: The Digital Histories and Digital Lives of Young Teachers in English Primary Schools, *Literacy*, 42(1): 10–18.

Graham. L. and Johnson, A. (2003) *Children's Writing Journals*, Royston: UKLA.

Grainger, T. (1997) Poetry From the Nursery and the Playground: Making Time for Rhythms and Rhymes, *Language and Learning*, 12–16.

Grainger, T. (1997) *Traditional Tales: Storytelling in the Primary Classroom*, Leamington Spa: Scholastic.

Grainger, T, (1998) Drama and Reading: Illuminating their Interaction, *English in Education*, 32(1): 29–37.

Grainger, T. (1999) Conversations in the Classroom: Poetic Voices at Play, *Language Arts*, 76(4): 292–9.

Grainger, T. (2001a) Drama and Writing: Imagination on the Page I, *The Primary English Magazine*, 6(4): 12–17.

Grainger, T. (2001b) Drama and Writing: Imagination on the Page II, *The Primary English Magazine*, 6(5): 8–13.

Grainger, T. (2003a) Let Drama Build Bridges Between the Subjects, *The Primary English Magazine*, 8(3): 8–12.

Grainger, T. (2003b) Let Drama Build Bridges to Non-fiction Writing, *The Primary English Magazine*, 8(4): 19–23.

Grainger, T. (2003c) Exploring the Unknown: Ambiguity, Interaction and Meaning Making in Classroom Drama, in E. Bearne, D. Dombey and T. Grainger (eds), *Classroom Interactions in Literacy*, Maidenhead: Open University Press, pp. 105–14.

Grainger, T. (2004) Drama and Writing: Enlivening their Prose, in P. Goodwin (ed.), *Literacy Through Creativity*, London: David Fulton, pp. 91–104.

Grainger, T. (2005) Teachers as Writers: Travelling Together, *English in Education*, 39(1): 77–89.

Grainger, T. and Goouch, K. (1999) Young Children and Playful Language, in T. David (ed.), *Teaching Young Children*, London: Paul Chapman, pp. 19–29.

Grainger, T. and Cremin, M. (2001) *Resourcing Classroom Drama 5–8*, Sheffield: National Association for the Teaching of English.

Grainger, T. and Pickard, A. (2004) *Drama, Reading and Writing: Talking Our Way Forwards*, Cambridge: UKLA.

Grainger, T., Goouch, K. and Lambirth, A. (2002) The Voice of the Writer, *Reading Literacy and Language*, 36(3): 39–142.

Grainger, T., Goouch, K. and Lambirth, A. (2004a) *Creative Activities for Plot, Character and Setting, 5–7*, Milton Keynes: Scholastic.

Grainger, T., Goouch, K. and Lambirth, A. (2004b) *Creative Activities for Plot, Character and Setting, 7–9*, Milton Keynes: Scholastic.

Grainger, T., Goouch, K. and Lambirth, A. (2004c) *Creative Activities for Plot, Character and Setting, 9–11*, Milton Keynes: Scholastic.

Grainger, T., Lambirth, A. and Earl, J. (2004d) *Creativity and Writing School-based Audit Analysis for the Creativity and Writing Project Consortia*, Canterbury: CCCU.

Grainger, T., Goouch, K. and Lambirth, A. (2005) *Creativity and Writing: Developing Voice and Verve in the Classroom*, London: Routledge.

Grainger, T., Barnes, J. and Scoffham, S. (2006) Creative Teaching for Tomorrow, Research report for Creative Partnerships.

Graves, D. (1994) *A Fresh Look at Writing*, Portsmouth, NH: Heinemann.

Grugeon, E. and Gardner, P. (2000) *The Art of Storytelling for Teachers and Pupils*, London: David Fulton.

Guildford, J.P. (1973) *Characteristics of Creativity*, Springield, IL: Illinois State Office of the Superintendent of Public Instruction, Gifted Children Section.

Guthrie, J.T. and Wingfield, A. (2000) Engagement and Motivation in Reading, in M. Kamil, P.B. Mosentahl, P.D. Pearson and R. Barr (eds), *Handbook of Reading Research Volume 3*, Hillsdale, NJ: Lawrence Erlbaum, pp. 403–22.

Hall, N. and Robinson, A. (1995) *Exploring Play and Writing in the Early Years*, London: David Fulton.

Hall, N. and Robinson, A. (1996) (eds) *Learning About Punctuation*, Clevedon: Multilingual Matters.

Hall, C. and Coles, M. (1999) *Children's Reading Choices*, London: RoutledgeFalmer.

Halpin, D. (2003) *Hope and Education*, London: Routledge.

Hardy, B. (1977) Towards a Poetics of Fiction: An Approach Through Narrative, in M. Meek, A. Warlow and G. Barton (eds), *The Cool Web*, London: Bodley Head.

Harrison, C. (2002) What Does Research Tell Us About How To Develop Comprehension?, in R. Fisher, G. Brooks and M. Lewis (eds), *Raising Standards in Literacy*, London: Routledge.

Heathcote, D. and Bolton, G. (1995) *Drama for Learning: Dorothy Heathcote's Mantle of the Expert Approach to Education*, Portsmouth, NH: Heinemann.

Hendy, L. and Toon, L. (2001) *Supporting Drama and Imaginative Play in the Early Years*, Buckingham: Open University Press.

Hickman, A. (2005) Who Should Ask the Questions? How Arts Partnerships Develop Children's Critical Thinking, in S. Ellis and K. Safford, *Animating Literacy*, London: CLPE, pp. 86–99.

Honan, E. (2008) Barriers to Teachers Using Digital Texts in Literacy Classrooms, *Literacy*, 42(1): 36–43.

Hughes, T. (1967) *Poetry in the Making*, London: Faber

Hull, R. (2001) What Hope for Children's Poetry?, *Books for Keeps*, 126: 10–13.

Hyland, K. (2003) *Second Language Writing*, Cambridge: Cambridge University Press.

Jeffrey, B. (2005) Final Report of the Creative Learning and Student Perspectives Research Project (CLASP), A European Commission funded project through the Socrates Programme, Action 6.1, Number 2002-4682/002-001. SO2-61OBGE. Milton Keynes: Open University Press, available at http://clasp.open.ac.uk (accessed 22 July 2008).

Jeffrey, B. (ed.) (2006) *Creative Learning Practices: European Experiences*, London: Tufnell Press.

Jeffrey, B. and Woods, P. (2003) *The Creative School: A Framework for Success, Quality and Effectiveness*, London: Routledge Falmer.

Jeffrey, B. and Woods, P. (2009) *Creative Learning in the Primary School*, Oxford: Routledge.

Jeffrey, G. (ed.) (2005) *The Creative College: Building a Successful Learning Culture in the Arts*, Stoke-on-Trent: Trentham Books.

Johns, J.L. and Berglund, R.L. (2006) *Fluency: Strategies and Assessment*, Dubeque, IA: Kendall Hunt.

Kamil, M.L. (2003) *Adolescents and Literacy: Reading for the 21st Century*, Washington, DC: Alliance for Excellent Education.

Kelley, M.J. and Clausen-Grace, N. (2007) *Comprehension Shouldn't be Silent: From Strategy Instruction to Student Independence*, Newark, DE: International Reading Association.

Kenner, C. (2000) *Home Pages: Literacy Links for Bilingual Children*, Stoke-on-Trent: Trentham Books.

Ketch, A. (2005) Conversation: The Comprehension Connection, *The Reading Teacher*, 59(1): 8–13.

King, C. (2001) 'I Like Group Reading Because We Can Share Ideas' – The Role of Talk Within the Literature Circle, *Reading, Literacy and Language*, 35(1): 32–6.

King, C. and Briggs, J. (2005) *Literature Circles: Better Talking, More Ideas*, Royston: UKLA.

Kress, G. (1997) *Before Writing: Rethinking the Paths to Literacy*, London: Routledge.

Kress, G. and Knapp, P. (1992) Genre in a Social Theory of Language, *English in Education*: 26(2): 2–11.

Kress, G. and van Leeuwen, T. (1996) *The Grammar of Visual Design*, Routledge: London.

Kwek, D., Albright, J. and Kramer-Dahl, A. (2007) Building Teachers' Creative Capabilities in Singapore's English Classrooms: A Way of Contesting Pedagogical Instrumentality, *Literacy*, 41(2): 66–73.

Lambirth, A. (2002) *Poetry Matters*, Mini-book Series 15, Hertfordshire: United Kingdom Reading Association.

Lankshear, C. and Knobel, M. (2003) *New Literacies: Changing Knowledge and Classroom Learning*, Buckingham: Open University Press.

Lewis, M. and Wray, D. (1995) *Developing Children's Non-fiction Writing: Working with Writing Frames*, Leamington Spa: Scholastic.

Lewis, M. and Tregenza, J. (2007a) Beyond Simple Comprehension, *English 4–11*, 30: 11–16.

Lewis, M. and Tregenza, J. (2007b) *Beyond Simple Comprehension, Project Report and Case Studies*, Horsham: West Sussex Education Authority.

Littlefair, A. (1991) *Reading All Types of Writing*, Milton Keynes: Open University Press.

Lockwood, M. (2008) *Promoting Reading for Pleasure in the Primary School*, London: Sage.

Luce-Kapler, R., Chin, J., O'Donnell, E. and Stooh, S. (2001) *The Design of Meaning: Unfolding Systems of Writing*, Changing English, 8(1): 43–52.

Mackcy, M. (2002) *Literacies Across Media: Playing the Text*, London: Routledge.

McNaughton, M.J. (1997) Drama and Children's Writing: A Study of the Influence of Drama on the Imaginative Writing of Primary Schoolchildren, *Research in Drama Education*, 2(1): 55–86.

Malaguzzi, L. (1998) History, Ideas and Basic Philosophy: An Interview with Lella Gandini, in C. Edwards, L. Gandini and G. Forman (eds), *The Hundred Languages of Children*, 2nd edn, Greenwich, CT: Ablex.

Mallett, M. (1991) *Making Facts Matter*, London: Paul Chapman.

Marsh, J. (2004) The Techno-literacy Practices of Young Children, *Journal of Early Childhood Research*, 2(1): 51–66.

Marsh, J. (ed.) (2005) *Popular Culture, New Media and Digital Literacy in Early Childhood*, London: Routledge Falmer.

Marsh, J. and Millard, E. (2000) *Literacy and Popular Culture: Using Children's Culture in the Classroom*, London: Paul Chapman.

Marsh, J. and Bearne, E. (2008) *Moving Literacy On: Evaluation of the BFI Lead Practitioner Scheme for Moving Image Media Literacy*, Leicester: University of Sheffield and United Kingdom Literacy Association.

Marsh, J., Brooks, G., Hughes, J., Ritchie, L., Roberts, S. and Wright, K. (2005) *Digital Beginnings: Young Children's Use of Popular Culture, Media and New Technologies*, Sheffield: University of Sheffield.

Martin, J. (1989) *Factual Writing: Exploring and Challenging Social Reality*, Oxford: Oxford University Press.

Martin, T. (2003) Minimum and Maximum Entitlements: Literature at Key Stage 2, *Reading Literacy and Language*, 37(1): 14–17.

Maybin, J. (2006) Locating Creativity in Texts and Practices, in J. Maybin and J. Swann (eds), *The Art of English: Everyday Creativity*, Basingstoke: Palgrave Macmillan and the Open University, pp. 413–33.

Maynard, S. MacKay, S., Smyth, F. and Reynolds, K. (2007) *Young People's Reading in 2005: The Second Study of Young People's Reading Habits*, London and Loughborough: NCRCL, Roehampton University and LISU, Loughborough University.

Medwell, J., Strand, S. and Wray, D. (2007) The Role of Handwriting in Composing for Y2 Children, *Journal of Reading, Writing and Literacy*, 2(1): 18–36.

Medwell, J., Wray, D., Poulson, L. and Fox, R. (1998) *Effective Teachers of Literacy: A Report of a Research Project Commissioned by the Teacher Training Agency*, Exeter: University of Exeter.

Meek, M. (1985) Play and Paradoxes: Some Considerations of Imagination and Language, in G. Wells and J. Nicholls (eds), *Language and Learning: An International Perspective*, London: Falmer Press.

Meek, M. (1988) *How Texts Teach What Readers Learn*, Stroud: Thimble Press.

Meek, M. (1991) *On Being Literate*, London: Bodley Head.

Mercer, N. (2000) *Words and Minds, How We Use Language to Think Together*, London: Routledge.

Mercer, N. and Littleton, K. (2007) *Dialogue and the Development of Children's Thinking*, London: Routledge.

Moll, L., Amanti, C., Neff, D. and Gonzalez, N. (1992) Funds of Knowledge for Teaching: Using a Qualitative Approach to Connect Homes and Classrooms, *Theory into Practice*, 31: 132–41.

Mroz, M., Smith, F. and Hardman, F. (2000) The Discourse of the Literacy Hour, *The Cambridge Journal of Education*, 30(3): 379–90.

Myhill, D. (2001) Crafting and Creating, *English in Education*, 35(3): 13–20.

Myhill, D. (2005) Writing Creatively, in A. Wilson (ed.), *Creativity in Primary Education*, Exeter: Learning Matters, pp. 58–69.

National Advisory Committee on Creative and Cultural Education (NACCCE) (1999) *All Our Futures: Creativity, Culture and Education*, London: DfEE.

Neelands, J. (2000) Drama Sets you Free, or Does it?, in J. Davison and J. Moss, *Issues in English Teaching*, pp. 73–89.

Nestlé Family Monitor (2003) *Young People's Attitudes Towards Reading*, Croydon: Nestlé Family Monitor.

Nicholson, H. (2000) Dramatic Literacies and Difference, in E. Bearne and V. Watson (eds), *Where Texts and Children Meet*, London: Routledge.

Nueman, S.B. and Celano, D. (2001) Access to Print in Low-income and Middle-income Communities: An Ecological Study of Four Neighborhoods, *Reading Research Quarterly*, 36(10): 8–26.

Office for Standards in Education (OfSTED) (2002) *The Curriculum in Successful Primary Schools*, HMI 553, October, London: OfSTED.

Office for Standards in Education (OfSTED) (2003) *Expecting the Unexpected: Developing Creativity in Primary and Secondary Schools*, HMI 1612, available at www.ofsted.gov.uk (accessed 12 June 2006).

Office for Standards in Education (OfSTED) (2007) *Poetry in Schools: A Survey of Practice, 2006/7*, London: OfSTED.

O'Neill, C. (1995) *Drama Worlds: A Framework for Process Drama*, Portsmouth, NH: Heinemann.

O'Sullivan, O. and Thomas, A. (2000) *Understanding Spelling*, London: Centre for Language in Primary Education.

Pahl, K. (2007) Creativity in Events and Practices: A Lens for Understanding Children's Multimodal Texts, *Literacy*, 41(2): 81–7.

Park, N. (dir.) (1993) *The Wrong Trousers*, Bristol: Aardman Animations.

Pennac, D. (2006) *The Rights of the Reader*, London: Walker Books.

Pirrie, J. (1987) *On Common Ground: A Programme for Teaching Poetry*, Sevenoaks: Hodder & Stoughton.

Poetry Archive, The, available at www.poetryarchive.org/childrensarchive/home.do (accessed 13 June 2008).

Powling, C. (2003) Introduction, in C. Powling, B. Ashley, P. Pullman, A. Fine and J. Gavin (eds), *Meetings with the Minister*, Reading: National Centre for Language and Literacy.

Powling, C., Ashley, B., Pullman, P., Fine, A., Gavin, J., *et al.* (eds) (2005) *Beyond Bog Standard Literacy*, Reading: National Centre for Language and Literacy.

Prentice, R. (2000) Creativity: A Reaffirmation of its Place in Early Childhood Education, *The Curriculum Journal*, 11(2): 145–58.

Pressley, M., Wharton-McDonald, R., Allington, R., Block, C.C., Morrow, L., *et al.* (2001) A Study of Effective First Grade Literacy Instruction, *Scientific Studies of Reading*, 5(1): 35–58.

Purcell-Gates, V. (1988) Lexical and Syntactic Knowledge of Written Narrative Held by Well-read-to Kindergartners and Second Graders, *Research in the Teaching of English*, 22(2): 128–60.

Qualifications and Curriculum Authority (QCA) (1998) *Can Do Better – Raising Boys Achievement in English*, London: QCA.

Qualifications and Curriculum Authority (QCA) (2005a) *Creativity: Find It, Promote It! – Promoting Pupils' Creative Thinking and Behaviour Across the Curriculum at Key Stages 1, 2 and 3 – Practical Materials for Schools*, London: QCA.

Qualifications and Curriculum Authority (QCA) (2005b) The National Curriculum in Action: Creativity, available at www.ncaction.org.uk/creativity/about.htm (accessed 12 December 2008).

Qualifications and Curriculum Authority (QCA) (2005c) *English 21 Report*, London: QCA.

Qualifications and Curriculum Authority (QCA) (2008) *Personal Learning and Thinking Skills: The New Secondary Curriculum*, London: QCA.

Raison, G. (1997) *Writing Developmental Continuum*, Port Melbourne: Rigby Heineman.

Rideout, V.J., Vandewater, E.A. and Wartella, E.A. (2003) *Zero to Six: Electronic Media in the Lives of Infants, Toddlers and Preschoolers*, Washington, DC: Kaiser Foundation.

Roberts, P. (2006) *Nurturing Creativity in Young People: A Report to Government to Inform Future Policy*, London: DCMS.

Robinson, M. and Ellis, V. (2000) Writing in English and Responding to Writing, in J. Sefton Green and R. Sinker (eds), *Evaluating Creativity: Making and Learning by Young People*, London: Routledge.

Robinson, M. and Mackey, M. (2006) Assets in the Classroom: Comforts and Competence with Media Among Teachers Present and Future, in J. Marsh and E. Millard (eds) *Popular Literacies, Childhood and Schooling*, London: RoutledgeFalmer, pp. 200–20.

Rose, J. (2009) The Final Report on the Review of the Primary Curriculum, London: DCSF.

Rosen, H. (1988) The Irrepressible Genre, in M. Maclure, T. Phillips and A. Wilkinson (eds), *Oracy Matters*, Milton Keynes: Open University Press, pp. 13–23.

Rosen, M. (1989) *Did I Hear You Write?*, London: André Deutsch.

Rosenblatt, L. (1978) *The Reader, the Text, the Poem: The Transactional Theory of Literary Work*, Carbondale, IL: South Illinois University Press.

Rosenblatt, L. (1985) The Transactional Theory of the Literary Work: Implications for Research, in C. Cooper (ed.), *Researching Response to Literature and the Teaching of English*, Norwood, NJ: Ablex.

Rothery, J. (1985) *Teaching Writing in the Primary School: A Genre Based Approach*, Sydney: Department of Linguistics, University of Sydney

Rumelhart, D. (1980) Schemata: The Building Blocks of Cognition, in R. Spiro, B. Bruce and W. Brewer (eds), *Theoretical Issues in Reading Comprehension*, Hillsdale, NJ: Lawrence Erlbaum.

Rumelhart, D. (1985) Towards an Interactive Model of Reading, in H. Singer and R. Rundell (eds), *Theoretical Models and Processes of Reading*, Newark, DE: International Reading Association.

Sedgwick, F. (2001) *Teaching Literacy: A Creative Approach*, London: Continuum.

Sharples, M. (1999) *How We Write: Writing as Creative Design*, London: Routledge.

Shayer, M. and Adey, P. (2002) *Learning Intelligence: Cognitive Acceleration Across the Curriculum from 5–15*, Buckingham: Open University Press.

Smith, A. (2007) In What Ways Can a Creative Pedagogy Feed Narrative Writing?, unpublished MA dissertation, Canterbury Christ Church University.

Smith, F. (1982) *Writing and the Writer*, London: Heinemann.

Smith, L.L. and Joyner, C.R. (1990) Comparing Recreational Reading Levels from an Informal Reading Inventory, *Reading Horizons*, 30(4): 293–9.

Soalt, J. (2005) Bringing Together Fictional and Informational Texts to Improve Comprehension, *The Reading Teacher*, 58(7): 680–3.

Spiro, J. (2007) Teaching Poetry: Writing Poetry – Teaching as a Writer, *English in Education*, 41(3): 78–93.

Sprackland, J. and Coe, M. (2005) *Our Thoughts are Bees: Writers Working in School*, Southport: Word Play.

Sternberg, R.J. (1997) *Successful Intelligence*, New York: Plume.

Sternberg, R.J. (ed.) (1999) *The Handbook of Creativity*, New York: Cambridge University Press.

Styles, M. (1992) Just a Kind of Music: Children as Poets, in M. Styles, E. Bearne and V. Watson (eds), *After Alice*, London: Cassell, pp. 73–88.

Styles, M. (1998) *From the Garden to the Street*, London: Cassell.

Taylor, B.M. and Pearson, P.D. (eds) (2002) *Teaching Reading: Effective Schools, Accomplished Teachers*, Mahwah, NJ: Lawrence Erlbaum Associates.

Taylor, B.M., Frye, B.J., and Maruyama, G.M. (1990) Time Spent Reading and Reading Growth, *American Educational Research Journal*, 27(2): 351–62.

Taylor, P. and Warner, C.D. (2006) *Structure and Spontaneity: The Process Drama of Cecily O'Neil*, Stoke-on-Trent: Trentham

Twist, L., Schagen, I. and Hodgson, C. (2007) *Readers and Reading: The National Report for England 2006*, Progress in International Reading Literacy Study (PIRLS), Slough: National Foundation for Educational Research.

United Kingdom Literacy Association (UKLA)/Qualifications and Assessment Authority (QAA) (2004) *More than Words: Multimodal Texts in the Classroom*, London: QCA.

United Kingdom Literacy Association (UKLA)/Qualifications and Assessment Authority (QAA) (2005) *More than Words 2: Creating Stories on Page and Screen*, London: QCA.

Vass, E. (2004) Friendship and Collaboration: Creative Writing in the Primary Classroom, *Journal of Computer Assisted Learning*, 18: 102–11.

Vygotsky, L.S. (1978) *Mind in Society*, Cambridge, MA: Harvard University Press.

Wagner, B.J. (1998) *Educational Drama and Language Arts: What Research Shows*, Portsmouth, NH: Heinemann.

Wallas, G. (1926) *The Art of Thought*, New York: Harcourt Brace and World.

Walsh, C. (2007) Creativity as Capital in the Literacy Classroom, *Literacy*, 41(2): 74–85.

Warrington, M., Younger, M. and Bearne, E. (2006) *Raising Boys' Achievement in Primary Schools: Towards a Holistic Approach*, Maidenhead: Open University Press.

Watts, R. (2007) Harnessing the Power of Film in the Primary Classroom, *Literacy*, 41(2): 102–9.

Wells, G. (1986) *The Meaning Makers*, London: Hodder & Stoughton.

Wells, G. (1999) *Dialogic Inquiry*, Cambridge: Cambridge University Press.

Wells, R. (2008) Dancing into Writing: Adventures into the World of Abdhi, *English 4–1*, 33: 9–13.

Whitehead, F. (1977) *Children and Their Books*, London: Macmillan.

Wilson, A. (2005a) The Best Forms in the Best Order? Current Poetry Writing Pedagogy at KS2, *English in Education*, 39(3): 19–31.

Wilson, A. (ed.) (2005b) *Creativity in Primary Education: Theory and Practice*, Exeter: Learning Matters.

Wilson, S. and Ball, D.L. (1997) Helping Teachers Meet the Standards: New Challenges for Teacher Educators, *The Elementary School Journal*, 97(2): 121–38.

Winston, J. (1998) *Drama, Narrative and Moral Education*, London: Falmer Press.

Woods, P. (1994) *Critical Events in Teaching and Learning*, London: Falmer Press.

Woods, P. (1995) *Creative Teachers in Primary Schools*, Buckingham: Open University Press.

Woods, P. (2001) Creative Literacy, in A. Craft, B. Jeffrey and M. Liebling (eds), *Creativity in Education*, London: Continuum, pp. 62–79.

Wray, D. and Lewis, M. (1997) *Extending Literacy: Children Reading and Writing Non-fiction*, London: Routledge.

Wray, D. and Lewis, M. (2001) Developing Non-fiction Writing: Beyond Writing Frames, in J. Evans (ed.), *The Writing Classroom: Aspects of Writing and the Primary Child*, London: David Fulton.

Wray, D., Medwell, J., Poulson, L. and Fox, R. (2002) *Teaching Literacy Effectively in the Primary School*, London: Routledge Falmer.

Writing Together (2006) *Bringing Writers into Schools: A Practical Guide*, London: Booktrust.

Zephaniah, B. (2001) Poetry Writing, in J. Carter (ed.), *Creating Writers: A Creative Writing Manual for Schools*, London: Routledge.

Zipes, J. (1995) *Creative Storytelling: Building Communities, Changing Lives*, London: Routledge.

INDEX